DON'T SHOOT!
WE'RE REPUBLICANS!

Memoirs of an FBI Agent

Who Did Things His Own Way

Jack Owens

Published in the United States by
History Publishing Company
Palisades, New York

LCCN: 2009925524
ISBN-13: 978-1-933909-67-7
ISBN-10: 1-933909-67-6
SAN: 850-5942

Owens, Jack, 1944 Nov. 19-
       Don't shoot! : we're Republicans! : memoirs of an FBI
agent who did things his own way / Jack Owens.
       p. cm.
       Includes index.
       LCCN 2009925524
       ISBN-13: 9781933909677
       ISBN-10: 1933909676

       1. Owens, Jack,--1944 Nov. 19- 2. United States.
Federal Bureau of Investigation--Officials and employees
--Biography. 3. United States. Federal Bureau of
Investigation.--History--20th century. 4. Criminal
investigation--United States.   I. Title.

HV7911.O94A3 2009   363.25'092
                             QBI09-600092

Printed in the United States on acid-free paper

9 8 7 6 5 4 3 2 1

3 9082 11515 1444

First Edition

DEDICATION

To my wife, Patricia, the love and anchor of my life. Her devotion and understanding made it possible for me to disappear into the Bureau or into a writing pad. She was always there when I came back. Her passion is my lifeline.

ACKNOWLEDGEMENTS

I am deeply grateful to Don Bracken, my publisher, for his fearless sense of humor and faith in me. He saw a book where others would not tread.

My steadfast and artful editor, Leslie Price Hayes, saved me from myself, smoothly untangling the knots and bedlam that I threw in the path of the reader. She gracefully put her foot down precisely where it was needed.

I am indebted to Arthur Deutcsh and Theron Raines for their encouragement and wise counsel over many years. Claire Gerus, my Arizona buddy, believed that another book about the FBI was not one too many. In San Francisco, Jeevan Sivasubramaniam was never too busy to accept my calls or second my efforts.

My dearest friends and FBI colleagues, Leon Sizemore and Luther Brannon, always had my back and shared many of the adventures in this book. We broke a lot of bread together and never took ourselves too seriously. They appeared early in my career and never left. They shared my belief that the best meal was right after an arrest. There are no finer gentlemen or more accomplished agents.

Bob Sligh taught me the back roads and intrigues of counterintelligence. He was decisive and brilliant, with unfailing judgement and instincts. A mentor of the highest order, and a solid infield glove.

My former neighbor and SWAT team leader, Starley Carr, shaped every crisis with a calm and steady hand. I would not rappel until he secured my gear. Which gave me a start the time he laughed as I backed over the edge.

Others ran the Bureau marathon with me, always supportive. Of the many, here are a few: Jeanette Banks, Alvin Berry, Peter Bodkin, Jim Brandt, Steve Brannan, Bill Branon, Jimmie Brown, Barbara Brown, Billy Bryan, John Bochnak, Michael Byrne, Bob Bunch, Jackie Carrico, Sidney Caspersen,

Sherolynne Coachman, Roel Carranza, Beau Coleman, John Colvin, Ben Cumbie, Ashley Curry, Craig Dahle, Lonnie Davis, Will Deffenbaugh, Richard Deslauriers, Lill Dill, Frank Evans, William Fleming, Danny Garnett, Gregg Gilliland, Frank Grider, Don Groghan, Oliver Halle, David Heaven, Beverly Holder, Lucy Hoover, Douglas Hudgel, Gwynne Hupfer, Dave Jernigan, Paul Johnson, Jane Koshutko, Gerald Kelley, Al King, Ronald Klug, Bob Kuykendall, Mandy Lavender, Lee Leggett, Mel Leigeber, Larry Long, Margaret Long, Roy Long, Mary Jo Lorino, Jeff MacDonald, Kevin McPartland, Bill Malone, Wayne Manis, David Martin, Patsy Martin, Tammy Mathis, Lorenza Moore, Tom Moore, G. Wray Morse, Jim Morton, Cecil Moses, Bob Nelson, Betty Norris, Tina O'Connor, Ginger Odom, Pete Odom, Steve Odom, George Pare, Chuck Pierce, Richard Procop, Jim Procopio, Paula Ragusa, Marshall Riddlehoover, Glenn Rotenberry, Bob Rolen, Frances Self, Paul Shea, Bill Sievers, Alton Sizemore, Frank Slapikas, Kelli Sligh, Herb Smith, Gary Steger, Larry Sylvester, Bill Temple, Bill Teigen, Lloyd Warnken, Dale Watson, Brenda Williams, Lynn Williford, Eric Wilson, Tom Wiseman, Don Wright, and Billy Yessick.

Like every successful organization, the Bureau produces men and women with moxie, pluck, and vision. Such were the leaders who shaped and nurtured my career: Ralph Miles, Lewis Barnett, and William Westberg. Although I recruited Janice Windham into the FBI and had more experience as an agent, she became my supervisor and a damn fine one. Courageously, she did not shrink from putting her stamp on her more senior charges.

The Denver FBI tempered my impetuous flights as a first office agent, while twenty-nine years in my beloved Birmingham added the seasoning that I cherish. To the Bureau men and women in Colorado and Alabama, I salute you.

Former Birmingham police officers Earl Melton and Joe Warden, and former Birmingham Chief of Police, James Parsons, unselfishly devoted all of their considerable savvy and street experience to making an FBI venture successful. They taught me a great deal, and I treasure their friendship and the years we worked and played together.

Federal, state, county, and local law enforcement in Colorado and Alabama kept their doors open and their hands outstretched during my entire career. They gave me far more than I gave them. Thank you.

My children provided the love and sanctuary that I needed away from law enforcement. In order of their arrival: Brett, Duane, Deke, Stacey, Laura, and Molly. They enriched my life beyond measure, and did not hesitate when I signaled them to steal home into the teeth of a waiting catcher. Their mothers have never forgiven me.

My daughter-in-law, Corinne, and sons-in-law, Warren and Clay, did not take away my children. Instead, they gave me another daughter and two more sons.

Always in my thoughts are my grandchildren, Rachel, Allyson, Slayton, Dylan, McCabe, Allen, and Mary Helen. They think that I'm wise and all knowing. They are not yet old enough to know better.

I raise a glass in tribute to my irreverent mates in New Agents Class #17, 1969, and our dauntless counselors, Charles Parkis and Fred Brown. Humor and love of the Bureau bound us together far more than fifth floor commandments.

Finally, in memory of my brother, Bob Owens, who was my better in every respect save longevity, and Bob Rogers, a peerless FBI Irishman whose scorn I feel whenever I'm tempted to take an elevator instead of the stairs. They are missed with every sun.

TABLE OF CONTENTS

Foreword ix
Prologue 1

PART ONE

Chapter 1: Origins 7
Chapter 2: Beginners. 11
Chapter 3: Basic Training 15
Chapter 4: Hogan's Alley. 25
Chapter 5: Graduation 27

PART TWO

Chapter 6: Denver. 31
Chapter 7: Learning the Ropes 35
Chapter 8: Softball 43
Chapter 9: A Real Pro 45
Chapter 10: Transferred. 49

PART THREE

Chapter 11: Birmingham 55
Chapter 12: Motivation. 61
Chapter 13: J. Edgar Hoover. 71
Chapter 14: Big Shoes to Fill. 81
            Part 1: L. Patrick Gray 81
            Part 2: Clarence Kelley. 83
Chapter 15: The Young and the Restless 87
            Part 1: Doing Foolish Things. 87
            Part 2: Volkswagen Arrest 93
Chapter 16: Crime Resistance 101
Chapter 17: The Atlanta Child Murders 109
Chapter 18: William H. Webster. 121
Chapter 19: A Perfect Moment in an Imperfect World 129

Chapter 20: Don't Shoot! We're Republicans! 131
Chapter 21: And Then Came Molly 135
Chapter 22: Foreign Counterintelligence. 139

PART FOUR

Chapter 23: Headlights. 157
Chapter 24: Area Code 215. 165
Chapter 25: Prison Hymn. 171
Chapter 26: William S. Sessions 181
Chapter 27: Lincoln and Grant. 187
Chapter 27: Assassination of a Federal Judge 191
Chapter 28: Louis J. Freeh. 203
Chapter 30: Colin Powell 209
Chapter 31: Talladega Uprising. 213
Chapter 32: Dogcatchers. 221
Chapter 33: Beer for Breakfast. 225
Chapter 34: Losing the Recruiting Wars 229

PART FIVE

Chapter 35: Hitting the Wall. 233
Chapter 36: Retirement. 241

FOREWORD

It is a good thing that Jack Owens has written a book about himself. I have always felt that he should be a character in a book—now he is.

I came to know Jack Owens when we moved in across the hall from each other in the "new" men's dorm at Concord College in 1962. I was a sophomore and Jack was a freshman. We were team-mates on the 1962-63 Concord College Mountain Lion football team. That team became the first West Virginia Intercollegiate Athletic Conference Champion football team in the history of Concord College. This was the first of many victories that would mark Jack's life, *Don't Shoot! We're Republicans!* is only the most recent.

It is not surprising to me that Jack became a law enforce-ment officer. Neither would I have been surprised if he had de-cided to be an IBM computer salesman. He just has that look about him—great smile, short hair (at least it was in those days), a winning personality, and looks good in a white shirt and dark suit. The FBI was a great fit for him.

Don't Shoot! We're Republicans! gives the reader an insight into the life and work of one FBI agent that describes his Bureau as "... loafers, not wing tips." While the tone is often light and the relating of the stories is humorous, do not be misled. Regardless of how few FBI field officers and agents have died in the line of duty, it is still a dangerous job and one I am happy that brave young Americans, like Jack Owens, are still willing to take on.

Being from West Virginia myself, I like the fact that he works in references to our state. Although he and his family are Alabamans now, we still claim anyone who can refer to Jenkinjones (a small town in McDowell County, West Virginia) with a straight face. The coal fields of the Mountain State are dotted with coal camps and places with funny little names—Jenkinjones is just one, but that is where Jack is from and West Virginians note things like that.

When I read this book, I was reminded of a story that occurred following the O.J. Simpson trial, where it seemed pretty clear that some evidence had been planted by the police. I was talking on the telephone to a friend in law enforcement (twenty-plus year veteran) and I said, "Did you ever hear of any of your fellow officers falsifying evidence in a case?" There was a long pause on the line and finally he said, "Well no, at least not against anyone that didn't deserve it." Somehow, that same flavor comes through in the stories Jack relates.

This is a very readable book. The chapters are short and the action is fast-paced. I think you will come to know and appreciate Jack Owens and his fellow agents. What you will see is that, notwithstanding the seriousness of the work, FBI agents are like most of the rest of us. They gripe about the working conditions, the boss, the pay and … the working conditions! The men and women who populate the pages of this book are real, and, while that sometimes makes their actions seem a little ordinary, that is also what adds to the reality of the book. I hope the one person that comes through to you is Jack Owens.

Of course I have an advantage over the casual reader. I have known Jack Owens for over 45 years. Jack was a defensive back and tailback and I played on the offensive line. We shared the ritual agony of pre-season football two-a-day drills under a hot southern West Virginia sun. Our school was small and the travel budget for the team was equally small. We rode Trailways buses over the winding roads to our away games and half the team showed up sick to their stomachs. The team was few in number so most players traveled and most players got in the games. The down side of that was the Monday film session when the head coach graded each player's performance and subjected everyone (except a couple of stars) to a humiliating critique. The only good thing was that the room was dark so no one could see your embarrassment. Jack Owens was prepared for the FBI bureaucracy on the playing fields of Athens, WV.

Jack and I were also fraternity brothers. I was already an active when he pledged and it was one of my duties to prepare him to be a good "Frater." Like everything else in his life, Jack plunged into his role and outdid everyone by climbing a flagpole in Hinton, WV to "liberate" a West Virginia State Centennial flag during rush week. And what would be a college man's career without a "panty raid?" Yes, there was one of those in Jack's life too.

I left Concord College (now Concord University) in May, 1963 and lost touch with Jack and most of my other teammates until much later. In 1980, I had the great good fortune to be elected to the U.S. House of Representatives from West Virginia's Third Congressional District. During my time in Congress I saw the FBI in action on a number of fronts. Some of my close friends and colleagues had been FBI agents before their election to Congress. I worked closely with the FBI office in West Virginia on clearances for political appointees. And, of course, we had briefings on a number of topics. I had no idea that Jack was with the Bureau or that another teammate from Concord, Ancil Sparks, was an FBI agent also. Neither of us would have believed how the other turned out.

During that period Jack Owens and his fellow agents were dealing with the tragic Atlanta Child Murders—a case that gripped the nation, he was also dealing in foreign counterintelligence and critiquing the performance of two FBI Directors, William Webster and William Sessions. You will be interested in his take on both men.

Jack and I caught up with each other in 1987 when Concord invited the 1962 team back to campus for a 25 year reunion of the first Championship. It was great to see everyone again. We all checked each other out to see who was in the best shape. Jack certainly was in the running for the top spot. As it turned out, Concord also invited the team from 50 years before and Jack's

Dad was part of that team, so having father and son honored on the same day was pretty special.

Much later, when one of our teammates, Wayne Hicks, was inducted into the Concord University Athletic Hall of Fame, Jack and I reestablished our relationship. We began to correspond fairly regularly and I came to see another side of Jack, as a retired agent, grandfather, and a stalwart in the community. To my great shock, I also found out that he had been a participant in the TV show, "Big Brother." The more I thought about it, the less bizarre it seemed. Just another dimension of a very interesting person.

One of the challenges Jack faces in writing a memoir is how to portray his colleagues—especially the ones he likes. A writer realizes that anything in black and white can come back to haunt him. How does he make the character come alive and yet be believable? In recommending Jack Owens and *Don't Shoot! We're Republicans!* I am confident that you, the reader, will know more about how one of America's most famous institutions, the FBI, really functions. You will also get acquainted with my friend Jack Owens. I think you will like both pretty well.

—*Mick Staton,* President-Capitol Link, Inc.

"I know it looks like I'm movin', but I'm standin' still."
—*Bob Dylan,* Not Dark Yet

"You do not rise by the regulations, but in spite of them."
—*Winston Churchill*

PROLOGUE

You become a junkie in the Federal Bureau of Investigation, get high on adrenalin, black coffee, and sleeping with your ears open. You do all night surveillances in a dark car surfing the good time FM, and killing the doom light so you can open the door and pee out. For variety, you get out of the car, stretch, and pee on the Bureau tires. You stay awake talking to your partner about what an asshole your boss is. The FBI lives on gripes and stale air. Show me a better way to spend thirty years.

One night, because we had nothing more pressing and we were itching for adventure, three carloads of agents drove out of Birmingham and up the west side of Alabama into northeast Mississippi, hunting two fugitives who were joined at the hip. One, a dude named Singleton, was wanted for killing a convenience store manager in Alabama during a robbery, shooting him for the fun of it. Singleton collected coins and was a regular at numismatic shows, where he stole coins he couldn't buy. The other fugitive I'll call Thompson, a run-of-the-mill car thief. It was June, 1978. I'd been an agent for nine years and was certain I knew everything there was to know about everything.

It was darker than the inside of a snake's butt in rural Mississippi. We were a long way from home in a caravan of dull cars, feeling our way over unfamiliar roads, talking loud, comparing notes on the office stenos, invincible and full of ourselves. Every time we got out of the cars or rolled down the windows,

1

elephant mosquitoes came at us like lava. No one wanted to stir. I longed for peanut butter and beer, resigned to a long night of it.

My partner was Luther Brannon, an Alabama native who'd once driven a school bus in Talladega County, hauling Pat, my future second wife, to her primary grades. Luther, who could be a hardass, had once stopped the bus in order to kick his kid brother Arlan off for misbehaving. The incident so affected Arlan he became a mortician.

Luther Brannon was six years older than me, a difference that had never meant squat to us. We were friends as well as colleagues, saw the world as one big landscape of University of Alabama football victories. Luther and I loved the Crimson Tide more than we hated Auburn. The only glitch in our relationship was Luther's thick, wavy black hair, which left me cold and bitter. I was receding on top and would have killed Luther for his hair. He was a supervisor, one of the few desk jockeys in the FBI who was worth a spit, so I didn't hold that against him. Luther never ordered the agents on his squad to do anything that he wouldn't do himself, which was why he was holed up with me in some deep south moonscape.

I sat shotgun in the Bureau Pontiac, Luther had the wheel. The engine idled while we parked off the side of the highway a ways east of cotton country in the Mississippi Delta. Luther checked a road map with a pin light, consulted it out of boredom because he always knew where he was.

The FBI radio barked with a warning from agents miles away that the two fugitives were headed toward us in a wrecker towing a Mustang. You could usually trust what you heard on the Bureau radio, so Luther and I pulled across the road to block both lanes. The two FBI cars behind us did the same. We were lined up and exposed on the highway like toes in a sandal.

I put the emergency blue light on the dash and flipped it on, turned the interior of the Bureau car into a blue light special at K-Mart. Luther and I squinted as the bright light rotated in and out of our eyes.

The FBI radio went silent. What the hell did that mean? Where were the fugitives?

I ran my fingers along the stock of the M-79 grenade launcher resting on my lap. The business end was wide and looked like a grouper with indigestion. It was loaded with a round that could take out the windshield of a car and anyone behind it. The 79 smelled of Hoppies cleaning fluid and oil.

I looked down the highway. Headlights appeared in the distance. I clicked off the safety on the 79. I had to pee. Luther picked up the radio mic. "Quarter mile away," he said into the radio, which might have been heard in Natchez or in Detroit and not by the agents in the two cars directly behind us. You never knew about the reach of Bureau radios. They were influenced by sunspots, menstrual cycles, rings around the moon, the tides down on the Gulf. Coaches in the press box and cons on death row had better communications than the FBI.

The headlights down the road grew as the tall wrecker bore down on us at high speed. Luther grunted. He never said much, whether he was leading an arrest team or laying sheet rock. Luther had a knack for home improvement and laying pipe.

The wrecker didn't slow one bit. It wasn't going to stop. We could back off the highway and get out of the way, or we could stay put. My side of the car faced the wrecker, so I was hoping Luther would decide to back into the next county.

I looked at Luther. Our car didn't move. Luther took his hands off the steering wheel and gripped his .38 service revolver. We were in a Pontiac, playing chicken with a wrecker. I braced for impact.

The wrecker swerved off the side of the road, towing a fish-tailing Mustang. The agents behind us opened up on the wrecker as it flew by, fired a dozen rounds, a hundred rounds, I didn't know. The wrecker dissolved into a row of oversized taillights up the Mississippi hardtop, the half-dead Mustang in its wake.

Luther let loose a stream of profanities, gunned the Pontiac up the road after the wrecker. The other Bureau cars fell in behind us. We were going 90, but the wrecker stretched its lead. No way a wrecker with a tow could haul like that. We ate some sharp turns on the two-lane and the blue light flew off the dash. I left it on the floor. Never liked the damn things.

The Pontiac came out of a curve and Luther buried the brakes to keep from running past the wrecker and out of Mississippi. We stopped next to the driver's side of the abandoned wrecker, its doors open, engine running. FBI bullet holes peppered the door.

I jumped out and aimed the M-79 into the empty cab of the wrecker. I had an urge to waste the interior just for the hell of it. I didn't though. It wasn't worth the endless paper work explaining to FBIHQ why I'd gone to war against the empty front seat of a truck. There wasn't hide nor hair of the fugitives. No blood in the cab. No nothing.

Luther joined me, gun drawn. We stood there getting our bearings. There were thick woods in front of us. A wall of trees absorbed the headlights of the wrecker and the Bureau Pontiac. The other Bureau cars pulled in and lit up the place further. The woods were black as Mississippi tar. The fugitives had run off. We debated whether to pursue the fugitives or find an all night diner. Pursuit won, but the vote was close.

More FBI arrived, local cops too, and Mississippi State Police. Luther and I and a dozen other agents spread out and walked into the thicket of briars and needles. The long Bureau flashlights made us easy targets. We walked for a quarter mile or so, kept our voices down but made noise anyway, stepping on underbrush, announcing ourselves. The whole scene sucked. We had little hope of finding the fugitives in the dark. Plus, there were critters in the woods, just as there are fish in the ocean. I don't like to go into the woods or the ocean. Roughing it for me is running out of ice.

Luther called a halt to the search. We walked back to the highway to await daylight, then had another go with dogs and helicopters. I was glad to be out of the woods.

The sun brought heat, bloodhounds, and the FBI air force, piloted by agents flying a helicopter and a single engine plane over parts of Mississippi, Alabama, and Tennessee. There was no trace of the fugitives. The hounds lost their noses, the Bureau planes went to hangar. We stood down, exhausted. I had fire ants, mosquito bites, and a poison ivy leaf up my sleeve. I was not happy.

It was mid-afternoon when news came from McNairy County, Tennessee, just above the border with Alabama, that one of the fugitives, Thompson, had ridden a motorcycle into a rain-drenched field of honeysuckle trying to make his escape. The mud closed in on his tires and slowed him down. In desperation, he gunned the engine and attempted to run down a McNairy County Deputy Sheriff, who agilely stepped to the side of the cycle and swung the stock of a shotgun at Thompson's head, knocking him off the bike and into the mud, unconscious.

Six months later, the second fugitive, Singleton, was spotted by agents at a coin show in Huntsville, Alabama. He escaped again, fleeing to his girlfriend's place at a small motel in Florence, Alabama. He came out of the room later that night to get more beer and to call his wife. Luther Brannon had an arrest team waiting for him. I was downstate attending to something else and missed the fun, darn it. Singleton, who'd vowed never to be taken alive, was taken alive.

When Luther and the other agents arrived back in Birmingham, I joined them for a celebration at a local joint. Luther picked up the tab as usual. You can't have this kind of fun practicing law.

PART ONE

CHAPTER ONE

ORIGINS

I was born in Texas, raised in West Virginia, my draft board was in Pennsylvania, and I was about to graduate from the University of Alabama School of Law.

This personal information gave the FBI fits when it did the background investigation on me after I applied to be an agent at the start of my senior year in law school in the fall of 1968. The Bureau had to interview people in all those places, a small army of agents knocking on doors asking about my character, associates, reputation, and loyalty to the United States, or CARL, in Bureau speak. They must have said nice things about me.

My appointment letter signed by J. Edgar Hoover came in the mail in March, 1969. He ordered me to report for new agents class on June 23, 1969, in Washington, D.C.

The night the appointment letter arrived, I put on dark clothes and committed a burglary. I waited 'til midnight, quietly raised a dust-covered window and crawled into a warehouse across the street from my three-bedroom apartment in the married students complex at the University of Alabama. My accomplice, my younger brother Bob, was visiting us at the time. We had one flashlight between us.

The warehouse was full of the university's condemned furniture. I needed furniture. Bob helped me get it. We made off with a couple of easy chairs, a few end tables, a floor lamp, and a battered four-drawer empty file cabinet. There were lots of other goodies we just couldn't squeeze out the window, and the doors were padlocked. I regretted leaving a wonderful wooden desk that had character and a hundred years.

The next day, workmen from the university took axes and chopped up everything in the warehouse. My wife, Ginni, and I joined other married students and watched. It was sad. All that fine old furniture cut to pieces. I asked the University if I could buy a few pieces in the warehouse. The answer was no; it had to be destroyed; someone in Montgomery said so; there were no provisions for selling it; no forms for such a thing.

My brother left town right after the burglary. He'd heard bad things about Alabama jails.

Relaxing in one of the easy chairs my brother and I had pilfered, I listened to the stereo and watched my two small sons, Duane and Brett, play on the living room floor. They both had their mother's dark Italian looks. Ginni sat nearby in the other chair from the warehouse heist. My wife gently scolded me for stealing the furniture. What if the campus police had caught us? What would the FBI have done?

I told her that the Bureau wanted men with moxie. She pointed out that I didn't know a damned thing about the FBI other than what I'd seen in movies. She was right.

When I first saw Virginia Bonnie Madonna walking down the hall at the start of school in Fall 1960, I thought she was the Italian exchange student I'd been hearing about. She was fifteen, beautiful, exotic looking, long black hair, olive complexion. Her dad was second generation Italian-American, and her mom, pure Irish. She and her family had moved from New York to West Chester, Pennsylvania. She was low-key, calm, never raised her voice, and I loved her New York accent. She was an accomplished artist, and her drawings and paintings were remarkable. She was the only girl I knew who wore blue-green clothes and wanted to live in Alaska.

Ginni and I began dating the summer after I completed my freshman year at Concord College in West Virginia. She was fun, always up for a good time and ready to drive anywhere. She was terrific on the dance floor, too, an essential asset because I loved to dance. I did not date girls who could not dance. One evening I took Ginni to a drive-in movie and inadvertently pulled in next to her parents. We shrieked and sped away. Her parents laughed. Ginni and I went dancing.

We fell in love that summer, and I missed her when I returned to college in the fall. She accepted my invitation to come to Concord College for homecoming; I played in the game and Ginni sat in the stands with my friends. We partied all night with fellow TKE fraternity brothers and their dates, we watched the sun rise over Hinton Lake, and I showed her the West Virginia Bicentennial flag I had liberated from its flagpole there the previous spring as part of a fraternity rush stunt.

Being a full-time student without a job did not stop me from asking Ginni to marry me, and I proposed in the spring of 1964. We were married in a Methodist church in West Chester and honeymooned in Atlantic City, New Jersey.

I've always been interested in history and politics, so I decided to transfer from Concord College to American University in Washington, D.C. to be closer to the national political scene. Ginni and I moved to Baltimore. Ginni enrolled in art school while I commuted to American to complete my B.A. in Government. Then I summarily announced I was going to law school at the University of Alabama, and she did not object. We had our first son, Brett, just before I began my law studies in Tuscaloosa. Ginni, after a few days of homesickness, quickly adjusted to the Deep South. We lived in married housing without air conditioning. Our second boy, Duane, followed a year later. I disappeared for three years into the law library and left the care of the boys to Ginni. She steadfastly encouraged me in everything I did, even though she had to curtail her own artistic dreams and ambitions to take care of the boys and the house. She didn't even complain about the suffocating Alabama heat.

✶ ✶

So here I was with my letter of appointment from FBI Director J. Edgar Hoover. I'd never thought about a career in the FBI or any other law enforcement agency. Two of my uncles were cops in the coal fields of West Virginia. They broke up fights in bars and pool halls, and dodged firebombs during strikes around the mines. One of them directed traffic when the drive-in let out. I didn't want any part of that. Hoover's FBI was another matter. The Bureau had juice and glamour, and a worldwide rep for winning. Being an agent carried clout and glory. White-collar college boys with guns, wingtips, and badges. It looked like a lot of damn fun. Plus, I wouldn't have to take the bar exam.

At twenty-four, I signed on and loaded my stolen furniture in a van.

My yearbook photograph, University of Alabama School of Law, Class of 1969.

CHAPTER TWO

BEGINNERS

My first insight into the *real* FBI is a pair of shoes. I've just taken my alphabetically assigned seat in a classroom with fifty other new agents. It is June 23, 1969 and we are New Agents Class #17, or simply, NAC #17. It's our first hours of training, our introduction into life in the Bureau. Our classroom is located on the sixth floor of the Old Post Office, known as the OPO, a Washington landmark along Pennsylvania Avenue. The building has an atrium that reaches to the sky, the entire height of the building. The Bureau's Washington Field Office, WFO, has the second floor. The Voice of America, once headed by Edward R. Murrow, is on the first floor.

The class counselors are veteran agents William Brown and Charles Parkis. Brown takes the floor and welcomes us to Washington. He warns that agents should wear wingtip shoes in the best American and Bureau tradition. He smiles when he says this. I look down; Brown is wearing loafers. I know I've taken the right job.

I stand with my classmates and swear an oath to uphold the Constitution. When the class mingles over a break, I notice that many of the agents do not have accents, that is, they're Southerners, like me. Those *with* accents seem like all right stand-up guys and Coke drinkers, but they seem in a hurry. They complete forms quicker, rush their speech, raise their hands faster, and finish ahead of me at the urinals.

There are other NAC's training up and down the halls. NAC #17 are the rookies this week, but in fourteen days a new class will be sworn in, letting us off the hook as the latest fresh meat. The FBI will hire a thousand new agents during the spring, summer, and fall months of 1969, another thousand in 1971, the largest hiring frenzy to that date in Bureau history. President Nixon wants a beefed up FBI to combat organized crime. In two years, there will be Watergate, and agents will be investigating organized crime in the Nixon White House.

The agent sitting next to me in class is Jim Procopio from New York City. He's full of himself, confident, ready for bear like most New Yorkers. We hit it off right away. He doesn't blink when I tell him about watching a high school buddy lose his virginity to a hooker one night in a hotel on the upper West Side. You can't ambush guys from the City; they're always ahead of you. Jim tells me he's never heard of the University of Alabama School of Law. I tell him we have a library to go with the traffic light.

I become fast friends with classmate Ed Tickel. He's from the South with a background in chemistry, the son of a veteran FBI agent, and married with two daughters. Tickel has an oversized personality and sense of humor, and drives a souped up Chevy he built from the ground up. He's fun to be with. We fall in with Richard Procop, also a family man and a former cop from San Diego, and Tickel invites Procop and me for a ride through the D.C. streets after class. He says he can talk his way out of speeding tickets, and regardless, can outrun anything the Metropolitan Police Department has on the road. I immediately accept Tickel's invitation. Procop, the ex-cop, mumbles something and edges away from us.

The counselors hand out badges, the gold shields we'll carry for the rest of our careers. The number on the back of mine is 5362. The front of the badge displays an eagle over an engraved *Federal Bureau of Investigation*. The counselors tell us not to pin on the badges but to buy leather cases for our suit pockets.

The first day consists mainly of fifty-minute lectures with ten-minute breaks. I have numerous opportunities to size up my classmates, decide that I'm the youngest at 24 and one of the few lawyers in the class. Most agents come from backgrounds in business, the military, law enforcement, sales, or education, even though the FBI touts itself as being a club for lawyers and accountants. The basic requirement was at least a college degree. Hoover demanded it. Many agents had far more education than BA or BS degrees. Cops and other federal law enforcement could not match the credentials and communication skills that agents brought to the job.

Although our backgrounds are diverse, we blend nicely behind the metal classroom desks, conforming to the Bureau's cookie cutter: fifty-one clean cut, short-haired white guys in dark suits, white shirts, and quiet ties. Many of us are married. There are no hippies, no anti-war demonstrators. I support the war in Vietnam, but don't care to fight in it. I'll carry the flag in the FBI, keep the home front safe, protect West Virginia from Virginia, arrest draft dodgers and deserters who don't want to go to Vietnam. The class has one thing in common: we all have driver's licenses. I look forward to speeding around in one of those roomy, black Bureau Fords.

Seven of us wear glasses, mine appearing the thickest. I cheated on the eye exam during the medical exam to enter the Bureau: when the Army doctor at Ft. McClellan took a long lunch and left me in the waiting room, I helped myself to his office and memorized the eye chart. The FBI was looking for agents who showed initiative.

One of my classmates, Michael Irwin, was captain of the Penn State football team. He reminds me that State beat Bear Bryant's Alabama squad in the 1958 inaugural Liberty Bowl in Philadelphia. I tell Irwin the reason I went to law school at the University of Alabama was to watch the Crimson Tide play. Irwin laughs, says he can't think of any other reason to go to Alabama. I tell him that Penn State is a cow college like Auburn.

The first day creeps along with a numbing array of boring speakers handing out endless forms that choke the life out of your writing hand. Ink is the narcotic of the FBI. Before dismissing class, the counselors say we should think of ourselves as *special,* that Mr. Hoover himself set the right tone for characterizing the high caliber of men who become FBI agents. When asked by a reporter to define the average agent, Director Hoover replied, "There *are* no average agents."

I join Ed Tickel and others for rounds of beers at a bar in the Harrington Hotel, where most of the class is staying, and which has been an FBI all-round agents' hangout for decades because it's cheap and close to FBI Headquarters. The Bureau calls this *temporary quarters.* We will split our time between the city and the FBI Academy on the Marine Corps Base at Quantico, Virginia. The Academy is a three-story brick building on Main Side at the Base. We'd be there off and on for three of the sixteen weeks. FBI firing ranges are ten miles away, deep inside the Base.

Some of the married agents in the class have their families with them in apartments. To save money, Ginni and the boys stay with her parents in North Carolina until I finish training. I kind of put them on hold while I revel in being in the Bureau, and only see them twice during the entire four months I am at Quantico. I just want to do this thing, it seems to me at the time, and I have little patience or interest in anything or anyone else.

After numerous drinks at the Harrington bar, Tickel decides not to test his Chevy against the D.C. police that evening. We drink into the night, new agents armed with beers and badges.

CHAPTER THREE

Basic Training

NAC #17 changes classrooms later in the first week. We move from the OPO down Pennsylvania Avenue a few blocks to the fifth floor of FBI Headquarters in the Department of Justice building. Our classroom is just down the hall from Mr. Hoover's office, and he got his first look at us during one of our ten-minute hall breaks. We relax and shoot the breeze, lean against the walls, drink Cokes, mill around in circles. No one in the class sees Hoover sizing us up; if we had, we would have braced ourselves. Only a fool would irritate J. Edgar Hoover.

We file back into the classroom. Our two counselors, Brown and Parkis, follow us in. Parkis tells us in a grave voice that Mr. Hoover is not pleased, not pleased at all. Parkis seems on the verge of tears. Brown is hiding his face behind one of those thick FBI manuals; I suspect he is laughing. Parkis says that Director Hoover is put out with the way we are starting our careers. We were not *aggressive* in the hallway. Agents are always *aggressive*, even on breaks. Mr. Hoover has ordered that NAC #17 be more *aggressive*.

Mr. Hoover has the disquieting habit of observing our class without our seeing him. Example: I join classmates for sandwiches in the Department of Justice courtyard at noon. We sit in and out of the shade, shoot the breeze, and watch the ladies. Hoover spies some of us toting our lunches in brown bags, and he is not

15

pleased. The word comes down to our counselors to put an immediate stop to this brown-bagging heresy. Minutes after The Word comes down about brown bags, Brown and Parkis tell us that Director Hoover will not tolerate agents carrying their lunches in brown bags. Brown bags are unprofessional. The practice must stop now! Today! *Agents don't brown-bag!* There are sounds of shoes against paper as we slide our bagged lunches farther under our metal chairs. I covertly push mine under Procop's desk.

We've just begun our lives as agents, and we've already pissed off J. Edgar Hoover. Stories circulate around the class about new agents disappearing overnight during training. They were there one day, gone the next. Nothing was ever said about why they vanished. I visualize a midnight visit from the Director's men, flashlights in my face, ordering me out of the FBI because of unbecoming, unaggressive, un-Bureau-like behavior around the Coke machines. I resolve to spend my breaks in the toilet.

J. Edgar Hoover had headed the FBI since 1924, and agents feared him and his unlimited power—he would fire you on impulse or transfer you on a whim—but he had turned the FBI into a tight-ass, disciplined operation from top to bottom. He hired damned good people and dared them not to perform. Hoover's unrestrained power put fear in agents and kept it there. Screw up and you were gone or working in some backwater. I played the game and did the paperwork because I wanted to be an FBI agent. But something also happened to me along the way, my thirty years on the street. Case after case, arrest after arrest, one confession and signed statement after another, I realized that our way, Hoover's way, got results.

Ed Tickel and I go bar hopping at night after class, sample the downtown taverns in Washington, a city the Bureau refers to as the SOG, *Seat of Government*. One evening after drinks we make our way to the garage where Tickel shelters his Chevy. The first thing I notice is that there is no carpet on the floor of the Chevy. Tickel warns me he's replaced the entire floor of the car with a lighter metal, which puts out enough heat to light up your soles. I think he's kidding.

Tickel's a free spirit, a glad-hander and arm squeezer who never meets a stranger. His charismatic personality has made him the most visible and popular guy in NAC #17. The D.C. women love his dark good looks and Southern accent. He stops women on the street or in elevators or over lunch and says, "Hi, I'm Ed Tickel." He's then off and running, one woman after another on his arm. I shake my head in amazement. His wife is out of the know back home.

Tickel deftly handles the floor stick shift and runs the Chevy through its paces. Washington's Constitution Avenue is a straight-away, which Tickel treats like a drag strip. The floor quickly heats up and I lift my feet.

We finish cruising the city and head out of town. Tickel opens up the Chevy on I-95 south, buries the needle against the right side of the speedometer. The Chevy blows away every car on the interstate. I stick my feet up on the dash because the floor feels like white heat. Tickel laughs at my discomfort. I don't worry about Virginia State Troopers because we're FBI agents and Tickel is invincible. I'm confident he could preach his way out of hell.

It's very late when we get back to the garage. I call Ginni at home and tell her I've had a typical day in the FBI.

We bunk eight agents to a room in the dorm at the Academy on the Quantico Marine Corps Base. Storage space is severely limited, so we pretty much live out of our suitcases. We spend most of our training time in our Washington, D.C. apartments, so it's no big deal roughing it at Quantico. We sit in a classroom in ties and white shirts when we're not out on the firearms ranges in our painter's gray. Classes eye each other suspiciously and don't mingle, content to ignore each other in the spirit of tribes.

All dorm rooms at the Academy have gray metal trash cans. The cans are shiny and pristine, as though no trash has ever soiled them. They are crisp and clean like the Bureau. A worn type-written note is tacked on the door of every dorm room. We are warned that the floors must be swept at all times, surfaces must be free of dust, including any exposed metal, head and foot, on the eight single bunk beds in each room. Then the kicker: *Trash cans must be free of trash* for daily room inspections by the Academy staff. The maintenance crew empties the cans periodically, but not always ahead of the inspections. This presents a problem: what the hell do we do with the trash?

We get it: the FBI does not like trash. We hide trash anywhere we can before inspections. Cracker and candy wrappers, empty Coke cans, banana and apple peels, all are stowed out of sight or flushed down toilets. Afterwards, we gently deposit trash in the beautiful metal cans.

It's our first day of firearms, and we're two weeks into the four months of training. We spent days in the classroom dry-firing revolvers with handles painted red to show that the firing pins have been removed so they won't fire. Now it's the real thing. The entire class is lined up on the blacktop in the July heat on the FBI Firearms Ranges deep inside the Marine Corps Base at Quantico, Virginia. The immaculate and manicured ranges are ten miles away from the three-story red brick FBI Academy building where we bunk, eat, and sit with government-issue ballpoints for classroom lectures.

The FBI issue Smith & Wesson .38 six round revolver feels like dead weight in my right hand. We're about to fire our first FBI bullets, and all weapons are pointed downrange toward upper torso targets twenty-five yards away. I know the revolver is going to kick and make noise. There's cotton in my ears.

I have never fired a gun. There were no guns in the house when I was growing up in West Virginia and Pennsylvania. My dad was a football coach, a college professor with a love for politics and labor unions, who did not hunt or fish. My mother taught third grade and has a passion for books and the English language. My younger brother and I grew up in a gym and on the sidelines of football games. The talk at dinner was about first downs, FDR, and Shakespeare. I don't know when deer season begins or how many weeks you can shoot wild turkeys.

All fifty-one members of NAC #17 are dressed in range gray pants and shirts. We look like house painters. I'm nervous about this firearms stuff, worried that I'll shoot my foot off. I hear distant rifle and artillery fire. The Marine ranges are not far away; the Corps is preparing its officer candidates for Vietnam.

"Ready on the right," our instructor says from the tower at the back of the range. I cut my eyes to the right. The class is lined up nicely, strung out in our grays like Pickett at Gettysburg.

"Ready on the left," the instructor continues on the PA system from the tower. I look to the left. All is well on the left. I'm not out too far or behind.

"All ready on the firing line," the instructor announces.

Although I'm a lefty in kicking, batting, holding a fork, turning magazine pages from back to front, combination locks, and knocking my brother around, I decide to shoot right-handed. The reason is the way the FBI teaches firearms. The instructors give detailed pointers on how to grip and fire a .38 revolver. As an afterthought, they say, "And you left-handers, it's just the opposite." Since I write and throw right-handed, it's no big deal for me to shoot starboard side. I figure that anything *left* is out of fashion in Hoover's FBI.

The temperature is in the nineties There's no shade on the range. Sweat rolls off my forehead. My glasses fog up. I hold my breath, which, we are told, is integral to good shooting, but I may have started too early. I'm nearly out of breath. I need to breathe. I wish the instructor would hurry up. My arms are extended toward the target twenty-five yards away. "Fire!"

I cock the .38 with my thumb, single-action firing as instructed. Single action is a shorter trigger pull, making it easier to keep the sites on the target. After we've practiced more, we'll fire double-action, which is pulling the trigger all the way back without cocking.

I put pressure on the trigger. Guns go off up and down the line. They sound like fire-crackers. My gun suddenly fires. You should be surprised when the gun goes off, the instructors said. I wonder how damned surprised I'm supposed to be. Right now I'm too surprised.

It gets quiet on the range. I look at my target, and there's no sign of me—no bullet hole. I steal a look at other targets. My neighbors have holes. Something is wrong with my gun.

"Holster your weapons," the tower commands. I shove the .38 back into my Bureau-issue tan leather Sloan holster. My right arm shakes from muscle tension. I'm too uptight; I need to relax and cool it. Classmate Wilbur Ramsey, a high school teacher and football coach from Tennessee, is all smiles. His round is dead center in the target body mass. I hate people from Tennessee.

I shake my arms trying to get loose. I picture Marshal Dillon on Gunsmoke, arms at his side, ready to kick ass. The tower starts up again, ready on the right, ready on the left. I look down the site of the revolver. The shiny blue barrel is dancing without a partner. My nerves have gone south. I feel as though I'm attending my own execution.

On command, I cock and squeeze off a round, re-holster, look down range and pray. My prayer is answered. I plugged the left arm of my victim. It's not a kill shot but I'll take it.

We have an hour for lunch, which usually bleeds into more than an hour, but no one's keeping score out here in the woods. The kitchen specializes in hot lunches, because we eat breakfast and dinners back at the FBI Academy, Main Side. The food is excellent and served cafeteria-style. We sit in our grays and have at it, then mosey over to the shade under trees near the chow hall across from the ranges. The grass and grounds are maintained to perfection, neat, buttoned up, a showplace for VIPs who come here from all over the world to watch us shoot. We don't have visitors today, just other classes at various stages of firearms training. We ignore them and congregate at the horseshoe pits under a grove of trees. Tickel and I usually partner up, win more than we lose. The city guys, many of them Yankees, are pathetic at horseshoes. They grew up playing stickball or hockey. We play horseshoes, relax and shoot the bull, waiting 'til it's time to fire again.

NAC #17 now feels quite at home at the firearms ranges. We're six weeks into training, ten to go. I'm shooting well, plenty good enough to qualify on the timed revolver courses. The black-top firing lanes are hot in the summer. The courses are set at distances of 60 yards down to 7 yards. The average distance in Bureau gunfights over the years has been 7 yards, just 21 feet, which seems uncomfortably close to me. Hell, it's not even a first down.

We shoot standing, prone, kneeling, and from the hip. Cover is simulated by firing from behind barricades, removable wooden poles set up on the range. We take turns firing the courses and watching each other shoot. There's plenty of peer pressure with everyone staring at you. You try not to shoot the barricades themselves, but I've done it, denying like hell.

No one in the class has yet fired a *Possible,* the Bureau term for a perfect score. Shooting a *Possible* requires that you put all 50 rounds into the K-5 or kill area of the body mass silhouette target. It's a big deal in the FBI. A memo goes into your permanent personnel file at Headquarters, and you get an atta-boy letter from Mr. Hoover. Your photograph standing next to the perfect target is published in *The Investigator,* the Bureau's in-house monthly magazine. The closest I have come is a 92. I would never again shoot any better than that in my career. Tickel and Procop are damn good shots, shooting in the high nineties. The instructors score our targets, but not before we've had a close-up look at them. If you're having a bad day shooting, you can freshen up your score by punching strategic holes in your target with a black government-issue ballpoint pen, which looks wonderfully like a hole made by a .38 bullet.

The class fires wad cutter bullets instead of regular bullets, which the Bureau calls *service* ammunition. Service ammo is for the street. Wad cutter has a flat nose and is for target practice only. It is not something to toy with. Wad cutter will kill you.

I give full credit for my proficiency in firearms to our primary instructor, Bob Cohrs. He's in charge of NAC #17 at the range and is assisted by other instructors when we fire. The firearms gurus at Quantico take turns guiding classes through training. These guys are seasoned hands and remarkable marksmen, profane, tobacco chewing old Bureau. They are assigned permanently to the range, one of the FBI's cushion jobs. They landed this plum by doing something in the field to please Director Hoover. Once anointed, instructors tend to stay at Quantico forever, lifetime appointments like federal judges. Cohrs is ours for the duration of our training. He has a Yankee accent, but not New York. He won't tell us where he's from.

"It won't fucking kick," said Bob Cohrs, the firearms instructor for NAC #17. He nonchalantly held a Thompson submachine gun in one hand. "You can fire it off your fucking chin," he said. Yeah, well, fucking show me, I thought. I was certain the big gun would recoil like crazy.

The class was on one of the firearms ranges at Quantico, and we all watched as Cohrs expertly fired the Thompson from every conceivable position, including his chin. He demonstrated the proper grip, taking charge of the weapon like you'd manhandle a truck without power steering. If you don't lean forward when you fire a burst of rounds, feet widely spaced, left foot forward for right–handers, the Thompson will climb into the heavens, the rounds walk right up a wall. If you get a pansy grip on the Thompson you could shoot at someone coming through a door and take out the ceiling light instead.

The class took turns firing the Thompson, clip after clip of .45 rounds that left big holes in the targets. Cohrs went through the nomenclature of the gun, tore one down and put its many pieces back together in no time. He showed us diagrams of the Thompson and mentioned its storied history in the FBI. I had images of movie gangsters and 1930s G-men in wide-brimmed hats going at each other from cars with running boards.

After the class got thoroughly familiar with the Thompson, Cohrs took us under one of the open air sheds. We practiced disassembling and assembling the weapon over and over. We then paired off for a test on the old wooden tables that smelled of Hoppies, the liquid gun cleaner. Each team had a weapon; Tickel and I were partners. Cohrs told the class to tear down the Thompson, put it back together and be quick about it.

Tickel had grown up firing the Thompson, since his dad was an FBI agent. Tickel flew at the gun and had it broken down in no time, our table littered with its innards. I looked busy and didn't get in his way. He completed assembling the gun in no time. We stood smugly by as the other teams finished up.

I looked down. There was an ever so small metal piece about to scream for attention. A piece from the guts of the Thompson. Tickel quickly pocketed it, slapped me on the shoulder in triumph. You had to love the guy. Somewhere in the bowels of an FBI gun vault, there's a Thompson submachine gun that won't fire. Don't look at *me*.

✷ ✷

Cohrs relishes the F word. His foul mouth stings like a bumble bee coming after you off the tar-coated train trestle in Jenkinjones, West Virginia.

We fired the rifles all morning and would pick up where we left off after lunch. Cohrs says to be ready to fire at 100 yards.

The class does a slow walk in the heat across the grass from the horseshoe pits to the rifle range. A tunnel borders the left edge of the rifle range. It's not really a tunnel, but a grass-covered hump in the landscape that's used to store ammunition and to serve as a walkway to the 100-yard and 200-yard targets. It's climate controlled and cool in order to keep the ammo happy, and a refreshing stroll for us out of the Virginia heat. There's plenty of headroom in the tunnel. You walk past endless boxes of ammo and naked light bulbs that constantly burn overhead. When I'm in the tunnel, I get a twinge of WWII history, imagining that I'm with the British in the tunnels of Gibraltar or beside MacArthur in the underground maze at Corregidor. I'm full of shit.

I join a dozen or so members of the class and walk through the tunnel to the 100-yard targets. We spread out in the butts, the safe pit area below the targets. When we fire, half the class is in the butts while the other half fires the rifles. Those in the butts raise and lower the metal frames holding the targets, checking to see where the rounds went. We raise long poles with different colored discs, or paddles, the size of a tennis racket head to show the shooters the location of their bullets. Viewed from the firing deck, the paddles poke up and down like ground hogs. A red paddle is for bullets in the kill area of the target. The paddle called

"Maggie's Drawers" is pink, meaning the shooter has missed altogether.

Today, while waiting for Cohrs to finish lunch in the range cafeteria, the class has an inspired idea. We decide to play a trick on Cohrs by turning the targets upside down on the rifle range. We quickly turn all the black silhouette targets upside down, leaving them in the lowered position where they can't be seen from the tower. Giddy with anticipation, we head back through the tunnel to the firing deck. We emerge from the cool into the furnace of a Quantico August. In high spirits, we mill around the covered hardtop rifle deck waiting for Cohrs.

He shows a few minutes later, gives out the assignments for who will shoot first and who will man the butts at 100 yards. Luckily, I'm going to be shooting first. Half the class heads into the tunnel to the butts. I settle into a firing position on the rifle deck.

We wait for Cohrs to get comfy in the range tower, where he sees all. From the rifle deck, we give each other knowing smiles. In the tower, Cohrs has a PA system to announce his commands, and a telephone to the butts. We can see Cohrs through the open tower window. The PA is on and we can hear him on the phone. I grin and face the targets.

"Raise the targets," Cohrs commands into the phone.

The targets slowly rise. They squeak on the way up. I sneak a peek at Cohrs. He's focused on down range. The silhouette targets rise into full bloom, waists first, then the heads.

No one says a word. Twenty-five upside down targets at 100 yards. I'm about to bust. Everyone looks at Cohrs. He eyes the targets, expressionless. He carefully pulls out a fresh cigar and bites off the end. He spits out a piece of tobacco, removes a silver lighter and ceremoniously lights up. He slowly puts the lighter away, draws deeply on the cigar. Smoke fills the tower and spills out into the humidity. Every eye is on Cohrs. He takes the cigar out of his mouth.

"All right gentlemen," he says. "Stand on your fucking heads and load."

CHAPTER FOUR

HOGAN'S ALLEY

The head of the firearms ranges at the FBI Academy during the NAC #17 summer of 1969 was the legendary Bureau figure, George Zeiss. Zeiss was a big man, well over six feet, handsome, with a full head of graying dark hair. He might have played tackle for the Washington Redskins. Standing in front of a seated class of new agents, Zeiss took up a room by himself, rolling his head from side to side. He spoke to the heavens and to Hoover and to us. He looked like an agent, whatever that was, and had been handpicked by Hoover to collect the assassin of Dr. Martin Luther King, James Earl Ray, from Scotland Yard in England where he had been captured, and transport him back to Memphis to stand trial for the murder of Dr. King. Photographs of Zeiss in manly control of the handcuffed Ray were in newspapers around the world. TV coverage was endless, the John Wayne-like Zeiss just the ticket for the image-obsessed Hoover. Zeiss was no dummy. He knew not to hot dog it too much, or else he'd anger Hoover. The Director did not like individual agents getting more publicity than Hoover himself, or the Bureau. Zeiss always gave credit to Hoover for the FBI's successes. With a thousand new agents being hired in 1969, Zeiss couldn't personally handle all the classes, so he delegated to subordinates like Bob Cohrs.

The official name for this training class was Surprise Target Course, but agents knew it simply as Hogan's Alley, a block of storefronts like you'd find in any USA town. Agents trained by walking slowly past the storefronts to confront *shoot* or *don't shoot* situations armed with .38 revolvers loaded with blanks. The idea was for an agent to walk down the alley with his gun holstered and be confronted with life-sized friendly or unfriendly cardboard figures in the windows and doors of the alley. You had to make on-the-spot decisions about whether or not to shoot.

One hot summer day right before lunch, NAC #17 lined up for its training session at Hogan's Alley. We milled around in our gray uniforms out of sight of the Alley and waited our turns to be called one at a time. You couldn't watch your classmates until after you'd finished the course. The whole point was to confront and react. Zeiss sat in the ground level booth alongside Cohrs. The pop-up targets were controlled from the booth. Cohrs had the mic for the PA system. Zeiss liked to watch agents make asses of themselves at Hogan's Alley. Before taking the walk down the Alley, we studied mug shots of bad guys so we'd know their faces if they showed themselves along the Alley. I waited my turn.

I left the staging area when my name was called, felt the butterflies suck on my stomach, and headed down the Alley. Classmates who'd already taken the course were in the bleachers living it up watching the agents who followed them. I wished I'd been first. Cohrs' voice barked over the PA ordering me to start. I grew more nervous. I could hear the buzz of my classmates in the stands waiting for me to screw up. I slowly walked down the side-walk that paralleled the Alley. I was confronted by cardboard figures in windows and doors, drew my weapon each time, stopped, fired or didn't fire, and continued. I was correct each time, shot bad guys, didn't shoot innocents. I was nearly finished.

A bad guy flashed into view in a doorway. I drew, fired, holstered, smug as hell, and then looked again. The bad guy I'd just shot had his arms in the air to surrender.

There were hoots and catcalls from my classmates. Deaf and dumb from embarrassment, I barely heard Cohrs say something or other about fucking up. Zeiss was laughing. I went up in the stands to hide and heckle the next guy.

CHAPTER FIVE

GRADUATION

NAC #17 did not go quietly through the four months of training. We rebelled against the FBI's dress code, the suffocating white shirt, dull tie uniform. Toward the end of training, we organized a *colored shirt* day for a session in the Old Post Office classroom. Hoover was out of sight down Pennsylvania Avenue at FBIHQ and didn't have an office in the OPO; he wouldn't see us.

Our class counselors got wind of what we were planning and pretended not to know. They had loosened up considerably since that first day, Parkis especially, the counselor who wore wing tips. He laughed along with us, while Brown in his loafers had always seemed a rebel. We came to realize they had nothing to gain by shepherding NAC #17, and we grew to respect them and covet their friendship. We also wouldn't have done anything to get them into real trouble. They looked the other way on *colored shirt* day.

I wore a blue buttoned-down shirt—not very radical, but blue was the only other color I owned. Classmates wore yellow, green, and one even showed up in purple.

We filed into the classroom high up in the OPO atrium wearing 51 non-white shirts. The other new agent classes up and down the hall stared at us in disbelief. They looked dull and washed out in their Bureau whites. We thought we were hot stuff, peasants revolting against the Czar. If Hoover ever found out about the colored shirts, nothing was said to us about it.

Tickel and I continued to speed around Washington in his hot Chevy, daring the Bureau gods to find out about it. We partied with other classmates at the two swimming pools on the roof of our apartment complex in downtown Washington. A few weeks before the completion of training in late September 1969, every member of NAC #17 received his assignment to one of the Bureau's 59 field offices. We were about to morph from agents-in-training to First Office Agents, FOAs. The class was in a festive mood. We were all going to make it through training unless someone screwed up in a major way.

We walked one by one to the front of the classroom in alphabetical order through a gauntlet of catcalls. It was fiesta time high up in the Old Post Office. The counselors were in a great mood also, having survived the minefield of being close to Hoover without being fired. They handed out sealed business envelopes with our names typed on the front. We opened the envelopes like it was the Academy Awards.

The FBI's largest field office, New York City, where one out of every eight agents worked, was off the table. The Bureau didn't send FOAs to New York, at least officially. Hoover wanted us to get experience in a smaller environment where we would receive more individual supervision, although Headquarters could send agents, including FOAs, anywhere it wanted. New York was always in need of manpower because so many agents quit after being there a while, or resigned before even reporting. There were no salary allowances for the high cost of living in the City, and no one in the class wanted to go there, including the New Yorkers. When my turn came, I walked to the front of the class and tore into my envelope: *Denver.* Yeah! I was pleased. I'd never been to Colorado. Hell, I was ready to go anywhere because I liked this job so much. I also loved not having to practice law. Tickel was transferred to San Antonio, and Procop, the ex-cop from San

Diego, was also going to Denver. City after city came up, sending the class in all directions around the U.S.

Butte, Montana, on the other hand, was a dreaded place for agents. It was an ugly city with a large copper quarry in the middle of town, a dull, lifeless Bureau venue in terms of interesting cases. No one in NAC #17 wanted to go to Butte. Hoover knew that Butte was a shit hole and sent agents there who had screwed up. The class would sing the mangled lyrics to the Four Seasons classic: "I'm working my way back to Butte, babe."

One by one we walked to the front of the classroom to receive our assignments. We got to the last agent, Frank Zapalac, known affectionately as Zappy. No one had gotten New York or Butte. Zappy opened his envelope. Butte. The class roared. Zappy gave us the finger.

NAC #17 did not formally meet Hoover during our tenure in training. I was disappointed. He was an historic figure and a national icon. We did not get to experience the official *handshake* with Hoover in his office, a decades old FBI tradition endured by new agents. He had discontinued the practice in 1969 because of the historic number of agents hired that year, one thousand in all. I was confident that I would do well shaking his hand and introducing myself, but our two counselors knew the perils of walking into the Director's office. Agents had been fired for not *looking like an agent,* whatever that meant. Rumor was that agents had been fired for having sweaty palms during the handshake. There was a rumor that a new agent had been axed because his head was too small. Neither counselor would confirm the pinhead rumor, but counselor Brown cat-grinned when I asked him, so I knew it was true.

All fifty-one members of NAC #17 completed training. No one flunked out or disappeared overnight. The Bureau's creed mirrored that of the University of Alabama football coach Paul "Bear" Bryant: *Be good or be gone.*

There was no formal graduation ceremony to mark the end of training. We finished class one afternoon in the Old Post Office and that was it. We milled around saying goodbye to each other and to the counselors. I had really bonded with some of my classmates, and had affection and respect for Parkis and Brown. We promised to write and keep in touch through the FTS, the Federal Telephone Service, connecting the fifty-nine FBI field offices around the country. We couldn't have conceived of it at the time, but many of us would not see each other again. Our careers took us on paths that kept us apart. We'd been through four intense months of preparation for a life-changing job, and it was time to get on with it. We evacuated Washington, D.C. *en masse* and scattered to our respective field offices. Procop and I headed separately for Denver with our families.

The last thing I did in training was to sail a paper airplane off the sixth floor of the OPO. I watched it float aimlessly in the hot air of the atrium 'til it disappeared into the second level of the FBI's Washington Field Office.

PART TWO

CHAPTER SIX

DENVER

I drove to Denver in the family car and checked into a motel, "temporary quarters". Ginni and the boys flew into Denver's Stapleton Airport several days later. After registering at the motel late that first afternoon, I immediately changed into a suit and drove to the Bureau's perch in a high-rise building downtown on Stout Street. I was keyed up, ready for bear, armed with a .38 revolver and special agent credentials showing my face next to *FBI* in bold blue letters. I was thoroughly confident that I could do the job.

I walked into the office through the reception room, showed my creds and was escorted by one of the receptionists to the fugitive squad area where I'd been assigned. I met my supervisor, who introduced me to the other agents, many of them fellow FOAs. The agents and clerks were friendly, including the old timers. One FOA, Bob Rogers, would become a life-long friend. Richard Procop, my NAC #17 classmate, had not yet arrived in Denver with his family. He had been assigned to the organized crime squad, so we would not be working together on a daily basis.

My supervisor told me to spend the next few days finding a place to live, then report back ready to get to work. I was given a wooden workbox filled with cases assigned to me, most of them fugitive investigations, either deserters from the armed forces or Selective Service violators who were trying to evade the draft.

31

Vietnam was sucking up American blood and treasure in the fall of 1970, an increasingly unpopular war with young men subject to the draft, particularly college-age students. There were thousands of young men around the country who opposed the war in Vietnam and violated federal law by circumventing the system to stay out of the armed forces. One of my law school classmates at the University of Alabama had low grades after the first year, dropped out of school, went into the Army, and was killed in action in Vietnam. His twin brother graduated with me and entered on duty as an agent several months after I started. A third classmate also became an agent in 1969. There were years when the University of Alabama led the nation in supplying agents to the FBI.

I moved my family into a small basement apartment on South Irving Street west of downtown Denver. It was two bedrooms and cramped, but we knew it would be only a year before I was transferred to my second office. I'd be an FOA for twelve months.

I was assigned to an experienced agent my first full day on the job. He was going to be my training agent for two weeks before I struck out on my own. I would help him work his cases and he would assist on mine. The agent I drew was the spitting image of former president Lyndon Johnson. Johnson was essentially forced from office because of Vietnam. The joke in the Denver FBI office was that the Johnson look-alike was going to be assassinated. None of the agents wanted to be near him in public.

I hit the streets with him the first day. We worked an impersonation case, a "47 matter" in Bureau parlance, an investigation of a guy who had identified himself as an FBI agent in a downtown store and had requested financial records. The store became suspicious and called the office when the guy showed phony-looking credentials.

Agent impersonators agitated Hoover no end. He rightly wanted the public to rely on our authentic credentials, and only those. Hoover would not even permit agents to carry business cards because anyone could have cards printed with the letters FBI on them. Those three letters could not be used without Bureau permission.

On the way back to the office, the agent asked me about my background, so I tested his sense of humor. I told him I was from Birmingham and that I loved Alabama Crimson Tide football. Yeah, I loved the Tide so much I was going to issue a Government Travel Request, a GTR, and fly myself to Alabama at FBI expense to see the Tide play Tennessee in two weeks. Headquarters will never catch on to it, I assured my training agent. I also intended to issue a GTR in a month or so to see Alabama play Auburn in Birmingham. Damn, these GTRs were a hot item, I said. I leaned back in the BuCar with a satisfied look on my face.

I had a new training agent the next day.

I was assigned to an experienced agent who looked like Audie Murphy, the World War II Medal of Honor recipient who became a Hollywood star. How did I get so lucky as to be assigned two celebrity look-alikes in the Denver FBI? I rode with Audie Murphy to interviews on his cases, 52 matters, thefts of government property, the only investigations assigned to him. These cases were boring and made for a long day. Audie liked the slow pace of these cases, but I didn't. I wanted to chase folks and arrest them. He didn't want any part of my fugitive cases. I was itching to get away from him and on my own. I accompanied Audie into countless government office buildings, including the VA Hospital, where typewriters and TVs went missing. It was like watching paint dry.

One Friday afternoon, I got a lesson in winding down for the weekend. I was riding shotgun with Audie in downtown Denver when a FOA came on the FBI radio seeking assistance on an arrest of a deserter. Excited by the thought of going on my first arrest, I reached for the microphone to tell the FOA we would assist him. Audie grabbed my wrist. He shook his head *no*. Audie said the FOA had to learn not to stir the pot on a Friday afternoon. Too many things could go wrong and spill over into the weekend. Agents didn't make arrests on Friday afternoons, Audie told me. I thought he was full of baloney. I'd never heard of any such FBI practice. I didn't like it one bit, but I was new and I went along. I'm still ashamed of it. When my two weeks were over, I never worked with Audie Murphy again.

No other agent responded on the radio to the call for assistance by the FOA that Friday afternoon. He got a cop to help him make the arrest. It was not the Denver FBI's finest hour.

Nor mine.

During the year we lived in Denver I worked crazy hours tracking fugitives around town and up and down the Rockies. I loved it. I went to work, missed time at home when I *could* have been at home, and went looking for work that could have waited; I volunteered to assist other agents in their arrests and interviews. I wanted to be everywhere at once. I more and more put the Bureau first at the expense of spending time with my family. It was the start of a habit I came to regret. The truth is, I wanted to be everywhere but home.

CHAPTER   SEVEN

LEARNING THE ROPES

Part One

I got off to a bad start the second week in Denver when it
snowed a foot and I misjudged the time it would take to drive
into the office. I was late. The Special Agent in Charge, the SAC,
called me into his office and told me to get snow tires and never be late again. He eased up, made allowances because I was
from Alabama. I didn't tell him that I had driven for years in the
northeast.

The SAC had been in the FBI for ages, was the poster boy
for the Bureau in Colorado and Wyoming, the two states covered
by the Denver field office. He looked every bit the G-man, with
a full head of distinguished gray hair and a neatly trimmed mustache. Because he was a close friend of Director Hoover, the SAC
was the only agent allowed to wear a mustache. He made speeches
and showed up at bank robberies to be photographed by the press
and give interviews. In Hoover's FBI, only the SAC could speak
for a field office with the local press.

The Denver FBI office had several dozen FOAs, the Bureau's
version of a kindergarten for field training new agents. We worked
together and partied a lot, had a hell-raising time tearing around
the city and state. I was assigned to the fugitive squad and spent
my days tracking down and arresting draft dodgers, deserters, and

other federal bad guys. Classmate Procop was thriving on the organized crime squad.

My best friend, Bob Rogers, was an ex-Marine who had been in NAC #16 back in Washington. I hadn't met him during training because the classes didn't mix. Bob was married and had no children at the time. He was a man's man, a Marine captain in Vietnam, a Notre Dame graduate and an Irish Catholic New Yorker. His father ran a neighborhood bar in Manhattan. Although our backgrounds were quite dissimilar, we were examples of the grits-and-Pope mixture decking the halls of the FBI. The Bureau was overrun with Southern Protestants and Catholic Yankees.

Bob was a stand-up guy, smart, street wise, and a patriot. I immediately liked and enjoyed his oversized, in-your-face personality. We shared a love of books, history, and the armed forces. I was a Navy junkie, an Annapolis reject because my eyes were bad. Bob said Annapolis was full of pussies.

Bob loved Notre Dame football and was as obnoxious about it as I was about the Alabama Crimson Tide. The Irish had never played Alabama in football in 1969, so Bob and I had endless arguments about which team was better and had the more illustrious tradition. I pointed out that the two teams couldn't play each other in a post-season bowl game because the Irish refused to play in bowls. What a sack of manure I told Bob. The Catholic Fathers who ran the school said that bowls interfered with final exams. Bob said *so what*. Alabama was not Notre Dame.

Rogers and I worked fugitives together and spent our days successfully going after them, followed by long bouts of drinking beer and singing our schools' fight songs. I couldn't match him at the bar or on the track, nor in racquetball either. Our wives became close, the steady hands when we'd had too much grog. Bob and his wife served as a second set of parents to my two sons.

Bob and I teamed up early one morning for another go at arresting folks. After signing in at the office, we headed out in a Bureau car, BuCar, and had coffee with other FOAs at a downtown restaurant. Hoover prohibited coffee drinking on duty and there were no coffee pots in the FBI. Coffee wasted time, Hoover proclaimed. Which made drinking coffee on duty that much more fun. Agents couldn't work out on Bureau time either, but Bob and I paid no attention and hit the gym regularly. Screw Hoover, FBIHQ, and their stupid rules.

Rogers and I had our sights on a fugitive out of Texas based on leads from the Dallas FBI office. We drove east on Colfax Avenue through traffic lights and congestion. Colfax was straight as an arrow and went on for miles like Broad Street in Philadelphia. After a few dry holes trying to find our fugitive, we stopped at a restaurant where the fugitive was thought to have worked at one time. We didn't think he could possibly still be there, so we intended to go through the motions, interview the owner, then have lunch.

Bob and I walked into the crowded restaurant and came face to face with the fugitive. He was waiting tables at the front. There was no doubt who he was. Bob and I grabbed him and told him that he was under arrest. He protested and denied his identity. We braced him, pushed him up against a door for a spread eagle and a search, releasing him for just a split second. Trouble was, it was a swinging door and he bolted out onto the street.

Bob and I burst out of the restaurant right on his tail. The guy sprinted down the sidewalk in full view of a carefree Denver lunch crowd. People jumped back to get out of the way as two guys in suits ran after a guy in a waiter's uniform. Bob and I sprinted side by side, arms pumping, knees high. The fugitive had picked the wrong two agents to challenge. Bob and I worked out on a track every day. We were itching for a chase.

We chased him for one block, then two, not gaining on him, but not losing ground either. My suit coat felt like a straightjacket holding me back, so I yanked it off and dropped it on the sidewalk. Don't ask me how I did this while running at full speed. I have no memory of taking it off.

After a few more blocks the fugitive tightened up and slowed down, worn to a frazzle, as my grandmother would say. Bob and I ran right up his back and threw him to the sidewalk, yanked both his arms behind his back, palms out. Bob cuffed him.

A marked Denver Police unit braked to a stop along the curb right next to us. A uniform got out, covered us with his gun and demanded to know what the hell was going on. Bob and I yelled that we were FBI making an arrest. *Show me something!* he said. Bob removed his agent credentials and flipped them open for the cop to see. I reflexively reached for my credentials but they were back there somewhere in my coat. Jesus! If I lose those credentials I'll be explaining the rest of my career, if I had a career. One of the biggest screw-ups in the Bureau was to lose your creds.

The cop holstered his weapon. *Need a ride?* he said.

Bob and I loaded the prisoner in the police unit. Bob got in the back with the prisoner and the cop drove them back to the restaurant where we'd left the BuCar. My heart was pounding from anxiety about my creds. I quickly retraced my steps on the sidewalk looking for my coat. I envisioned some dude finding my agent credentials and taking home the souvenir of a lifetime. Hoover would look into my file and remember an agent who brown-bagged his lunch and wasn't aggressive on breaks. I'd be in Butte in two days.

I ran up the sidewalk, spied my coat on the ground up ahead. Pedestrians walked by it like it wasn't there. I picked it up and rammed my hand inside, pulled out my credentials. There is a god.

After I retrieved my suit coat and credentials, Bob and I delivered our fugitive into the custody of the U.S. Marshals and hit the road. He was no longer our problem. We celebrated with a leisurely lunch and headed to the courts for some covert racquetball.

The U.S. Marshal deputies searched the fugitive, now prisoner, and locked him up in a holding cell until he could be transported to the city jail. They missed one small item in his pockets: a dime. While mulling his fate in the solitude of his cell, the prisoner removed the dime and used it to unscrew the screws holding the air duct vent in place in the wall. He quietly climbed inside the vent and crawled through the duct to the nearest opening.

One of the secretaries in the office of the United States Attorney was busy typing when she was startled by the air duct vent falling out of the wall. She stared in disbelief as a guy crawled out of the vent, calmly dusted himself off, smiled and told her in a business-like voice that he was working on the heating unit in the building. He apologized for the fuss, bid her farewell and left.

Bob and I finished our racquetball match, another miserable loss for me, and headed back to the office when word came over the FBI radio that our prisoner had escaped. We thought it was a joke. The office scrambled to find the escaped prisoner. Bob and I combed the city far into the night without result. We stopped by bars along Colfax Avenue and handed out photos of the fugitive. One bartender was my informant. He promised to keep an eye out. I didn't believe we had a chance in hell to nab our guy again. Would he be so stupid as to hang around Denver in a bar while the entire Denver FBI was looking for him? I'd be headed back to Texas if I were him. Either that or Mexico.

The following night the office called me at home to report that my informant had phoned to say that our man was enjoying drinks in a bar on Colfax at that very moment. My first reaction was to jump into the family car, pick up Bob at his place and speed to the bar. I couldn't do that because of an arcane FBI rule forbidding agents from taking BuCars home after work or con- ducting any business in one's personally-owned vehicle. I came within an inch of saying *up yours* to those stupid rules. Instead, I drove to the office, picked up a BuCar, then collected Bob at his apartment. The fugitive was long gone by the time Bob and I ar- rived at the bar.

I never saw or heard about that fugitive again in my career. He's still free as far as I know. Bob and I also never told the Bureau that we'd braced a guy against a door that opened out onto the street. It's all in how you write it up.

Part Two

The Denver FBI office had a load of experienced, savvy agents who knew their stuff. They solved bank robberies, thwarted kid- nappers, hunted down fugitives, and stayed in the knickers of Colorado's organized crime family. I admired those older agents, tried to emulate them, and sucked up to them.

My NAC #17 classmate, Dick Procop, was assigned to one of the office sages, Bill Malone. I envied the time Procop spent with Malone working organized crime. I picked Malone's brain at every opportunity, and sought his approval. He was generous with his time with me and the other FOAs. Veteran agents "Red" Nelson and Bob Bunch were cunning and accomplished investigators who took time to serve as mentors to the rookies in the office. I observed everything those guys did. I was grateful to them for giving me some seasoning.

Bunch had cut his law enforcement teeth in an Oakland PD uniform, got his detective's shield before switching to the feds. He worked bank robberies and was a street animal through and through. I wanted to be like him.

Bunch showed me how to conduct a proper line-up of suspects that would stand up in court under cross-examination. You had to put people of the same race and approximate age, height, and weight as the suspect in a line-up for viewing by a witness. Everyone in the line-up had to repeat verbatim what the suspect said in the bank during the robbery. Bunch used agents, cops, and anyone he could corral to stand up with a suspect in a line-up. He assigned witnesses to me and other FOAs to take them through the line-up process and interview them afterwards. Bunch was an agent's agent.

The unwritten rule in the Denver FBI office was that First Office Agents, FOAs, were not allowed to make arrests without calling in experienced agents. The rule was breached more than followed. FOAs made numerous arrests without the assistance of veteran agents.

Bob and I left the Denver office one fine Colorado morning and drove the BuCar west of town to the city of Golden where Coors beer was brewed. We were looking for a fugitive and made a few stops in neighborhoods where he'd once lived and worked. Another agent, an FOA, came on the FBI radio and requested assistance on an apprehension of a deserter. Bob responded on our radio, said we were close by and would help.

The supervisor who handled fugitives came on the air and waved us off, saying he wanted more experienced agents to join the arrest, and directed two veterans to respond to the FOA's request. Bob hit the ceiling, burning mad at the supervisor. I was steamed, too. Bob fumed all day, hadn't cooled off by the time we got back to the office. It didn't help our dispositions that we hadn't located our own fugitive that day. We headed straight for the supervisor's office when we got off the elevator. The supervisor's door was open. We walked in and confronted him.

Bob demanded to know why we'd been waved off an arrest. He didn't shout, but his deep New York accent carried, and I figured the secretary as least could hear us, probably others. Bob walked around the supervisor's desk and stared down at him, looking like he was going to strangle the guy. FOAs did not challenge supervisors in the FBI.

The supervisor calmly reminded Bob and me of the rule that FOAs could not make arrests alone. Bob told him he was a Vietnam vet and an FBI agent and to *never* call him off an arrest again. I knew we were toast. I agreed with Bob, supported him by being present, but I didn't have the balls to hurl heat at a supervisor. *Fired for insubordination* swirled in my head. If we were lucky, we'd just receive letters of censure instead of being fired. The supervisor didn't say a word. He looked grim but unfazed. He motioned toward the door with his head and sat back down in his chair. Bob and I left and walked down the hall to our desks in the agents' bullpen. I wondered how much time they would give us to clean out our stuff.

The supervisor never wrote up the incident. As far as I know, he never said a word about it to anyone. Bob and I suffered no repercussions. Thereafter, we had numerous dealings with the supervisor and he didn't bring up the incident. He was cordial and businesslike, a professional through and through, and we respected him for it. During the remainder of the time we had left in the Denver office, we were not waved off an arrest by that supervisor or any other boss in the office. I never did beat Bob in racquetball. Give me a Notre Dame graduate New York Irish Catholic Marine Corps veteran, and I'll show you a friend for life.

New Agents Class #17, July, 1969, in the courtyard of the Department of Justice, FBI Headquarters, Washington, D.C. I'm in the front row, second on the left. Ed Tickel is front row, fourth on the left. Sixth from the left, fourth row, is Jim Procopio. Richard Procop is top row, fourth from the right. William Brown is first on the left, top row, and Charles Parkis is last on the right, top row. The class entered on duty June 23, 1969, and completed training September 26, 1969, when we reported to our respective field offices all over the country. Procop and I were assigned to Denver.

CHAPTER EIGHT

SOFTBALL RIOT

The Denver FBI office fielded a softball team every spring. Our sponsor was a local bank that supplied the uniforms and equipment. The game was fast pitch in the very competitive Denver Metro League. Although we had the name of the bank tattooed on our uniforms, everyone knew we were FBI. Our roster was made up of FOAs and a Deputy U.S. Marshal who pitched. He took a lot of abuse from the other deputies for associating with us. The marshals thought the FBI was arrogant and overrated. We viewed the marshals as glorified prisoner custodians and courtroom janitors. The deputy on our roster was a great guy who fit right in with a team of agents. He once flew back to Denver from an assignment in Kansas City just to pitch a night game. I still don't know how he pulled that one off.

The Denver office had a long tradition of winning softball seasons, with each new crop of FOAs under the gun to carry on the tradition. The FBI and the bank expected us to win.

A line drive singles hitter, I led off at the plate and played first. We had a good hitting lineup and a tight infield. Practices were fun and the games even more so. Bob Rogers, a stick-ball veteran from the streets of New York, said softball was for girls and refused to join the team. He came to the games to razz us.

We won a lot more games than we lost, which fed our already inflated FBI egos. We were rowdy and cocky, full of our-

43

selves. There was no quarter given in the Metro League. Although I'd grown up in an athletic family and had played many sports, I'd never seen heckling of opponents as bad as what we experienced in Denver softball. The personal attacks from the other dugout were unmerciful, and we fired right back. The catcalls and ridicule went on the whole game, and we gave as good as we got.

One night a batter hit a grounder to the infield and I took the throw at first. The runner ran smack over me at the bag, knocked me to the ground and my glasses went flying. Pissed, I went after the guy, but the umpire separated us. Profanities were exchanged between the teams, and things got hot. I wanted revenge against the jerk who had knocked me down. Playing first, I was nearest the other team's dugout when we were in the field. During infield warm-ups, I told our shortstop to throw a ball over my head, to aim it at the asshole who'd run over me when he came out of his dugout. Our shortstop let one fly. I made no attempt to catch it and it slammed into the dugout, just missing the guy's head. It was obvious what had happened, and the other team said they'd get back at us.

The next time we came to the plate, their pitcher threw one right at the head of our batter and that was it. Both dugouts emptied and the teams tore into each other. I tried like hell to get to the guy I was after, but I got tangled up in other scuffles. I don't think a fist landed anywhere, just a lot of cussing and rolling around in the dirt, a comical elementary school-level circus. Bob Rogers was laughing in the stands and had to be restrained from coming on the field to join the fun. The umps finally restored order, but not before the cops arrived. Several uniformed Denver officers came on the field and warned both teams, said they'd haul all of us off to jail if a fight broke out again. When the cops were told that the guys playing on the bank team were FBI agents, they shook their heads and stalked off.

CHAPTER NINE

A REAL PRO

I grew tired of losing to Bob Rogers in racquetball, so I started playing guys I could beat. One of them, Ben, was a veteran G-man who had worked cases all over the country. I challenged him to a racquetball match on the ancient courts tucked away at the top of the Colorado Springs YMCA.

The match started badly for me because Ben didn't know he was supposed to roll over and decompose. He hung in point for point, breathing hard but hammering away. Ben sounded asthmatic, a deplorable wheeze that was distracting. He came at me 'til I got out of breath myself.

When it was his serve, I positioned myself in the back court near the left wall where he liked to place the ball. I countered with a ceiling shot or a low cross-court that kept Ben's old legs churning. Somehow he would get to the ball while gasping for breath and seemingly on the very threshold of death. He called time out after time out, more than allowed by the rules, which I overlooked because he was so damn old. He drank water and toweled off every few minutes, his shorts and shirt soaked with sweat. It was during one of those frequent rest periods that he told me about his days in Mississippi in 1964 when the hick bullies in the coward-infested Klan killed three civil rights workers and buried them deep in a dirt dam near the small town of Philadelphia. Those bodies might still be resting there if an informant hadn't tipped the FBI in exchange for one of the richest payoffs in Bureau history.

Ben and I resumed our match, where my lead was surprisingly thin in the high altitude of Colorado Springs, with Pike's Peak visible everywhere in town except the racquetball courts just under the roof of the YMCA. Hanging on the edge of needing last rites, Ben continued his story about the murders, saying that Hoover sent swarms of agents into Mississippi to dehorn the kluckers, who suffered mentally from inbreeding and watching their coon dogs lick their own testicles. The Klan diverted their eyes away from the dogs' crotches long enough to make threats against FBI agents, boasting they'd gun down an agent as soon as they caught one off by himself without the other smart-mouth federal boys around.

The YMCA courts echoed with racquets and testosterone as Ben won points that he shouldn't have won, resting on a knee after he scored. He mumbled to himself when he was down on the sweat-worn hardwood floor, wheezed, leaning on one knee then the other. He looked like he was taking communion for the last time, then would slowly stand and drive another serve into my left side. Every time I thought I had him, he'd call time, look to the heavens and launch back into his story about the civil rights murders.

One night near Philadelphia, Mississippi, FBI agents learned that these cousin-loving inbreeders in the Klan (which included some local law enforcement) had gathered without their diapers (their sheets) at a restaurant that doubled as a pool hall. They were boozing it up and making threats to kill agents. They parked their shotguns and rifles in the corner along with their tiny little dicks while they shot pool and slopped gravy.

The Bureau gathered itself, Ben told me while bent over sucking racquetball air. Agents, including Ben, headed to the Mississippi establishment that was part eatery and part pool hall, walked in loaded for bear and circled the room with the red necks inside the circle and the agents outside the circle like Indians in a Western. Ben, who sounded to me like he needed an ambulance to climb to the top of the YMCA and save him, racked a Bureau shotgun and told the mental deficients that if any one of the Klan laid a hand on an agent he and the rest of the agents would *kill every motherfucking one of them.* Which ended threats against FBI agents by the KKK in the state of Mississippi.

I regained my serve but not my wind. I didn't let on to Ben that I was tired. I gave him one low ball after another, balls that screamed off my racquet, balls he couldn't possibly get to but did, and I began to see why this old guy scared the bejesus out of those Mississippi kluckers.

I beat Ben that day. Barely. I resolved to play a younger guy the next time around.

The winning Denver FBI softball team, summer, 1970. The brawl with another team during a game ended in a draw with the arrival of the Denver Police. With apologies to unidentified teammates, kneeling L-R: I am 4th, Ken Hayes, Bill Bernius, Jim Supan. Standing, L-R: Dale Farmer(2nd), United States Deputy Marshal, David Patton, Mike Byrne, Ed Lee, Tom Watmon.

CHAPTER TEN

TRANSFERRED

The transfer rule handed down by Hoover from Washington stated that FOAs would remain in their first field assignments for one year before being transferred to their second offices. Agents were on probation for one year after they began duty in the FBI and could be fired for most anything that didn't sit well with the office brass or with Hoover and his layers of supervisors at FBIHQ. They didn't have to give a reason to can you. Pack and be gone. After your year was up, supervisors theoretically needed a concrete reason to fire you, but don't bet on it. I looked forward to easing past my year of probation without incident, then awaiting the assignment to my second field office.

Agents played games with Headquarters about where they were transferred. The game was played on a field called the Office of Preference list, or OP. The military called it the *dream list.* Agents had four-letter words for the OP system because it didn't work. You filled out a form listing your choices of Field Offices where you'd like to be. The list was maintained at Headquarters. It could take fifteen years or more to get your OP. The magic phrase out of Headquarters concerning an OP transfer or any transfer was *Needs of the Bureau,* which justified whatever FBIHQ wanted to inflict on agents in the field.

The Wizard of Transfers hid out behind a curtain in a room at FBIHQ. He didn't show himself because agents would have killed him. He occasionally tested the waters, appearing unannounced at in-services for street agents at the Academy. He would begin his presentation by saying that the Office of Preference system was there to help them, causing a stampede to get at his throat, led by agents from New York who rarely got their OPs, couldn't get out of NYC, mortgaged and taxed over their heads, their youth slipping away in the commuter traffic, going gray in the Holland Tunnel.

Although I'd only been an agent for a little over a year, I'd been around older agents long enough to get that the OP list was a joke. I offered my theory about a monkey throwing darts at a map of the U.S. to decide where agents were transferred.

There was a pattern to FOA transfers out of Denver in 1969 and 1970. Most were going to California, which was terrific. All four of the California offices were desirable Bureau venues. Knowing they were not going to be sent to any office they placed on the OP list, FOAs disguised their real preferences. If you wanted to be in San Diego, you listed Los Angeles or Sacramento, or San Francisco, any office but where you actually wanted to go. Going to the South was out of the question. No FOA in Denver had ever been transferred to Dixie. No one knew why. I wanted to work in Birmingham, Alabama but was certain that wouldn't happen. Hoover never sent rookie agents to their home states. I bided my time waiting to be transferred, worked cases, partied, and lived it up.

I made plenty of arrests of fugitives during my first year in the FBI, recovered stolen federal property, bagged thieves who'd taken stolen motor vehicles across state lines, and stalked bank robbers. Denver was a hell of a lot of fun.

One night my NAC #17 classmate, Richard Procop, and I followed an 18-wheeler clear across the vast tabletop of east Colorado into an equally flat Kansas. We hadn't intended to drive all the way to Kansas, but you go where the case takes you.

An informant had stated that the big rig was carrying a load of stolen cigarettes and was going to stop somewhere east of Denver to pick up more stolen merchandise. Procop and I intended to follow the truck until it stopped for more booty, then nab the thieves for an even bigger recovery. We drove and drove into the night, far from Denver and out of range of the office radio. We hadn't intended to cross into Kansas. We couldn't pick up the Kansas FBI radio and realized we were in a no-man's land of federal radio coverage where no supervisors could reach us.

It was liberating and an adventure that we brought to a close somewhere in Kansas in the dead of night. Because we were hungry and needed to pee, we stopped the damn truck. The driver was cooperative and puzzled about our interest in him. He readily opened the back of the truck and revealed a load of refrigerated food. No cigarettes. No stolen merchandise of any kind. We thanked the driver and drove to the nearest all-night diner.

A few days later in Denver, over beers with other FOAs, Procop and I let slip what we had done. Bob Rogers laughed and ask me whether I'd ever seen a load of cigarettes transported in a refrigerated truck. I told him the Irish sucked.

My first year anniversary came and went, and on June 23, 1970 I was off probation. Bob Rogers called me at home one weekend in August 1970. The phone call was one I had been anticipating. My transfer to another office had arrived by mail from Hoover at FBIHQ. Bob playfully cursed and fussed that I must have *connections* and *juice* somewhere at Headquarters. I told him to shut up and give the news to me. He said I didn't deserve preferential treatment and could go straight to hell. Then he told me: Hoover had transferred me to Birmingham. Exactly where I wanted to go! Unheard of for an FOA. The transfer gods had smiled on me. I had taken a calculated risk. I was one of the few Denver FOAs who did not favor the West Coast on the OP list. I hadn't indicated an office of preference at all; I had left it blank, putting my fate in the hands of the Transfer Wizard in Washington—the monkey. It worked.

The SAC playfully told me to get the hell out of Dodge before Headquarters realized they had actually transferred an agent to where he wanted to go. I brought all my cases up to snuff so they could be re-assigned to another Denver agent. I also packed a Denver telephone directory to take with me to Birmingham as a reminder not to be stupid in my work: I'd spent time in Denver searching for a guy I wanted to interview, querying informants, searching motor vehicle and driver's license records, knocking on doors, going over arrest sheets, consulting the stars, and coming up empty. In frustration, as an afterthought, I looked in the phone book. He was listed.

There was a farewell party for my family and me in Denver. We had a grand and yet bittersweet time, and headed for Alabama in the family car at daybreak the next morning. I would miss the many fine people who'd broken me in and put up with all my mistakes. You never forget your first office in the FBI. It's a womb. You're not really born in the Bureau until you reach your second office. I would particularly miss Bob Rogers, my best friend and partner on many investigations. I trusted him and valued his friendship. His transfer had been delayed because of the birth of his first child, a girl. I was with him at the hospital shortly after she was born. He handed out cigars and said she would be the first female to play football for Notre Dame. I said that girls were *already* playing for the Irish.

Ed Tickel, my close friend from NAC #17, was transferred to Tampa. He was damned happy about that, blew into Florida with his family with the same zeal that I had heading for Birmingham. My NAC #17 classmate, Richard Procop, who spent the year in Denver with me, was transferred to Milwaukee, then on out to the small FBI resident agency at Green Bay.

Ginni was as surprised and pleased as I was to be heading back to the south and to Birmingham. We celebrated and packed. The movers had our furniture, including the spare tire from the family car—I had to remove the spare to make room for other stuff in the trunk—who needed a spare anyway? I knew what I was doing. Hell, I was an FBI agent! If I was invincible, so was my damn car.

So naturally, we had a flat on I-20 in the wilds of west Texas at high noon. The temperature was hotter than Texas tar in August, and there was no shade. No nothing. I hitchhiked to find the nearest gas station, leaving Ginni and the boys in the car running the air conditioning. I returned one hour later in a service truck, with a new tire and my tummy full of water and Dr. Pepper. Other than that, I was empty-handed. In other words, to be perfectly frank, I just never *thought* to bring beverages and refreshments for my waiting family. It was becoming real clear that this mid-twenties FBI agent was not into being a husband or a family man.

We zoomed through Texas, and made it to Birmingham in no time. No sense tempting the dart monkey.

I am firing a shotgun, the basic law enforcement weapon, at the FBI Academy, Quantico, Virginia, during the sixteen weeks of new agents training in the summer of 1969. Classmate Jim Procopio is on my right. This is the same range where the class turned the targets upside down to play a joke on firearms instructor Bob Cohrs. FBI Academy firearms instructors and ranges are among the finest in the world.

PART THREE

CHAPTER ELEVEN

BIRMINGHAM

I tucked Ginni and the boys into the Birmingham Motel and headed for the office. We would search for a house in the coming days. It was early September 1970. I was no longer a First Office Agent. I stood in the lobby of the 2121 Building in downtown Birmingham and waited for an elevator to the fourteenth floor, my new FBI home. The Bureau had the entire floor. It was 6:30 in the morning on a fine Alabama day.

Two guys came into the lobby and stood next to me. I knew they were Bureau. They were squeaky clean in their wing tips, white shirts, and dark suits, both over six feet tall and in their late twenties—straight out of central casting. They looked at me. My hair was a tad long and I was wearing a sport coat and loafers.

One asked if I was going to fourteen? I said yes. Their faces lit up. Was I the new agent from Denver? I smiled and we shook hands. The one with sandy hair introduced himself as Leon Sizemore. Leon said the other agent was Starley Carr, known as Abner because he looked like the cartoon character, L'il Abner. I looked at Carr, and damn if he *didn't* look like L'il Abner. He was a bruiser. Leon was thinner, quick on his feet, a ready smiler from Oklahoma. Abner was a Missouri boy, country drawl and all. Like me, Leon and Abner were in their second field office assignments, and had been transferred to Birmingham earlier in

1970. I took to these two guys straight off, like I'd just met my blood brothers.

The elevators were slow. Leon and Abner said I might as well begin with a Birmingham FBI tradition of walking up to the office on the fourteenth floor instead of taking the elevator. I thought they were kidding and gave them a look that said so. They grinned and headed for the stairs. We walked through a heavy gray metal door into the stairwell. We started climbing. Leon said he was a former pharmaceutical salesman and Abner had coached high school football in another life. I said that the FBI was the only job I'd ever had. I told them I had two boys, and they said they each had two kids. The Bureau was a rumor sponge so they already knew I was a law school graduate from 'Bama, and I'd been recruited by the agents in the Tuscaloosa FBI office. They wanted to know how on God's earth I had gotten to Birmingham in Mr. Hoover's Bureau, where no agent was transferred anywhere near his preference.

We kept walking up the stairs, and the three of us were getting out of breath. It was hot in the stairwell, and we were sweating. Why were these guys blown out like flat tires if they climbed the stairs every day? A light went on. I'd been set up, but the joke wasn't on me, because they were fried.

We finally reached the landing on the fourteenth floor, the Bureau's home. We collected ourselves, caught our breath, looked at each other and laughed like crazy.

We limped into the office. I was introduced to a few people, all of whom knew I was scheduled to arrive. We walked into the bullpen where the agents had their neatly arranged gray metal desks. It looked just like the bullpen in Denver, the same set up as in all Bureau offices. I was comfortable right away. Leon pointed to my desk near the window, a superb view of Birmingham from fourteen floors up. The desk was bare except for a wide government-issue desk calendar, typical for FBI offices because desks had to be cleared off when agents left the office; you couldn't leave your paperwork out on your desk if you weren't there. The clerks had their work areas separate from the agents, the stenographers had their own space, the secretaries' offices were next to the supervisors, with a closed files section tucked away in a far corner. All FBI offices followed the same strict arrangements and procedures, a Hoover trademark.

I sat down and got the feel of the place. The desk drawers were locked as required. I'd get a key shortly, Leon said. He and Abner huddled with other agents who stopped by my desk to introduce themselves and welcome me to Birmingham. Everyone was friendly; they all knew that an agent was under transfer from Denver. An older agent, with years of Bureau wars etched on his unsmiling face, walked right for me and asked straight off why I was sitting at his desk? Everyone looked at me and laughed. I laughed along with everyone else and surrendered my desk to its rightful owner, who loosened up and directed me to my real desk with less of a view.

Ginni and I found a house in lovely, suburban Homewood, and bought it. We got pregnant a few months after settling in. Ginni wanted a daughter and had gone ahead and picked out a name for her: Bonnie Jean. Instead, Deke was born in June of 1971. Ginni cried when she first saw her third baby boy; she decided not to get pregnant again, joking that she did not require four sons in order to prove she couldn't deliver a daughter.

I was assigned to the fugitive squad in Birmingham, same as in Denver. The Bureau liked to sic its young agents on fugitives because our bodies were still under warranty. We could do with little sleep and random food, bounce back ready for the next all-night all-day manhunt. It was exactly the work I wanted, tracking down federal bad guys with a posse of Leon and Abner, and later my pal Luther Brannon, the Alabama native who transferred in from the New York city office in 1972 with his wife and two young daughters. Luther said that from the time the one thousand agents arrived in the New York office every morning, they spent the rest of the day trying to figure out how the hell they were going to commute home.

It sucked being an agent in Manhattan. You were lucky to cover two leads a day because of the traffic congestion, riding city buses and subways to get around on Bureau business. The work was exciting and there was plenty of it, but the cost of living and the commuting were unbearable. An agent's salary, around eleven thousand dollars in the early '70s, practically put you on food stamps in New York. You had to live in New Jersey to save money, and the Jersey commute was a nightmare. Taxes were low in Alabama and the Birmingham commute was a joke. Luther was in Birmingham to stay.

The Birmingham FBI office was eaten up with keeping statistics on agent accomplishments. Sheets were posted on the bulletin board with weekly updates on how many arrests each agent made and the number and value of recovered stolen vehicles and property. You could walk across Alabama on the tops of out-of-state stolen cars because of Alabama's antiquated title law. You could buy a truck license tag at the county courthouse with a bill of sale that was written on a strip of toilet paper or the top of a shoebox. Alabama was a dumping ground for stolen vehicles, many of them straight off the assembly line in Detroit. I didn't care. I wasn't intoxicated with working stolen vehicle or property cases anyway. What I wanted was to hunt down and arrest folks with Leon, Starley, and Luther by my side, then hit a diner for coffee and grease.

The best week I ever posted in Birmingham totaled eight arrests, an office best. Many of them were draft dodgers or deserters who didn't want to fight in Vietnam. The case agents got credit for the arrests, while others on the arrest teams received an *assist,* like in basketball. The rule in the FBI was that an agent couldn't make an arrest alone. The Bureau didn't like cowboys, and the rule made for better safety in dangerous situations. It was not unusual to take five to ten agents to arrest one bad guy. Agents frequently had the luxury of planning arrests and raids, something that local law enforcement couldn't do, because cops had to react without warning to street crimes. It was far more dangerous to be a cop in America than an FBI agent. When I entered on duty in the FBI in June of 1969, only eighteen agents had been killed in the line of duty since the modern Bureau was formed under J. Edgar Hoover in 1924; a hundred or more police officers were killed every year in the U.S. Whether we admitted it or not, many FBI agents looked down on cops and called them "locals," thinking of them as low-paid, poorly trained, uneducated boobs. We worked with them when we had to, but we didn't always respect them. I, too, shared this low opinion of the locals early in my career, but I grew out of it as I grew up. I had a lot to learn.

After locating a fugitive, we would "hit" his house right before daybreak when he was asleep with his wife or girl friend. We would quietly drive up and park, splitting up to cover the front and back of the house, knock on the front door and then bust in a second later yelling *FBI!* As a perk, the case agent was always at the front. We would rush straight for the bedroom and into the startled expressions of reclining nudes: the fugitive and his woman. We would throw back the covers, untangle the couple, handcuff the guy on the spot and watch as his lady scrambled to put on clothes. If we were quick enough, we could let in the agents covering the back before the woman got completely dressed. After depositing the prisoner at the county jail, we would take breakfast at the closest diner.

I had become good at this kind of thing in Denver, and kept improving in Birmingham. Leon Sizemore, Luther Brannon, Starley Carr, and I stood astride Bureau immortality through our exploits. You just had to sit up and take notice. We cut a wide federal swath through northern Alabama. We were Masters of the Heart of Dixie, if not the Universe. The difference, though, between my buddies and me was that Sizemore, Brannon, and Carr were good family men who went home after work. They could put away the Bureau. Not me.

I started to get frisky early on. I could not get my fill. I became the Lone Ranger at night and on the weekends, had an affair, and dragged her down with me. I told Ginni lies about where and how I was spending my time, using my FBI buddies as cover. Of course, all the lying eventually strangled me, and Ginni found out. She forgave me, which only enabled me to continue seeing the other woman. When she confronted me again about the affair, I confessed and said I wanted out. She offered an easy divorce without contention, and that is how we ended our marriage. I've got to say, though, that the real love affair was with my work anyway, which I worshiped.

I moved into an apartment complex on the south side of Birmingham; Ginni and the boys stayed in the Homewood house, and she found a job. On December 23rd I called Ginni to set up how we would handle Christmas. There was no answer. I went over to the house, but no one was there. I finally got her on the phone at her parents' home on the coast of North Carolina, not far from Jacksonville. She told me she had decided to take the boys and move permanently to North Carolina to be near her parents. She would not be returning to Birmingham. I don't blame her. She deserved far more than I gave her.

I spent Christmas alone in my apartment, and had a *come to Jesus* talk with myself. My sons had moved six hundred miles away. If I did not re-order my priorities, I would never have a meaningful relationship with them.

CHAPTER TWELVE

Motivation

Local and state law enforcement nabbed their share of federal fugitives. They would notify the Bureau that they had a federal bad guy in custody at a local jail. FBI agents would then put a *hold* on the prisoner and claim credit for an arrest. A similar shell game played out when the locals recovered stolen motor vehicles that had been taken across state lines and into FBI jurisdiction.

For example, the Birmingham Police Department auto theft squad were damned good detectives. They harpooned scores of stolen cars and trucks being investigated by the FBI. We took our federal forms, dark suits, white shirts, and unmarked black cars to the big dirt lot at Kemp's wrecker service on the north side of Birmingham where the cops stored their recovered stolen vehicles. We eyeballed the vehicle identification numbers, VIN's, through the windshields of the stolen vehicles, and with a straight face claimed them as FBI recoveries. The Bureau fattened its arrest and vehicle recoveries this way, giving Director Hoover the statistics he needed to go before Congress each year to request an increase in the FBI's budget. All fifty-nine field offices had to report an increase every year in the number of arrests and vehicle recoveries. We accomplished this increase through our own good investigative work, with a usually unacknowledged major assist from local law enforcement.

Criminals make mistakes, which is a good thing, because how else would law enforcement catch them. Example: In 1972, one of the Florida FBI offices sent me a lead about a UFAP—an unlawful flight to avoid prosecution investigation. A thief had committed a crime in Florida and had fled the state, thereby committing a federal offense as well by crossing state lines to escape. In-state authorities, however, must issue a warrant and formally request that the FBI open a UFAP case to locate and arrest the fugitive, or agents will not spill out of coffee houses all over America to dog fugitives wanted by the locals. The jurisdiction issuing the warrant must agree to extradite the fugitive back to that locale after the Bureau apprehends him. Agents catch these desperados and the locals prosecute them.

The FBI is damned good at UFAP cases. We have the national resources and know-how to round them up by the bushels. I enjoyed going after UFAP bad guys because the cases were purely fugitive hunts involving manhunts and arrests with a minimum of FBI paperwork. They were mainlined right into your veins. Plus, UFAPs provided an opportunity to get involved in non-federal matters like local homicides and theft investigations that FBI agents wouldn't normally handle. Cops ridiculed the Bureau for not knowing squat about murder cases or the bread-and-butter street crimes that the locals routinely solve. My response to the locals is that the Bureau can't do all of your work for you. Call us when you run out of resources and ideas and we'll step in and clean up after you.

Fugitives on the run or trying to start a new life tend to fall back on vocations they've been trained to do. Politicians work as politicians and preachers work as preachers. If you're hunting them, look to their employment histories to catch them.

The request that came to me from a Florida FBI office on this particular UFAP was a *shotgun lead*, meaning it had been sent to many Bureau offices to have agents check construction sites where there was heavy machinery. The fugitive had a history of operating equipment that men loved when they were boys, some never growing out of it: steam shovels, bulldozers, earth movers. Following up on the lead, I visited construction and heavy machinery sites in the Birmingham area and ended up at a salvage yard in the northern section of the city. It was an overcast day with light rain.

The site had a tall crane. I parked the Bureau car and showed a photograph of the fugitive to the yard boss, who took one look and pointed straight at the glass-enclosed crane operator high above the ground. "That's him," the boss said, and asked what the guy had done to bring the FBI to a salvage yard in the rain. I said the operator was a thief from Florida and a federal fugitive. I could tell the boss hated to lose a good crane man. It reminded me of another one of my UFAP arrests of a chef in a fine Birmingham restaurant: I hauled him out of the kitchen at the height of the dinner crowd, leaving behind a distraught restaurant owner.

I considered a Lone Ranger approach to arresting the UFAP crane operator, grabbing him myself and taking all the credit. But those are cowboy tactics, and if you charge off alone John Wayne style, you end up doing paperwork explaining why you went solo. So I used the FBI radio in my BuCar to request assistance on an arrest.

The yard boss called the fugitive down from his perch atop the crane. I promptly arrested him on the spot in front of his boss, co-workers, and an army of FBI agents. *How did you guys find me?* the UFAP asked in the rain. I helped him into handcuffs, hands behind his back, the Bureau way. Criminals talk too much. They can't keep a secret. They brag about their crimes.

Regardless of how good the FBI looked in its yearly achievements, the cops knew what we were up to, knew our game, and grumbled that the most underrated thing in the world was a good crap, and the most overrated was the FBI. I didn't blame them. The cops could surely have educated me about the importance of motivation when making an arrest if I had bothered to ask them. I found it out on my own one morning tracking a federal fugitive in Birmingham.

The bad guy this time was an army deserter named Jones. The army wanted him back. I was assigned to locate and arrest him, what the FBI calls an *apprehension.* My buddies Luther, Leon, and Abner, were busy elsewhere, so I asked an agent I'll call Hammond to assist me in the arrest. Hammond was a First Office Agent, full of piss and starch. He fancied himself a go-getter in apprehending fugitives, a knock-down-the-door, take-no-prisoners G-man. He was also a sprinter; he said he could run down anything on two legs. Oozing testosterone and virility, Hammond answered the telephone by shouting into the receiver, "Hammond!" irritating the hell out of the rest of us.

Hammond and I rolled out into the neighborhoods in west Birmingham, drove up and down the streets and alleys frequented by the fugitive deserter Jones, places where he had girlfriends and family. We parked the BuCar and walked up an alley I thought might be promising. If anyone had asked us what we were doing strolling up an alley, I would have said we were meter readers.

It was my case and I called the shots. I handed Hammond a photo of Jones provided by the Army. The weather was mild and agreeable, layered with the usual Birmingham haze from the steel mills west of downtown. Birmingham called itself *The Magic City.* Yeah, now you see it, now you don't.

Hammond and I had not walked far down the alley. A guy came out of a back yard and headed up the alley toward us about two first downs away. I looked at him. Hammond looked at him. The guy looked at us. The three of us stopped dead in our tracks. It was the deserter Jones.

Jones was not wracked by indecision. He knew damned well we were not meter readers. He spun and ran hard and fast down the alley without waiting for us to announce ourselves as Representatives of the United States Government and that he'd better stop if he knew what was good for him. We immediately gave chase, the start of fun and games that no one in law enforcement ever wants to miss—two guys in suits chasing a dude in casuals.

Funny how selfish you can be at times like this. I completely forgot about Hammond and tore after Jones, wanting all the glory for myself. I'll wager that Hammond felt the same desire. I don't know what Jones was thinking. Everything was happening fast for me as I ran. The vision of my law school classmates sitting in those wretched law offices popped into my brain and vanished as quickly. The deserter Jones darted in and out of backyards, alleys and streets, in glorious imitation of a jackrabbit. Hammond and I split up somewhere along the chase, staking out our own routes on the heels of Jones, what my college football coach called *pursuit angles*. I can't tell you where exactly I realized that I was running through west Birmingham neighborhoods completely alone. I liked to run, and this particular experience of just running was not unpleasant, even in my suit. I might otherwise have assumed the state of rapture that comes over you when you mesh with the earth you're running on, find peace and get closer to God. But my near reverie was brought up short when I realized Jones was gone and people were staring at me from the safety of their homes and cars. I stopped, out of breath, dazed, and took stock.

What the hell was going on here? Something they don't teach you at the FBI Academy. I had just said hello to *motivation*. The deserter Jones was running for his freedom. He didn't want to go to jail, or worse: Vietnam. He had no desire to leave family, friends, and bedmates behind in the Magic City. Jones was highly motivated. Me, I was at work. I was an FBI agent. I was in the business of catching Jones and putting handcuffs on him, depriving him of the people and places he loved. If I didn't catch Jones today, I'd catch him tomorrow. My motivation was no match for Jones'. It was a lesson. I'm glad I learned that lesson early in my career. And where the hell was Hammond?

It's late Friday afternoon on a payday in the early 1970s. We're paid every two weeks. Our checks are placed at the register in alphabetical order where everyone signs in for duty each day, where the entire office can see how much you make.

The office bullpen is full of agents gearing up for the weekend. At five o'clock sharp we're going to adjourn to the Falstaff beer distributorship on the south side of town for unlimited free beer in the company's upstairs executive fun room furnished with an elegant dark wood bar and leather chairs. Falstaff liked the

Bureau because agents had recovered a truckload of stolen beer several years ago, and the company had been trying to make us drink it ever since.

In walks the Birmingham Special Agent in Charge, SAC Ralph Miles, the best boss I ever had in the Bureau. He's an agent's SAC, a great guy who leaves us alone, requires only that we do our work. We never want to let him down. He announces there's a 91, a bank robbery. He gives us the bank location on the south side, and we know exactly where it is because we pass it every Friday afternoon on the way to drink free beer at the Falstaff beer distributorship. Miles tells us to mount up.

Every FBI field office has an identical bank robbery response plan. The first agents on the scene enter the bank and quickly interview witnesses for descriptions of the robber and the getaway vehicle. Later arriving agents work outside the bank, canvassing streets and neighborhoods for information. An office supervisor assigns the robbery to a case agent, who controls the crime scene and interviews assignments.

The police are frequently the first law enforcement to arrive at a bank robbery. The FBI share bank robbery jurisdiction with police, but the locals back off and let us handle things once we get there. Cops have excellent evidence technicians and work inside the bank dusting for fingerprints, while agents conduct interviews. It could be an uneasy alliance between cops and agents after a bank robbery, each agency jealous of its prerogatives. Usually, however, we get along.

I'm assigned to one of the tellers, whom I interview at length. She is naturally upset and frightened because the robber had pointed a gun at her. She gives me a good description, which I pass on to the case agent. One of the agents picks up the film taken by the bank camera high up in a corner of the bank and drives it to the Alabama Air Guard wing at the Birmingham Airport, where the Guard lab will quickly develop the film for still photos of the robber.

After several hours of interviews and canvassing nearby businesses and neighborhoods, the agents head back to the office to regroup. We're angry at the bank robber for ruining our payday beerfest at Fallstaff.

We mill around the bullpen on the 14th floor of the 2121 Building and go over what we have, which is not much, only that a black male has robbed the bank. The robber is given the FBI designation of unknown subject, UNSUB. We don't yet have anything on the getaway vehicle. It is my experience that FBI agents are able to make a lot out of little, and that we'll catch this guy before long.

The photo clerk picks up the bank photos of the robber from the Alabama Air Guard at the Birmingham Airport, copies them at our office and hands them out to us. We now have excellent photos of a black guy wearing a ski mask.

It gets to be 9:00 p.m., then 10. We're still in the office. An informant calls to tell his agent handler that he knows who committed the bank robbery. A posse of agents scramble, but the lead proves to be false. So here we sit on a payday Friday night with no beer.

Another telephone call comes in. The boss, SAC Miles, takes the call, which I've seen him do before, because bank robberies, 91s, are dear to his heart. He takes every bank robbery in Alabama personally, which is the main reason we have an 80% solution rate on stickups. Miles is really a blue-collar union type of SAC. Most field bosses are eaten up with their own importance and don't do squat in the way of street work. Miles had started at the very bottom of the FBI as a file clerk in Savannah, Georgia. He never forgot his roots.

After taking the phone call, Miles walks into the bullpen to tell us that another informant has the robber located at a bar on Graymont Avenue near Legion Field, the football stadium where the Alabama Crimson Tide has won so many big games. The robber is buying drinks for the house and waving chunks of shiny new bills, bragging that the money is loot from a bank robbery. He's drunk and living it up. The informant provides a description of what the guy is wearing. We scramble out of the 2121 Building, caravan in BuCars to the bar at high speed, and roll up without fanfare. The case agent in charge of the bank robbery, the guy with the *ticket* in FBI parlance, assigns a team of agents to cover the bar exits. The rest of us head straight through the front door.

It's dark, noisy, and smoky inside, a good-time place. Music is blaring. The bar is full of black patrons. Heads turn as in we rush, a bunch of white agents in suits. We spot the robber right away, our UNSUB, wearing just what the informant said he was wearing. We surround the guy and his table of buddies. The case agent says *FBI,* stands the robber up, handcuffs him, arms behind his back, the Bureau way. He does not resist. No one in the joint protests or gets in the way.

The robber is puzzled: *How had we found him so fast?* I ask you, is the FBI good or what?

Fugitives in general, and Army deserters in particular, have a compelling desire to return to the womb; they miss their mommies. It's basic, understandable, and gets them caught. Example: A fugitive case was assigned to me, and I went straight to the guy's mother. I visited her often, let her see that I was not a monster, had coffee with her if she invited me in, told her that her son was better off not running and should go back to the Army if he was a deserter. He'd do well to face things rather than to keep running, rather than be forced to steal to survive, where he might be injured or who knows what. Mothers often saw the need for their sons to stop hiding, and would cooperate with me openly or covertly.

I worked an Army deserter investigation not long after I transferred to the Birmingham FBI. The fugitive had been raised in a city housing project in the eastern part of town. I visited the guy's mother and we got along well, but she wouldn't agree to help me catch him. One afternoon she called out of the blue from a pay phone to say her son was home asleep in his own bed. She pleaded with me not to tell him that she'd turned him in. I promised to keep her cooperation confidential.

I collected my trusted buddies, Abner, and Leon Sizemore, and drove to the red brick housing project where the mother of the deserter lived. Luther Brannon was busy, or I would have taken him along as well. I always wanted those three agents with me on an arrest; I had absolute faith in their judgment and professionalism. We were going to arrest one nineteen-year-old kid who did not have a criminal record other than running away from his Army obligations. He wasn't likely to be a problem. But you never knew: In the early '70s deserters led all types of fugitives in assaulting FBI agents.

We drove into the housing project in two cars and parked in front of the apartment. I sent Abner around to the back door because he was big enough to stop anything coming at him. Leon and I went to the front and I knocked on the door. I was the case agent, so I called the plays.

The mother answered the door. Not giving anything away, I told her we were looking for her son. She said he wasn't home and pointed upstairs with her finger. Going along, I asked if we could look around. She protested that he wasn't home and to stop bothering her, all the while pointing at the ceiling. She finally told us to come in, but continued saying we wouldn't find her son.

I fetched Abner at the back door and let him in, because you don't leave a member of your arrest team hanging, not knowing what's going on. The three of us went through the motions of searching the first floor; we knew there was no way out of the apartment from the upstairs. We walked up the stairs alert and ready to make the arrest. We thoroughly searched the entire upstairs in the small apartment, under the beds, in the closets, and behind the shower curtain. The deserter wasn't there.

I told Abner and Leon to stay put, and I went downstairs to the mother and gave her a questioning look without saying anything. She said loudly that her son wasn't at home and she didn't know where he was. She kept pointing up with an expression that said *keep looking, you dumb ass.*

It then hit me where he was hiding. I returned to the upstairs and motioned for Leon and Abner to stand close. I positioned myself and started talking to a large pile of dirty laundry in the hall, calling out the fugitive's name and telling him to come out of the laundry. He slowly emerged from the pile of clothes with a sheepish grin, and stood straight up like he was surfacing in a swimming pool, except that clothes fell off him instead of water. I asked Leon and Abner to take the fugitive outside and not to handcuff him 'til they got him in the car. They understood.

Downstairs, the mother hugged her son and gave him words of encouragement as he was taken away. I hung back and quietly thanked her. She had tears in her eyes. I touched her shoulder and left.

CHAPTER THIRTEEN

J. Edgar Hoover

There were really two FBIs. Every agent knew this. To the grunts in the field offices, the street agents who did the interviews and stirred the dust and looked under the rocks, the *FBI* meant themselves, the field, the investigators who did the actual work. The other FBI was Headquarters in Washington, *The Bureau,* as agents referred to HQ, a place for advancement-focused career supervisors and the politically appointed Director. When agents mentioned *The Bureau* in conversation with each other, they meant FBIHQ, not the FBI organization.

FBI Headquarters on Pennsylvania Avenue was like a turtle safe in its shell, a house of inertia and aversion to risk. It moved when it felt like it, and sometimes not at all, and was immune to exhortations and pleas from the field. It was the way Headquarters had always been, a culture unto itself, crammed with layers of supervisors in rooms without windows.

J. Edgar Hoover had been isolated for decades on the fifth floor of Headquarters. His world *was* Headquarters. He did not visit field offices. He did not make rounds. When he *did* come out of his Washington cocoon it was to play the horses at tracks in Florida and California or to take in the nightclubs and restaurants of Manhattan.

Agents met Hoover by going to his office for a handshake or a photograph. The signed photos were then mailed to the agents' field offices. Agents could also write Hoover and request an autographed photo. I wrote and requested one. It came back quickly. It was in his handwriting, or the handwriting of Helen Gandy, Hoover's longtime secretary, who had mastered his signature; we were never sure. My color photo showed a tight-lipped but benevolent looking Director sitting on a table wearing a light blue suit, white handkerchief neatly in place in his breast pocket. He held a book with a red cover. The handwriting read: *To Jack A. Owens, Jr., Best Wishes, J. Edgar Hoover, 3.2.71.*

Hoover was susceptible to flattery. You called him *sir* or *Mr. Hoover,* then got out of the way as he took off on a long monologue about past glories, particularly the gangster wars and the Communist menace. Hoover would get wound up and talk beyond the allotted time for appointments. Agents waiting to see him backed up in the reception room. My close friend, Leon Sizemore, exercising an agent's prerogative when he was working in the Quincy, Illinois Resident Agency, requested to see Director Hoover in person at Headquarters. The request was granted when Leon was attending a routine five-day in-service. Leon was excused from class the last day and headed for the Director's office on the fifth floor of the Justice Building. Leon's irrepressible personality instantly drew people to him. Strangers felt like old friends after a few minutes. Part of his charm was an inexhaustible reservoir of self-deprecating humor, and he was charming and mannerly to a fault.

Leon walked into Hoover's office and waited in the reception room under the stern gaze of Mrs. Gandy. The walls were covered with photographs of the Director with famous people, as well as cartoons depicting the bulldog-like Hoover as crime fighting hero. After a short wait, Mrs. Gandy's phone rang and she informed Leon that the Director would see him. Leon walked down an inner hallway past more photos and cartoons and into the Director's office, where Hoover shook hands and motioned for Leon to sit on a couch. The meeting was scheduled to last about five minutes. Hoover sat behind his large desk. They chatted a few minutes, long enough for Leon to work his charm. One of the phones rang. Hoover picked up the receiver and said, "Hold my calls." Hoover was under the Sizemore spell.

For the next hour, Leon answered questions about the type of work he was doing in the Quincy RA, and listened attentively as Hoover launched into the exploits of the early Bureau and the glories of arresting famous gangsters. As the meeting drew to a close, Hoover asked Leon about his OP, office of preference. Leon said Birmingham, which he had earlier calculated as a realistic choice given that he was from Oklahoma and his wife from Georgia, and given the severely restrictive FBI OP culture. Hoover closed the meeting saying he had to leave in order to have lunch with President Nixon.

The following week, now back in the Quincy RA, Leon received a call from the SAC in Springfield informing him he'd been transferred to Birmingham. He'd gotten his OP after only three years!

Hoover installed an internal record keeping system that was the most effective in law enforcement, local or federal, a system that he copied from the Library of Congress, where he'd worked as a young man. No one keeps records better than the FBI. Hoover got the Library's wonderful numbering system in his veins and modified it to fit the Bureau. Every federal matter investigated by the Bureau was given a number designation. For example, a bank robbery was a 91, a kidnapping was a 7, extortion a 9, theft of government property was a 52, and interstate transportation of a stolen motor vehicle was a 26, and so forth, up to nearly 300 violations by the year 2000. Each violation carried deadlines for investigation, forcing agents to do work on a timely basis and record it accurately. Hoover built the system over decades from the ground up, one piece of paper after another. He was demanding and fastidious about documenting investigations, filling files with evidence of not only the end result, but how we got there.

Hoover's methods earned my respect. The FBI won case after case in court; in fact, many cases never went to court because the defendants pleaded guilty after their lawyers looked at the evidence accumulated by the Bureau. I *never* saw an FBI case go to trial where there were questions about the defendant's guilt. We knew he was guilty. We had the evidence. We still had to prove it in court, and usually we did. The Bureau *won* in court.

Hoover's clout with Congress brought about the FBI's expansion. The Bureau had more violations to investigate and more assignments than all other federal law enforcement combined. It was the variety of work that made days in the FBI such a kick. The pay and prestige matched the fun. It was J. Edgar Hoover who secured and sustained high salaries for agents. Overtime was built into agent salaries, far better than what cops and other feds earned. Our high pay created envy and jealousy in the rest of law enforcement. Bureau put-downs by police, the ATF, and the U.S. Marshals were high sport. Screw 'em, I said. One on one, I didn't have problems working with other feds or cops on the street. I liked the work. They liked the work. We got along.

Hoover kept the FBI buttoned up. Only the SACs could talk to the press, but even then it was *no comment* for SACs unless Headquarters authorized it. Headquarters meant Hoover and his Crime Records unit, the FBI's propaganda machine that strangled negative press and polished flattering information or articles concerning the Bureau. Years after Hoover's death, I saw first hand the peril of giving SACs full reign in handling the press, a wide latitude that Hoover would never have granted. A Birmingham SAC with a big ego tipped reporters about an upcoming gambling raid in order to court favor with reporters and make the FBI and the SAC look good. There was a leak somewhere in the press, the bad guys were warned, and we arrived for the raid at an empty casino. FBIHQ transferred the SAC to Jackson, Mississippi and demoted him to street agent. He deserved it. Hoover would have busted him to Butte to empty trash cans.

Agents lived under the hammer of *Don't embarrass the Bureau.* Don't do anything in your official duties or private life that would reflect negatively on the FBI. It kept us all running scared. Hoover stood astride his creation ready to smother fires that singed or scorched the Bureau's reputation, suffocating agents and flames alike. He was tyrannical and all-powerful. He made the Bureau work.

Hoover refused to hire women as agents. His public position was that women couldn't physically handle the demands, the arrests. Hoover was wrong about women and minorities not being able to cut it as FBI agents. They have performed splendidly since the FBI woke up and began hiring them after Hoover died. His intransigence denied the Bureau the talents of a large segment of the American population, men and women who would have made a contribution to the FBI's many successes. The white male culture of the FBI, however, continued long after Hoover was gone. There were agents who simply would not accept women and minorities as qualified colleagues. Subsequent Directors have been committed to diversity, but the Bureau agent population remains predominately white male.

The FBI's Crime Records Division was responsible for honing the image of the Bureau's war against the menace of the Communist Party, USA, headed in the 1950s by American citizen, Gus Hall. In reality, Hall's group was ineffective and disorganized, and had never been a serious threat to national security; nevertheless, Hoover played the Communist card every time he went before Congress to request an increase in the Bureau's budget. He hammered the Commies in speeches, articles, and books, working the country into a frenzy over the internal Red menace. Hoover knew better because *the field told him so in its reports and investigations*. An agent told me in 1969 that he had devised plans to put sugar and salt into Gus Hall's gas tank.

On May 2, 1972, J. Edgar Hoover died of natural causes overnight in his Washington home. He was seventy-seven years old. He'd been Director of the FBI for forty-eight years. He was America's top cop and one of the most powerful men in the country. Indeed, he'd been the Bureau's *only* director since the modern FBI came into being when he took over in 1924. It was called the Bureau of Investigation then, a little regarded dot on the Washington landscape. Calvin Coolidge was President. Hoover methodically bent the Bureau to his will and turned a corrupt and inept federal investigative agency into the country's foremost law enforcement organization.

Although Director Hoover died in his sleep in his own bed, I did not hear about his passing until much later in the afternoon. I let myself in through the employee entrance to the Birmingham FBI office after covering some leads in town. The clerk working the switchboard said *He's dead.* I was immediately concerned that the SAC, Special Agent in Charge Ralph Miles, had suffered a heart attack; Miles was battling heart problems. It was *Mr. Hoover*, the clerk informed me. The Bureau no longer had a Director.

The agent's bullpen was buzzing: Would the death of Hoover mean the end of guard duty in the office? The eight hour shifts that agents rotated alphabetically, sitting in a chair or sleeping on a couch until your week was up? The end of standing guard? A monotonous, lifeless duty that kept agents off the street doing the real work of the Bureau, we viewed guard duty as another suffocating edict from Hoover's desk.

The day he died my most pressing concern was where to have a beer after work. I settled on the bar on the second floor of the 2121 Building, a hangout for agents twelve floors below the offices of the Birmingham FBI. I walked into the tiny bar crowded with agents and a few civilians. Abner was there, along with many other agent friends. The tribe had gathered to unwind, piss and moan, a Bureau ritual played out in bars all over America. We laughed and carried on as usual the day Hoover died. One of the agents, a paunchy, overripe veteran, leaned close to suggest that we tone it down because the civilians were watching to see how we would react to the loss of our Director. We should look distraught or something, the older agent said. We ignored him and partied on.

The truth was, nothing changed for street agents when J. Edgar Hoover passed away. We were the Bureau's grunts. We wanted to be left alone by the Director and the rest of his deskbound, paranoid wallflowers at FBIHQ. As we saw it, the *real* FBI was the fifty-nine field offices around the country, not the goons in Washington who pretended to speak for us. We viewed Headquarters supervisors as politicians who couldn't hack it on the street.

I personally didn't care who the Director was. I intended to take my BuCar out everyday and work my cases away from office supervisors and the gang at FBIHQ. Many agents shared this view. We also had a detached view of whoever was Attorney General at the Department of Justice, or President of the United States, for that matter. We were professionals, field FBI agents, and did not feel that political leaders should influence the way we did our jobs. Most politicians didn't know hoot about law enforcement. We were insulated and cozy inside the Bureau, and no outsider was going to reach in and stir things up. All we asked from Washington was a cost of living raise every January.

We speculated about who the new Director would be. We might get one of Hoover's minions, a career Headquarters animal who hadn't been on the street in ages. No one thought the mantel would fall on Associate Director Clyde Tolson, Hoover's forever companion; Tolson's function was to be Hoover's buddy. I never saw a communication with Tolson's name on it. He was old and feeble, perhaps in worse health than Hoover and was going down-hill. He didn't have the energy for the Director job. The more we drank in the small bar in the 2121 Building, the less we thought about Hoover's death and who would follow him.

Decades after Hoover's death, his image has been tarnished by break-ins that he authorized without judicial approval in the late 1960s and early 1970s against radical left-wing groups in the U.S., and by his personal animosity toward Dr. Martin Luther King, which took the form of surveillances of King's private and professional life, wire taps on the civil rights leader's telephones, and attempts to smear King with leaks from the FBIHQ about King's extramarital sex life. Hoover was also vehemently opposed to King's anti-Vietnam war speeches and activities, believing that the civil rights leader was a Communist sympathizer. When King was assassinated in Memphis in 1968, however, Hoover put aside his personal dislike of King and unleashed all the resources of the Bureau to find and prosecute his killer, James Earl Ray.

Perhaps nothing has so smeared the image of J. Edgar Hoover as the charge that he was a homosexual. If he played with men at all, one could speculate that it was with his companion, Clyde Tolson, whom Hoover made Associate Director of the FBI. They were together constantly in the office and out of the office, traveling to Hoover's favorite haunts in New York, Florida, and California. When Hoover testified before Congressional committees, Tolson sat next to him. When Hoover gave interviews to reporters, Tolson was there. When the Director ate lunch at the Mayflower Hotel and drank whiskey over steaks at Harvey's Restaurant on Connecticut Avenue, Tolson was with him. Whenever Hoover checked into a hotel, Tolson had a room nearby.

Tolson lived in a house just down the street from Hoover's N.W. Washington home. They rode to work together in an FBI chauffeured Cadillac, getting out of the car near the office so that they could walk the last few blocks to work. When sick, Tolson recuperated in Hoover's house. They were rarely apart. All this might seal the case for many of Hoover's detractors, however, I'm not convinced.

No one ever even hinted they had seen J. Edgar Hoover being intimate with Clyde Tolson or any other man. Not so much as holding hands or words or letters of love or intimacy: not the FBI clerks who came to Hoover's house every day to run errands and tidy up, nor his chauffeur, his housekeeper, nor his longtime secretary Helen Gandy, nor the higher ups at Headquarters who wanted his job, nor the hundreds of agents with whom I worked during my thirty years in the Bureau.

No photographic or audio record has ever surfaced showing J. Edgar Hoover dressed as a woman, or in sexual contact with Clyde Tolson or any other man. If such evidence existed, it would have floated long ago, because Hoover's many and voracious enemies would have made it public. In my opinion, evidence hasn't been published because it doesn't exist. Hoover's enemies were powerful men who hated and feared him because of what he had on them or what they feared he had on them in his private files. Eight presidents under whom Hoover served, big shots in the FBI who wanted his job, the shadow people in the CIA who loathed him, the KGB, and the Mafia, all would have ravaged him if there had been evidence that he preferred men in general or Tolson in particular.

I don't believe J. Edgar Hoover was gay, nor do I care; it doesn't concern me. I theorize that Hoover's sex drive and his passion were directed at the FBI he'd fathered. Hoover said publicly that the Bureau didn't have gay agents, but privately he kept the heat on looking for them. And as for heterosexuals, having sex outside marriage in the FBI could get you censured, transferred, or fired if an affair became public or arose in the middle of a publicized divorce. Hoover acted quickly in dealing with sex scandals and meting out punishment, while the Crime Records Division at FBIHQ kept it away from the press. The Bureau's image, and his own, was what mattered most to Hoover.

Evidence of Hoover's despotic style gradually disappeared after his death. The disciplinary transfers for small infractions, disrupting the lives of agents and their families, the firings for no good reason, abated. There was more allowance for agent mistakes, up to a point. Letters of censure were still handed out and agents fired. But the reasons had to be substantial and proven by FBIHQ.

The FBI, as Hoover fashioned it, and the way it is today, is not without flaws. Agents make mistakes in their personal lives, agents blunder in their professional lives, and some have committed espionage and betrayed the United States. Cases are lost and surveillances blown. Agents overstep and citizens' rights are violated. But the Bureau is the best at what it does. It's still the best-equipped and trained law enforcement force anywhere.

CHAPTER FOURTEEN

BIG SHOES TO FILL

Part One: L. Patrick Gray

L. Patrick Gray, a Republican operative from Connecticut and former submariner with no law enforcement experience, was quickly plucked out of obscurity by President Nixon to succeed J. Edgar Hoover as Director of the FBI. Gray came to Birmingham in the fall of 1972. My assignment was to get him into the 2121 Building and up the elevator to the Bureau's fourteenth floor office without fuss, to give his speech to the Birmingham office. His wife had accompanied him.

I led the way into the lobby to the waiting elevator, its door open. I let them go in ahead of me. They turned and faced the open door. They stared at the panel of floor buttons. I took the elevator key out of my pocket and walked in, ready to unlock the elevator and push the button for the 14th floor. I looked at the panel. Someone had punched all 14 floors. We were going to stop on every floor before the Acting Director of the FBI could get off and make a speech. We quickly took another elevator. If it had been Hoover, I would have been headed for Butte by the end of the day.

Gray was in his fifties and wore a Naval crew cut. He had warm blue eyes and was quite congenial in person. Later, he mailed me an autographed color photograph. He never mentioned the elevator.

Gray threw darts at some FBI traditions. Example: He lifted the ban on drinking coffee on duty, which hadn't been observed anyway, because agents drank coffee outside the office. But the *clerks* benefited, since they were stuck in the office all day and couldn't slip out to restaurants except at noon. Coffee pots sprang up all over the Bureau. The revolution had begun.

He eliminated *time-in-the-office*, TIO, record keeping, a Hoover invention that agents lied about every day. Hoover wanted agents to be out on the street working cases. The amount of time inside had to be short or you risked being called on the carpet for not aggressively working your cases on the street. Hurray for all that. The catch-22 here was that the paper work was extensive and required a considerable time behind your desk. So, we all fudged the time we recorded as being in the office. As an outsider taking a look at FBI practices, Gray rightly thought that TIO was bullshit and canned it.

He authorized physical training for agents while on duty. We could take an hour three times a week, whenever the workouts didn't interfere with our duties. I was secretly exercising daily. I didn't care what the Bureau rule was; I was going to stay fit.

Within months of taking over the FBI, Gray decided to hire women agents. The first female agent hired came out of the Marine Corps. Not surprising. The second woman, however, was a former Catholic nun, a rail-thin, attractive brunette. I later worked with her on recruiting matters and she was a fine agent. She and the former Marine conducted themselves in exemplary fashion under fishbowl scrutiny as pioneers in a male world. There were male agents who never accepted women as equals. Some guys just don't get it.

Gray started the long-overdue push to hire minorities in the agent ranks, particularly blacks and Hispanics. He also attempted to prune some of the top-heavy fat at Headquarters, but wasn't around long enough to move that mountain.

Although I'd been an agent for only three years when Gray came aboard, I was already deeply ingrained with the *us* and *them* attitude of FBI agents. There were two kinds of people: agents and those who weren't agents. I was suspicious of Gray because he wasn't one of *us*. He wasn't *of* the Bureau, and we hadn't experienced a director from the outside. It was simple: Hoover *was* the Federal Bureau of Investigation; Gray was not.

We had little faith in the top echelon at Headquarters, the circle around Hoover. They were out of touch with the real FBI. Yet we couldn't have it both ways: we didn't take to outsiders but were leery of Hoover's minions as well. I knew a few SACs who would have made good directors. Ralph Miles, the best SAC I ever had, could have run the Bureau. But it was never going to happen for a SAC, and we all knew it. The Director's job would become a political football. Presidents were going to install their own people at the top of the FBI, men they could trust.

This suspicion of Gray, a legman for Nixon and his pals and a man with no law enforcement experience, co-existed with our fear that we'd be even worse off if one of Hoover's cronies had been promoted to Director. Gray had a short Bureau career and never went beyond serving as Acting Director. He resigned after his Senate confirmation hearings did him in. Actually, Nixon did him in. Gray destroyed Watergate-related evidence on request of the White House. When he admitted that he burned the evidence in his home fireplace, he too, was cooked.

There would be no more J. Edgar Hoovers.

Part Two: Clarence M. Kelley

President Nixon appointed Clarence Kelley to replace the fallen Patrick Gray as head of the FBI, and in July, 1973 Kelley was sworn in as the Bureau's permanent replacement for J. Edgar Hoover. Kelley was the first former street agent to head the FBI. He'd retired from the Bureau after a 23-year career, and after leaving the Bureau, served as the Chief of Police in his hometown of Kansas City, Missouri, prior to his appointment as FBI Director.

Kelley was a big, broad-shouldered, thick-chested teddy bear. His massive hands looked like paws. He might have been cast as the square jawed Dick Tracy. Distinguished looking, with thick gray hair, he seemed to fill a doorway when he entered a room in a dark, tailored suit. He was easy in conversation, liked a good joke, would squeeze your shoulder or slap you on the back without warning, crowd in and lower his voice or throw his head back and laugh loudly. His voice was raspy from years of heavy smoking. He tapped unlit cigarettes over and over on his desk top, gesturing with them, hiding them in his large hands before suddenly lighting up.

I applauded Richard Nixon's decision to hire a former FBI leader, a guy who'd started at the bottom as a street agent. Kelley had been one of *us,* and that was damn good for starters. There were still people in the office who had remembered working under Kelley when he was a SAC stationed in Birmingham, and they were unanimous in their praise. Kelley ran the Birmingham office with an even hand and didn't suck up to Headquarters. The FBI had a director. I was pleased.

The beginning of Kelley's tenure coincided with the formation of the Bureau's Special Weapons and Tactics teams, SWAT, which Kelley supported and promoted. Birmingham was one of the first offices to form a SWAT team, and I was fortunate to be selected for it. Two of my fellow SWAT team members, Leon Sizemore and Starley Carr, aka, Abner, formed a tight bond and life-long friendships.

The initial training for SWAT required two arduous weeks at the FBI Academy, at Quantico, Virginia, followed by physical and firearms training and the sharpening of skills back home. With the exception of several brief intervals, I remained on the Birmingham SWAT team until January, 1992, when I reluctantly resigned due to conflicts with foreign counterintelligence cases I was working. SWAT training and operations provided some of the most exhilarating and fun days of my FBI career.

The need for FBI SWAT teams was evident after U.S. marshals, FBI agents, and police from the Bureau of Indian Affairs (BIA) were confronted with putting down an armed disturbance by several hundred members of the American Indian Movement (AIM) at Pine Ridge Sioux Reservation in Wounded Knee,

South Dakota, February, 1973. That standoff with the Indians showed that the FBI was unprepared for confrontations against armed groups and required highly trained, fast reaction teams on the scene.

The siege at Wounded Knee lasted until the Indians gave up in May, 1973. Two Indians were killed and others wounded. An FBI agent and a U.S. Marshal were wounded by bullets.

Two years later, in June, 1975, radical members of AIM ambushed and executed FBI agents Ron Williams and Jack Coler near Wounded Knee while the agents were searching for a robbery suspect, an Indian from the Pine Ridge Reservation. The coldblooded murders of Coler and Williams at close range while they were lying wounded near their Bureau vehicle incensed the FBI. We all wanted to go to South Dakota to hunt down the killers. Richard Held, the SAC of the Minneapolis field office, headed a team of two hundred agents who identified four members of AIM as responsible for the murders of agents Williams and Coler.

Two of the murder suspects at Pine Ridge were acquitted in a trial, and charges against a third were dropped. The fourth suspect, AIM member Leonard Peltier, was convicted of killing the two agents and is serving a life term. Peltier received mushy-headed sentiment from some members of the entertainment and recording industries like Willie Nelson and Robert Redford, who have campaigned over the years to have Peltier paroled. Their sentiment is misguided. I share the strong belief of other FBI agents that Peltier is a murdering sonofabitch who should have received the death penalty for executing the two agents, both of whom had families.

Kelley took over the FBI right after the U.S. began winding down its decade of fighting in Vietnam. The early years of my FBI career were effected by the Vietnam War in the sense that I worked scores of fugitive investigations involving Selective Service violators, draft dodgers, and deserters from all branches of the armed forces. I cut my teeth on these cases, developing skills in locating and arresting fugitives, and honing my interview techniques and street savvy.

I was to have many close-in dealings with Director Clarence Kelley in the coming years.

Kelley was a street agent at heart and never took himself too seriously, the sort of guy who'd spring for a pitcher of beer—a trait we admired dearly. Unfortunately, he got himself into a jam in late 1977 when it became public that he had accepted home improvements made by Bureau employees. The improvements were small, involving woodwork around windows. Kelley later reimbursed the government, but in the post-Watergate climate, the press went after him and he was heavily criticized by politicians. He resigned in 1978.

CHAPTER FIFTEEN

THE YOUNG AND THE RESTLESS

Part One: Doing Foolish Things

You could find most anything along 20th Street in Birmingham. It was the cream of the city's thoroughfares, flowing from the flagpole at Linn Park at it's northern end, past bank towers, hotels, and restaurants downtown, then under the broad expanse of railroad tracks where commerce became less and less active, dividing the city's north and south sides. 20th Street was less busy on the south side of the trains. The buildings were not as tall. There was a hotel called the Parliament House where President Nixon gave a speech, and where I helped guard his daughter Julie and her husband David Eisenhower.

A hill on 20th Street led up to a plateau running for a half dozen blocks before the street climbed steeply over Red Mountain past the cast iron statue of Vulcan, the iron man known as the symbol of the city. The plateau area contained the historic *5 Points South* district, the city's only Bohemian area, a fun and entertainment center of night clubs, restaurants, gays, hippies, pigeons, a magnificent old Methodist church, a grand Baptist Church, record stores, a quaint water fountain, and a legitimate theater.

One evening I parked my BuCar on 20th Street near *5 Points South* and entered a hotel looking for a fugitive. The hotel rented by the week. I had a lead from another FBI office that he might be staying at the hotel under an alias. The guy was wanted for inter-state transportation of a stolen motor vehicle, ITSMV in FBI lan-guage. He had no history of being A&D: armed and dangerous. I quietly showed my credentials to the front desk and confirmed that the fugitive was a guest at the hotel. I got the room number and went upstairs.

I was playing Lone Ranger when I should have had at least Tonto with me. I didn't care. The guy was there and I was going to arrest him. I had time to call for help or backup, which would have gotten Leon, Abner, or Luther there in no time; there was no need for me to sail solo.

I stood in front of his room and knocked. The fugitive opened the door. I made him from a photograph I was carrying. He readily admitted who he was. I stepped inside the room and told him he was under arrest. He was docile and unthreatening, small in stature. No alarms went off in my head.

The fugitive asked if he could collect his things. I agreed and stayed close to him as he put on a shirt. I intended to handcuff him after he got dressed. A black and white TV was on low vol-ume in the room. There was traffic noise outside on busy 20th Street. The room was clean and neat. The hotel wasn't cheap, so he had money.

He buttoned up his shirt and abruptly sat down on the bed. I should have told him to stand back up and turn around. I should have cuffed him with his hands behind his back, palms out, the Bureau way. He leaned back on his elbows, calm and unperturbed. He wanted to talk, he said. I stood over him, prepared to listen, and positioned myself so he couldn't kick me. Maybe he was go-ing to finger other fugitives or provide information on federal or local investigations. Maybe I'd use him as an informant inside the Jefferson County Jail or in federal prison. Lots of maybes.

He spread his elbows further out and stared at me. He seemed a little nervous now.

"So talk," I told him.

His right hand slid slowly under the pillow where I couldn't see it. I'd had enough. I told him to stand up. His right hand slid deeper under the pillow.

"Pull your hand away from the pillow." He froze.

"Get up!"

He slowly came out of the bed and got to his feet. I pulled him farther away from the pillow and turned him around. I yanked out my silver handcuffs and put them on him, arms behind his back, palms out. Holding on to him by the metal cuffs, I slid my hand under the pillow and removed a snub-nosed .38 revolver, a five shot special, the smaller brother to the six shot .38 Smith & Wesson I carried. I confiscated the .38. The fugitive gave me a condescending smile that conveyed: *You dumb ass. I nearly had you.*

I took him out of the hotel and drove him the mile or so to the Jefferson County Jail on the north side of town. After checking him in as a federal prisoner, I went to the FBI office a block away and sent teletypes informing Headquarters and other FBI offices that the fugitive had been apprehended without incident, which was partially true. I left out the part where I'd behaved like a damn fool and enjoyed it.

Birmingham is a long and narrow city running northeast to southwest hugging the contours of Red Mountain. The city was thick with stolen vehicles. The whole state was. Alabama was a dumping ground for stolen cars, the end of the rainbow for car thieves. There was no title law in the state. You could present a bill of sale at the courthouse written across most anything and receive a vehicle tag saying *Heart of Dixie.* Or you could just make up your own handmade cardboard sign with the message: *Tag applied for.* You could do that in Alabama, drive around for months with cardboard messages in your rear window: *Tag stolen; Tag lost; Tag on the way.* Or you could have no tag or cardboard sign on your vehicle at all. Authentic tags that had expired were also common. Renew the tag if and when you felt like it was as Alabama as football. This was America, wasn't it? Local law enforcement frequently shrugged, looked the other way, and didn't crack down on this mischief. Alabama was a forgiving place.

Lincoln Continentals were popular with interstate thieves. The vehicles were stolen right off the Lincoln assembly lines in Michigan and brought to Alabama for quick and easy profit. I had recovered several stolen Continentals by randomly running the vehicle identification numbers, VINs, on parked cars in the city. The raised VIN numbers were located on small plates on the driver side dash just under the windshield. I sometimes cruised looking for stolen Lincolns in the downtown area. When that area played out, I would work the east and northeast end of the city after dark, the beer joints frequented by rednecks with tattoos. I carried a flashlight so I could read the VINs at night.

It wasn't quite dark when I drove my BuCar into northeast Birmingham looking for stolen Lincoln Continentals. I headed up Roebuck Parkway past used car lots, bars, restaurants, and strip malls. Generally, the racial makeup of the neighborhoods showed blacks in the north and west, whites in the south and east.

Cruising Roebuck Parkway near Center Point one evening on the northeast edge of Birmingham, I spotted a light-colored Continental in the parking lot of a bar. I pulled in and got out of the BuCar. The bar looked rough. It had painted cinder block walls and neon beer signs in the windows, loud music from a jukebox, thick motorcycles, pickups, and beat-up cars crowding the parking lot. And a brand new Lincoln Continental.

I walked over to have a look at the VIN. I wore a light jacket to cover my .38 Bureau Smith & Wesson revolver, which set snug against my right hip in a black holster I'd bought from another agent. It had a strap to keep the gun secure in the holster. I'd retired the tan leather Sloan holster the Bureau had issued at Quantico due to one drawback: it didn't have a strap to hold the revolver fast. The .38 could easily fall out when you ran. I'd chased an escaped federal prisoner through a field in Colorado one afternoon, jumping a small stream in pursuit. My gun fell into the water, but I kept running and arrested the guy—without my weapon! I went to a better holster after I was transferred to Birmingham and kept the Sloan as a memento of my early days in the FBI.

Alone in the bar parking lot in northeast Birmingham, I turned the flashlight on the VIN plate just under the windshield of the Continental. I copied the long number on a note pad, retreated to the BuCar and radioed the Birmingham FBI office, using the call signal of 200. The night clerk answered my call. I read the VIN over the air. The clerk copied the number and told me to stand by while he queried NCIC, the National Crime Information Center computer, to see if the Lincoln was stolen.

I waited. Loud music continued from the bar. Customers came and went. The FBI radio operator reached out to me, calling my credential numbers: 3674. He told me the Lincoln was stolen. I thanked him and said 10-7. I went straight for the entrance to the bar. I opened the door and went in. The place smelled of beer, cigarettes, and bodies. I stopped, looked around, took stock. The room was small and jammed with men in work clothes. I could tell this was a neighborhood hangout. As to who belonged to the stolen Lincoln Continental outside, I didn't have a clue. I should have turned around, walked back to the BuCar and summoned help, but I didn't. When the jukebox music stopped between selections, I walked to the middle of the floor and stood like Caesar.

"Who owns the Continental?" I shouted. Everyone stopped talking and stared at me.

"FBI. Who's driving the Lincoln?" I said. My adrenalin was firing. I faced all directions at once.

A dude got up from his table and walked over to me through the cigarette smoke. *The Lincoln was his,* he said, *what of it?* I told him it was stolen and to come with me, and he did, without a whimper of protest.

Out in the parking lot, the Lincoln owner said he didn't know the car had been stolen, a story that panned out through further investigation. I had my doubts, but I never came up with the evidence to charge him. The FBI confiscated the car and the owner was out of luck. My supervisor in the office, a man twice my age with a hundred times more Bureau experience, dressed me up and down. He demanded to know why I had walked into a crowded bar alone when I could have easily gotten help from other agents. And why hadn't I at least waited until the owner came out to his car, as agents do in bank robberies. Agents don't go into a bank when a robbery is in progress; we wait for the robber to come out.

What in blazes were you thinking? he asked. A room full of bystanders, maybe even accomplices, there could have been resistance, innocent people getting hurt, me getting hurt. I didn't have answers for the supervisor. I left his office with half my ass.

The office bulletin board showed I had recovered a new Lincoln Continental. The stat was added to my monthly total of arrests and recoveries. My total was high. It had been another bigshot month for me. Never mind that I might have gotten myself pickled in a redneck bar. I was omnipotent. That's not how you spell *stupid,* but it is how you spell fun.

I didn't learn. I received a phone call one afternoon from an informant who said an Army deserter I was hunting was hanging out at a particular house, and that the guy was there right now if I was interested. The vacant one-level house was in a poor residential area in the heart of north Birmingham. Local tough guys used the house for gambling, passing drugs and women around, and dividing up the loot after robberies.

I drove into the neighborhood to get my deserter. I was Gary Cooper at high noon, a lone force for God and country. The difference was, Cooper had at least *tried* to get help before he faced Frank Miller. I guess adrenalin had seized control of me.

I parked the BuCar several blocks away where I could see the house and get a feel for the neighborhood. The deserter could have left the house through the back door and I wouldn't have known it; I didn't have the alley covered.

I collected myself and drove the two blocks to the front of the house, got out, adjusted my suit to cover my .38 revolver, and walked up to the house. It was summer, hot, the way Alabama gets hot in the summer. I heard men's voices inside the house through the screen door. I opened the screen door and walked through a bare front room to a doorway and into the middle of the house, into the middle of a group of men shooting craps.

The deserter was sitting on the floor leaning against a dirty wall. I kept my eyes on him and quickly guessed there were a half-dozen males with him. I smelled marijuana.

Everyone jumped up when I came in. They looked surprised. There was a radio going.

"FBI. You're under arrest," I said, locking eyes with the deserter. "Let's go," I commanded. The deserter didn't move. No one moved.

"Come on. We've got a car outside," I said. I had suddenly become *we*.

I didn't edge closer. I wanted the deserter to come to me, to separate him from the others.

He hesitated and then slowly walked over. I took his elbow and positioned him on my left side away from my .38. I guided him out, kept my hand on him and an eye over my shoulder. I took him out the way I'd come in.

Once in the sun, I could sense the neighborhood watching. I had the deserter face the door of the BuCar. I brought his right arm back, then the left, turned his palms out and put the cuffs on him, the Bureau way.

In the crush of deserter arrests during the Vietnam War in the early '70s, with assaults on agents mounting by the week, the paperwork on my collar sailed through Headquarters without comment. My stats for arrests swelled on the office bulletin board. There was no column for being reckless and foolhardy.

Part Two: Volkswagen Arrest

Alone, I point my 1964 Volkswagen Beetle east and head out of Birmingham to catch a fugitive. It's nearly sun-up on an Alabama Saturday, a day full of promise here in the Heart of Dixie. My quarry is an Army deserter I'll call Jerry Dale Watkins. He's hiding out with countless relatives in the backwoods hollows near the small town of Leeds, just a spit east of Birmingham. Jerry Dale is quick as a rabbit, a stealthy son-of-a-gun who knows the deep woods behind his clapboard house like the dirt under his fingernails. He's eluded me several times before today. This morning I'm going to try to catch Jerry Dale asleep with his wife or one of his girlfriends. The Watkins folks aren't violent, just elusive. They have no tolerance for incarceration. Trying to capture them is high sport.

I'm going to trap Jerry Dale with my beloved white VW Bug. It's stylish, sports a handle-operated sunroof and flower petals hand-painted on the fenders by the free spirit I bought the car from years ago. I'm not wearing the prescribed Bureau robes as I head out in a one-man posse. My dark suit with matching dark tie, the Hoover blues as agents call them, have been replaced by bellbottoms and a T-shirt. It's summer so I roll the metal sunroof back to get more breeze. A blue steel .38 Smith & Wesson with six rounds is parked on my right hip in a Bureau-issue Sloan holster. Silver handcuffs press against the small of my back. I'm on a mission, looking for glory by capturing a Watkins.

Agents are like bankers: We don't like to work on the weekends. So what the hell am I doing going after a fugitive alone in a VW on Saturday, my day off? The answer is innovative necessity in the face of Bureau cant that agents should not endanger themselves by making arrests alone or conduct FBI business in personally owned vehicles. Sometimes, though, you just have to create your own fun by capturing Jerry Dale in his lair. I've learned from failure that Jerry Dale is not going to be caught if I show up in a caravan of BuCars with a dozen agents dressed in Hoover blues. The dark Bureau cars with dull tires give off a federal odor that's not conducive to the element of surprise, which means Jerry Dale and his kin have already headed deep into the woods by the time we get close, aided by an army of dogs who raise hell and spread the alarm.

I head out of Birmingham on Route 78. Traffic is starting to build with the dawn. The big rigs pull out of the twenty-four hour coffee shops and haul ass toward Atlanta. I fall in with the eighteen-wheelers east of Irondale, then gear down and leave 78 for the mess of two-lane roads leading into the hollows in the hills beyond Leeds. Trees flank the narrow blacktop and bury me in the first shadows of the day. Some of the road signs have been shot up for target practice.

Something is wrong with the headlights on my Bug. There's a dark spot on the highway ahead of me that shouldn't be there. I pull over and get out to look. The right headlight is out, but

I figure the sun will be up before long. I drive on with the AM radio going and the windows down. The '64 VW Beetles have 40 hp engines and are the first editions to have gas gauges. There's plenty of fuel perking in the rear-mounted engine.

I run out of blacktop and take the dirt road that meanders up the hollow. The old Alabama mountains form the lower spine of the Appalachians. First light settles on the tops of the Alabama pines crowning the ridges off to the east. Agents used to drive the Bureau cars flat out up the hollow, using speed to trap Jerry Dale. Speed did not work. We also drove slow, easing into position to run Jerry Dale to ground. Slow did not work. Countless dogs raised the alarm regardless of the speed as we swooped in. This morning, my one-headlight VW bites into the pre-dawn stillness, as I pass one rundown house after another, a litter of half-eaten cars on cinder blocks, discarded hubcaps and tires, and the remains of some of the first armadillos to migrate all the way up from Texas. I drive by dogs who barely stir, an army of *not* barking hounds hugging the grassless yards and eyeing me with little interest.

I drive into Jerry Dale's yard and kill the engine. It's eerily quiet. The Watkins clan is not stirring. I ease out of the Bug and walk up to the house. There's a screen door to receive what little breeze the hollows offer in summer. I look inside the house through the screen. Three bare-armed adults lie asleep on a mattress just inside the front door, a man between two women, a sheet loosely covering them, comfortable as hell. Clothes and shoes are strewn about the wooden floor. I try the screen door. It opens and I quietly step into the house. There's a wonderful smell of collard greens. Standing over the mattress, I get a good look at the guy. It's Jerry Dale Watkins. He doesn't look like the photo I have of him in Army uniform. His hair is long and greasy, his face heavier. He's been gone from the Army a long time.

I tiptoe over and gently shake him so as not to rouse the women. I don't want them waking suddenly and screaming, scaring the bejesus out of us all.

Jerry Dale's eyes pop open and he sees me. He doesn't move a muscle. I admire his control. I whisper that he's under arrest.

Damn those greens are inviting. I haven't had breakfast. Jerry Dale wants to know in a whisper why the dogs aren't barking. I don't have an answer. He shrugs, curses under his breath, and comes out from under the sheet in his underwear. He also has his boots on. I figure the boots are a habit he's acquired in order to stay ahead of the FBI.

I order him to get dressed. Both women awake and raise up on their elbows, half asleep. I remember them from earlier failed raids to arrest Jerry Dale. One of them may be his wife, but who knows. Both women are nude.

Jerry Dale tells the women he has to go back to the Army. The women want to know where the dogs are. Jerry Dale reaches for a pair of jeans nearby on the floor, but I tell him to hold on. I examine the jeans for possible weapons, a knife maybe, but I don't find anything, and hand the pants to him. He deftly eases his tight jeans over his boots. Damn, I've never been able to do that; my jeans always get hung up on my shoes. He puts on a t-shirt and stands.

I inquire about the collard greens. They smell wonderful. He understands. We casually walk the short distance into the kitchen. A lone pot simmers on the stove. The wonderful aroma of greens is overpowering. I'm reminded of my grandmother's kitchen in the hollows of West Virginia and her magic with collards.

Hungry? Jerry Dale asks. I nod. I call a temporary halt to the arrest. A time out.

Jerry Dale collects two plates and spoons out some greens for both of us. We sit at an old table and devour the greens and a spread of cornbread, wash them down with cold milk.

The women dress and chat in the other room, something about the dogs. Jerry Dale says he cooked the greens himself. I compliment him. We finish a delightful breakfast. The arrest resumes. I bring out the handcuffs.

Not in front of my family, he requests, and assures me he won't try to escape.

I acquiesce. I've already violated most of the FBI's rules of arrest, what's one more?

Jerry Dale hugs both women and we casually walk out of the house. Some of the other Watkins women have gathered around the VW. They stand back and let us pass. I figure the men took to the woods once the word spread that Jerry Dale was under arrest.

Jerry Dale is momentarily taken aback by the presence of the VW and looks at me for an explanation. I tell him it's a long story. He shrugs and says a casual goodbye to everyone as though he'll be back before long. Which is not far fetched since Army deserters are recidivists. Although this is the first time that Jerry Dale has been caught deserting, I'm confident he'll try again.

I drive out of the hollow with Jerry Dale in the front seat. When the dirt road ends and we reach hardtop, I stop and put the handcuffs on him, hands behind his back, the Bureau way. We head toward Birmingham with the sunroof back and windows down. It's already hot. August is going to have its way with us.

Jerry Dale and I make small talk. I tell him about the bummed up right headlight. He thinks about this, lost in thought. I ask him why he walked away from the Army without permission. It was the food, he says, he hated Army food. Cooking is his passion. He's a good cook, he says with pride. The Army doesn't know fleas about preparing food. I suggest that he finish his hitch in the Army, then find his way into a fancy kitchen in one of Birmingham's downtown restaurants. He considers this and shakes his head. The Army isn't for him. He'll run again first chance, he says. Besides, he can't stand cities. He's content to do his cooking at home in the hollow. Then I'll be back for him the next time he deserts, I tell him.

We drive by a barbecue joint in Irondale and a Shoney's just inside the Birmingham city line. Jerry Dale casually informs me it would be easy for him to open the door and roll out of the VW to freedom, handcuffs and all. I tell him to go ahead. After a pause, we look at each other and laugh.

The little VW federal prisoner wagon putt putts past the small businesses along First Avenue North. The twin towers of the First National Bank building and the South Central Bell head-quarters rise up ahead in the morning heat.

I downshift the four-speed, fall in with the pickups, Fords and Chevys going past Sloss Furnace below the viaduct, on into downtown to the Jefferson County Jail, located on the top floors of the Jefferson County Courthouse on 21st Street North. The Bureau's fourteenth floor office is in a building half a block away. I know the weekend clerks are up there alone taking care of business while the agents have the weekend off.

I park the VW at the basement entrance to the Courthouse reserved for law enforcement, and guide Jerry Dale by the elbow out of the VW and through an unmarked door into a small drab room, where two Jefferson County deputies wearing their traditional brown uniforms check my FBI photo credentials. They give me a once-over. Deputies aren't used to an agent showing up with a prisoner on a Saturday, particularly an agent dressed in jeans.

Trying to look like the photo on my credentials, I don't smile. I'm all business. Jerry Dale seems amused by all this law enforcement tittle. Satisfied that I'm for real, the deputies admit Jerry Dale and me into the basement holding area next to the elevator. Following procedure, I lock my weapon in a safe, pocket the key and lead Jerry Dale into the cramped elevator. We take a slow ride up to the 7th floor to the jail itself.

The old elevator jolts to a stop, the door bangs open and we step out into the busy main prisoner receiving area. Uniformed deputies man desks or mill around. They look at Jerry Dale and me with little interest. The place smells of cleaning fluid, cigarettes, and yesterday's food. There is no air conditioning, which keeps the uncirculated August air at jungle temperatures. You can sweat through your clothes just thinking about a summer day in the Jefferson County Jail. Male prisoners are kept on the two floors directly below the top level of the Courthouse, which is reserved for women inmates.

I take Jerry Dale across the room to the check-in counter for turning custody of your prisoner over to County authorities. I shoot the breeze with a deputy as I quickly fill out the paperwork labeling Jerry Dale Watkins Federal property belonging to the U.S. Army. The County houses deserters until the military picks them up, sometimes weeks later. Army green may look more inviting to Jerry Dale after a spell in the Jefferson County Jail. I turn to say goodbye.

"I figured it out," Jerry Dale says.

"What?"

"Why the dogs didn't bark."

It was the *headlight*, he says. The *missing* headlight in that *tiny* car fooled the dogs. The FBI always comes up the hollow in big cars with big headlights. The dogs didn't paid no attention to some puny car with one headlight. "The FBI don't play fair," Jerry Dale tells me.

I thank Jerry Dale for breakfast and leave. I cross the street and surprise the FBI weekend clerks. "Is it Monday already?" they ask.

My report to Headquarters omits more than it contains: U.S. Army deserter, Jerry Dale Watkins, is in custody. I fail to mention I'd gone after him alone in a 1964 Volkswagen with one headlight out and an *Impeach Nixon* decal on the dash. Like most agents in the field, I think of Washington as a giant mushroom to be kept in the dark and fed a diet of manure.

After leaving the FBI office in the seasoned hands of the weekend clerks, I make a mental list of repairs for my VW mechanic. Fix this, fix that, I will tell him. Tune this and tune that. Don't repair the headlight.

The next time Jerry Dale runs away from his military obligations, I'll go into the Leeds hollows in my trusty Bug. If that doesn't work, I'll think up something different. Maybe ride in on a motorcycle or a mule. Anything to fool the dogs.

Members of the Birmingham FBI Crime Resistance Team pose in front of the news media with University of Alabama head football coach Paul "Bear" Bryant in Tuscaloosa, September, 1975. Bryant graciously participated in a public service promotion for Crime Resistance, an FBI crime prevention program. From L-R: Birmingham Police Officer Joe Warden, Agent Leon Sizemore, Coach Bryant, me, Birmingham Police Sergeant Earl Melton. The length of my hair and sideburns are a tad long by FBI standards.

CHAPTER SIXTEEN

CRIME RESISTANCE

In 1975 the FBI decided to fight crime by preventing it on the federal level. The cops invented crime prevention; the Bureau was going to show them how to do it. The program, called *Crime Resistance,* was the creation of John Coleman, a non-agent and top Kelley advisor whom Kelley had brought with him to FBIHQ from the Kansas City PD, where Kelley had served as chief before heading the Bureau.

The initial Crime Resistance program called for the marriage of two Bureau agents and two local cops from different locations. Leon Sizemore and I were thrown together again to be on the Crime Resistance team for Birmingham. We worked directly out of the office of the Birmingham Chief of Police, and only went into the FBI office to collect our paychecks. The Birmingham SAC did not like Leon and me being on our own, essentially out of his control, but there was nothing he could do about it. He was afraid of John Coleman.

So when John Coleman came to Birmingham to recruit two agents for his Crime Resistance team, I saw the opportunity for change and stepped forward. It was one of the best decisions I made in my career. Because Birmingham was a small FBI office, agents jumped into the middle of big investigations regardless of our specialties. There was spillover of assignments that provided variety. I remained on the SWAT team, but my focus was elsewhere.

Crime Resistance was a watershed in my career. The work took me off the street and into another Bureau world. I flourished. I'd begun to question my role and life as a grunt working criminal investigations. Sure, the chase and arrests still had allure, but I began to feel professionally empty and unfulfilled, losing the sense of accomplishment. As Peggy Lee sang, *Is That All There Is?* I wondered. There had to be more. I wanted something more mentally challenging that would take me where I'd never been. The FBI offered great variety, and I hadn't tapped into it.

Working away from the FBI office was a heady freedom unknown by Bureau agents. Our immediate boss was Birmingham Chief of Police James Parsons, whose down-home, southern boy demeanor masked a shrewd and decisive intellect and leadership style. Leon and I thoroughly enjoyed working under Parsons and with the two cops, Joe Warden and Earl Melton.

Given the inherent antagonisms, jealousies, and turf battles between the FBI and local law enforcement nationwide, you might have expected tension between two agents and two Birmingham cops working together every day. There wasn't. Leon and I got along straight off with Melton and Warden. We developed friendships that last to this day.

Our FBI leader, John Coleman, had California origins. He read widely, was an intellectual, and could converse on many subjects. His reserved and unsmiling demeanor contrasted with Kelley's openness. White-haired and in his sixties, Coleman was suave and debonair. He smoked English cigarettes and made frequent trips to Ireland to visit family. He had money and let his Bureau paychecks pile up in his Headquarters desk. Both men lived in buttoned up, tailored suits. Coleman wore colored shirts, Kelley stayed with Bureau white. When he visited Birmingham to sit down with Leon and me and the two cops about Crime Resistance, Coleman paid for our expensive dinners, then abruptly retired early to his hotel room. He never drank with us. His rooms were the best in Birmingham. He had little use for Headquarters supervisors; he once told Leon and me that if the FBI was the best in American law enforcement, think how bad the rest of the profession must be. Coleman made enemies in the FBI.

Join the Resistance was the slogan with which Coleman hatched the program. Crime Resistance was no more than a mirror of the crime prevention programs existing in hundreds of American and foreign cities, especially in the United Kingdom. Scotland Yard had been at it successfully for decades. The Bureau called it Crime Resistance, and we told the world that it was a different approach to getting citizens involved in preventing crimes. It wasn't. The cops knew it; they were on to us.

Coleman had a young assistant named Bill Brannon, a supervisor at Headquarters whose job was to oil the nuts and bolts of Crime Resistance. Brannon was in daily contact with the agents and cops, ensured that the paper work was correct and done on time, and traveled to the locations frequently to stoke the chiefs. Leon and I became fast friends with Brannon, a regular guy with a contagious sense of humor.

One night in the fall of 1975, the Birmingham 4, as we called ourselves, plus Bill Brannon, Coleman's assistant, were in Kelley's office at FBIHQ working on a report. We finished around 11:00 p.m. Kelley and Coleman had gone home long ago. We needed to get the report typed so Kelley could read it the first thing the next morning. I called the typing pool and told the head steno that I had an expedite matter for the Director to read early tomorrow. She told me the typists were busy but to bring the report down to her and they might or might not get to it by morning. I could drop it off she said. Thinking that she had misunderstood me, I reiterated that this was a matter for the Director, and had to be typed *immediately.* She repeated her answer, told me to leave the report with the steno pool. They *might* get to it. She couldn't promise.

J. Edgar Hoover had been dead for three and a half years when I made that call to the typing pool at Headquarters. When he ruled the FBI, it would have been unthinkable to shrug off a request coming straight from the Director's office.

One afternoon, during the 1970s hey-days of Crime Resistance, I accompanied Police Officer Joe Warden to the Bank for Savings Building. We went to the bank's basement to plead our case on a project we were working on as fellow members of the Birmingham Crime Resistance team. There I saw the most beautiful woman I'd ever seen. She met me with a firm handshake and unyielding eye contact. Her name was Patricia Vance. I was guessing she was in her twenties, tall, gorgeous, with long blonde hair parted down the middle.

Joe and I interviewed Pat, and she was impressively professional, knowledgeable, and steady in the presence of two law enforcement guys staring at her across her desk. She spoke in the elegant current of a well-educated southerner. She worked in the Marketing Department of the bank and operated the largest advertising sign in Alabama, a huge message board atop the Bank for Savings Building; you could see it from all over Birmingham, day or night. Joe and I wanted Pat to program messages on the board giving information about our Crime Resistance Program, and we were looking for a way to do it cheaply, that is, free. Pat listened without comment, letting us make our pitch.

There was one moment, while Joe was making a point, that I happened to glance in the corner and saw an Auburn umbrella leaning against the wall. Without hesitation, I looked at Pat and blurted out, "I *know* you didn't go to Auburn."

Pat fired back: "My husband is an Auburn graduate," drilling a hole through me with her dark brown eyes.

Joe stared me down. He was angry as hell that I interrupted him, and we both knew my question to Pat was unprofessional. Nevertheless, we secured a pledge from Pat that the bank would join the resistance by running our messages free of charge. Mission accomplished. We told Pat we would call her periodically with new texts for the signboard.

Outside Joe jumped me about the interruption, and I apologized. He broke into a smile and playfully slapped me on the shoulder. "FBI agents," he said.

Joe and I phoned in new texts to Pat for several months, and she was always well-versed and fun to talk to. We once had her welcome John Coleman and Bill Brannon to Birmingham on the sign. They were most impressed. We even ran Clarence Kelley's name across the board.

There were long periods when I did not talk to Pat on the phone. Leon Sizemore and I went to San Francisco on Crime Resistance duty as well as to other pilot cities, and went to FBI HQ to meet with Coleman and Brannon. We courted Governor George Wallace, Bear Bryant, and Auburn coach Shug Jordan.

When Crime Resistance phased out, I attended to other FBI duties. One day I was on afternoon surveillance in a van in downtown Birmingham, pointing the long lens on two New Left guys handing out the communist newspaper, *The Daily Worker,* when Patricia Vance walked smack dab into my lens. I took her photo as she passed by, and it interested me to note about myself that my juices flowed at the sight of her. I called her the next day and asked her why she was cavorting with communists. She said some of her best friends were communists. I asked her to lunch.

She walked in wearing a short purple skirt. Over cherry Cokes, burgers, sassafras, and moonbeams we caught up with each other's lives, including our marital statuses. She had left her husband and was living in an apartment with her infant daughter, Stacey. Her divorce was nearly final.

We started dating and I was totally smitten, love drunk, hell bent to marry her. Numerous lunches and dinners later, I finally got to meet Stacey, an adorable redhead, and soon began to cherish and love her as well. I missed my boys, and Stacey, who called me Jack, helped to fill the void.

Pat was a native of Talladega, Alabama, the oldest and tallest of four Gilbert sisters. Her father, William, raw-boned and handsome in his youth, was a World War II Army Air Corp vet. Tall, inquisitive, with black hair, he was a successful Talladega businessman, and it was clear that Pat had gotten her height and dark eyes from him. He had endless energy and wherewithal. He smoked cigarettes in a holder, á la FDR, while listening to Lawrence Welk on eight-track tapes. He was a hoot, and I liked him right away.

Pat's mother, Muriel, was a spirited, lovely, green-eyed woman who ran a tight domestic ship. She had to with four daughters. Pat was her mother's right hand and helped raise the other three girls. Pat's intelligence and talents were manifested in many ways: She landed an academic scholarship in math to Samford University in Birmingham, her soaring voice was much in demand in area churches, she played the clarinet in high school and was a splendid pianist, and she somehow acquired a soul-stirring and profound knowledge of mixed drinks. Her Rusty Nails glow with good cheer. Had she not dedicated herself to academic pursuits, I have no doubt she would have been much in demand as a bartender in area saloons.

After a Master's Degree in Microbiology from UAB and thinking about going to medical school, Pat opted to be a high school science teacher instead so she could spend more time as mother to Stacey. I admired her for that. In 1978 Brett, Duane, and Deke spent half their summer with me at my apartment, and the very first time they encountered Stacey she grabbed one of Deke's wooden airplanes and broke it. Deke didn't fret much over the broken airplane, and the boys and Stacey quickly bonded. Pat was terrific with my sons, and they responded by growing to love her.

Pat and I were married in Birmingham in a simple ceremony, on March 8, 1980. Stacey stood with us during the ceremony. We honeymooned for a week in Bermuda, and for the first time I heard Pat refer to herself as Mrs. Owens. It had a most gratifying ring to it. Still does.

During that two-year ride with Crime Resistance, Leon and I traveled to three other pilot cities, and to Headquarters to meet with Coleman, Brannon, and occasionally Director Kelley. We also spent several months in San Francisco in early 1976 to launch Crime Resistance in the Bay area. It was my first trip to San Francisco and I loved the place. The cop I worked with had been born and raised in the area, and he took me to some great local restaurants off the path. We took advantage of his moonlight job as head of security for a major downtown hotel. One night after work, we started at a bar in the basement of the hotel and worked our way up to the top, where we sat at a table with an incredible view of the city and Bay area.

I rode all day with the cop and local FBI agents, learned my way around the city in the way that taxi drivers and law enforcement do. Leon and I jogged across the Golden Gate Bridge and took long runs along the ocean side of the city and into Golden Gate Park. We got to know the mounted patrol headquartered in the Park, and used their locker room and showers. We played racquetball on the Army base at the Presidio, one of the most beautiful locations in the country, overlooking the Bay and Golden Gate Bridge.

There I was, feeling so proud, one of the Bureau's "experts" on crime prevention. While I was playing racquetball at the Presidio, someone stole my watch.

I never went back full time to reactive criminal investigations. I joined Leon Sizemore in recruiting and testing agent and clerical applicants. The work was most gratifying, particularly recruiting women agents, a stark contrast to the way I'd viewed applicant work as a new agent in Denver. In the mid '80s, I happily went underground into counterintelligence.

John Coleman reshaped the Crime Resistance program to target federal crimes as a purely FBI venture, and expanded it into every field office. Headquarters supervisors and street agents didn't believe in it, though, and it never really took off. The program didn't last much beyond Kelley's tenure as Director of the FBI. Agents today have never heard of it.

When the pilot program teams were disbanded in 1977, we returned to the Birmingham FBI office, where we now had to *straighten up and zip our flies* in the straitjacket of Bureau rules under the glare of the SAC.

I visited my sons as often as possible, driving the 1200-mile round trip in a Pontiac Bonneville I had bought, roomy enough to fit me and the boys. I was trying to make it work. Ginni wanted to restrict my time with the boys to short periods in North Carolina. I took her to court in Alabama and won the right to have the boys with me in Birmingham for half of each summer, and for Christmas every other year. Ginni adapted to the new rules and fully cooperated to make the boys available for my visits. She never tried to turn them against me.

Through the years I made dozens of trips from Birmingham across I-20, up I-95, and along State Rte. 41 to the North Carolina coast, to watch Brett and Duane surf and skateboard in competitions, and Deke play baseball, soccer, and football. I watched Deke play football, whether at home or away, every Friday. I came to know the back roads and tobacco country towns in eastern North Carolina. I drove all over the country in the trusty family GMC van to watch Deke play during his four years in college. I ran that van for sixteen years. The kids grew up in it. It never let us down. I matured in slow degrees as I tried to become a better father.

CHAPTER SEVENTEEN

THE ATLANTA CHILD MURDERS

May, 1981. FBI profilers from the Academy at Quantico, headed by the incomparable John Douglas, predict that the serial killer terrorizing Atlanta is an intelligent and sophisticated black male in his twenties, and not some other race because he's been able to find and dispose of his victims in African-American neighborhoods without standing out or drawing attention. The profilers say the killer is a police buff who owns a large police-type dog like a Doberman or a German Shepherd, and that he uses his car to transport some of his victims. Clothes and other evidence from the murder victims may be found in the car according to the profile, along with dog hairs. The killer believes he's smarter than law enforcement and, when caught, will relish the publicity and matching wits with police. He's been dumping bodies out in the open on land, which has led to incriminating hairs and fiber evidence. The FBI profilers believe the killer will start dumping the bodies in a river to wash away the evidence.

But I'm not thinking about the profile. I'm sick and tired of Waffle House coffee and their spongy toast. It's hours 'til daybreak as I sit in my BuCar near a bridge over the Chattahoochee River in Atlanta, Georgia. Atlanta is a big league city, a southeast hub for professional sports, Delta Airlines, and the worst traffic in Dixie. During the civil rights struggles of the '50s and '60s, Atlanta billed itself as *The City Too Busy To Hate,* in stark contrast to Birmingham with its fire hoses and Bull Connor. It has been said that the only thing wrong with Atlanta is that it is surrounded by Georgia.

The bodies of black children and young black adults have been showing up all over the Atlanta area for two years. People are afraid to go out of their homes, day or night. The body count is twenty-eight according to local police, and the Bureau has doubts that all of the victims are the work of the serial killer. The decision about the number of victims is above my pay grade. I'm one of two street agents on loan to Atlanta from Birmingham, two of a large number of agents pouring into Atlanta from southeast field offices. My lot is to sit from sundown to sunup with two Atlanta cops and watch a bridge across the Chattahoochee River on the hunch that the killer will show up and dump one of his victims into the river. Gregg Gilliland, the other Birmingham agent, is on duty one bridge upriver from my location. He's a First Office Agent, FOA, mature, a committed professional. I'll probably be working for him one day.

Young police cadets are stationed at water level watching and listening for a body to hit the water, one cadet under each bridge along the river, spending nights in pup tents in the Georgia heat fighting off mosquitoes and flies. These poor cadets have law enforcement aspirations and eagerly perform this wretched assignment without complaint. We have it easy in our cars.

This marriage of cops and agents on a series of murders would not normally come under the FBI's jurisdiction; however, President Carter, followed by President Reagan, decreed that the Bureau work this case, so here we are. Officially, we're hanging our presence on kidnapping and civil rights violations, but this is thin and everyone knows it. It was a good move politically for the White House to inject the FBI into this unsolved series of murders, especially for Carter, a Georgia native. The elephant in the room is that local law enforcement was not making much headway in solving the murders; locals and agents were thrown together in an uneasy alliance.

The two Atlanta cops in my BuCar are okay guys. We pass the nights talking about sports and our families, how the crazy hours and bad food make law enforcement a bitch. We over-coffee and under-sleep, our bodies confused by being awake under the moon and asleep during the sunlit daytime. We haven't pickled each other over which Atlanta radio station to listen to. They haven't expressed resentment of FBI agents who make a lot more money and who are running this damn nightmare because the Atlanta PD couldn't solve it. If anything happens at the bridges at night, we have orders to call the Atlanta FBI office first, not the PD. I can imagine how the cops don't like the Bureau messing in their sandbox, but these guys have not let on if it bothers them. They're good police.

This is the fourteenth and last night for us to watch the bridges. There are forty cops and agents involved. The Bureau gave it two weeks and we're winding down. When the sun comes up in a few hours, the bridges will be abandoned and some other strategy will be tried. At this point, I'm glad my part is nearly over so that I can go home to my wife and kids. Gregg Gilliland and I will be replaced by fresh FBI bodies who will attack the serial murders from another angle. The bridge I'm watching is well traveled even late at night. The cops and I don't hold much hope the killer will use this bridge as a dump site. Bell Telephone workmen labor near our bridge most of the night. The nights have been warm, so the cops and I alternate between air conditioning and rolling down the windows.

Just a few more hours and the shift will be over. I haven't heard from Gregg on the FBI radio tonight, which is not unusual; he's reserved and stays off the radio, focusing on his surveillance up-river at the Jackson Parkway Bridge over the Chattahoochee.

Even though Greg and I are agents assigned to the Birmingham FBI, on this assignment we are under the direct authority of the Special Agent in Charge of the Atlanta office, John Glover, the first African-American to head an FBI field office. When I reported to Atlanta two weeks earlier, I was curious about whether Glover was actually a good SAC or whether the Bureau just wanted the publicity to promote equal opportunity, especially in a southern city. However, watching Glover in action up close, I no longer have questions about his ability. He's a leader and not one of those candyass *managers* that pass for leaders around the Bureau. Glover personally gave the visiting agents an impressive briefing on the Atlanta child murders case. He could have come in the room, said *howdy,* and bolted. He didn't.

Glover is quiet and doesn't raise a fuss when he's giving orders to a room full of agents. The Atlanta brick agents tell me that Glover backs them up and that his word is good. I figure he's had to kick ass and suck up to get where he is, since the old boy network running the Bureau is white. Regardless, I like him. Perhaps, down the road, after he's savored the many SAC perks, he'll prove the argument for equality by becoming as big a jerk as many other FBI supervisors.

The two cops and I are in plain clothes in my unmarked BuCar for both comfort and strategy. We want to surprise the killer, not let him or anyone else know we're watching the bridges. Nothing has been reported in the media about what we're doing along the river. The lid is tight.

Except for the waitresses at the Waffle House. They made us straight off. Maybe because we come in at ungodly hours wearing jackets in May heat to cover our guns and handcuffs. Maybe it's the portable radio we bring into the booth, low volume, so we can hear the FBI traffic, especially from one of the police cadets on the river. Although we're in the Waffle House for only a few minutes at a time, the waitresses say things like, *it sure is comforting having you guys around, what with people coming in here drunk at all hours and running out without paying.* Or, *where's the radar gun going to be tomorrow?*

Gregg Gilliland and I have settled into a happy routine these last two weeks in Atlanta. As soon as we leave our respective bridges at sunup, we convoy into downtown Atlanta to eat steak and eggs at the International House of Pancakes near our hotel. Afterward, we sleep in separate rooms at the hotel for no more than five or six hours. Neither or us can sleep during the day. We get up around noon, eat a sandwich at a deli, then drive to the campus of Georgia Tech University for a workout. We run laps around Grant Field, Tech's storied football stadium. After running, we sunbathe in the bleachers, which is good for our morale since there are scores of coeds lying on towels and blankets in the stands.

After several hours of this uplifting surveillance, Gregg and I go over to the student center at Tech where we help ourselves to their weight room and tennis courts. No one challenges us; we're in good condition and don't look much older than the students. Gregg is a good athlete and we take turns beating each other in tennis. We finish our workout and return to our hotel rooms to shower and dress for the night ahead. Before reporting to our respective bridges, we select a nice restaurant, usually some franchise place like Steak & Ale, for a wonderful meal at government expense. We satisfy our big appetites, then head to the bridges for a night of it.

The two cops and I take turns selecting the FM or AM radio program for the evening, settle in, alternate dozing off. One of us always has an eye on the bridge and the Bell Telephone guys in hard hats.

An FBI agent I'll refer to as Mexican Joe, who is not a Mexican at all but a tall Texan with a big longhorn belt buckle, jeans and cowboy hat, frequently comes on the Bureau radio in the wee hours with a barrage of Spanish about something or other. I met him at the initial briefing in the Atlanta office concerning the bridge surveillance. He's out of the FBI's Columbia, South Carolina office.

Joe doesn't speak Spanish to anyone in particular during the night, and no Spanish comes back at him over the radio. He simply broadcasts for the benefit of a large audience of cops and FBI agents. I recognize a few Spanish words here and there—words like *senorita, pasto,* and *fugitive*—and I know that Mexican Joe has women, food, and fugitives on his mind. He holds forth in a slow Texas-style Spanish, coming on the radio without warning to talk or sing a Spanish song. He helps us slide through the night.

There's a pop of static on the FBI radio. Sounds like someone keyed a microphone, then didn't transmit. The two Atlanta cops and I quit talking and listen.

The radio comes alive again. Gregg reports that a station wagon stopped on his bridge, that the driver got out, unloaded something out of the back of the vehicle and dropped it into the river. *Something big hit the water!* jumps out of the radio. I don't recognize the voice. I later learned it was the police cadet on the shore under the bridge.

The two cops and I stare a hole through the FBI radio. I glance at our bridge, about 150 yards away. There are no stopped vehicles or pedestrians on it. I'm getting paranoid.

Gregg reports that the driver of the station wagon got back into the car and is driving off. Gregg is going to follow it.

The FBI radio dispatcher says 10-4, requests that Gregg keep giving his location, and that FBI and PD help is on the way. I'm wide awake, jumping to join in. The dispatcher directs units to assist Gregg. The cops and I stay put. We haven't been directed to leave. Gregg provides his location and direction as he follows the station wagon. He identifies it as an older Chevy and gives the Georgia tag number in an admirably controlled voice. The driver isn't doing anything kinky like slowing down, speeding, or violating one-way streets.

The station wagon takes I-285, the beltway around Atlanta. Other units catch up with Gregg and fall in behind him. He advises that they are in position to stop the vehicle. Radio FBI Atlanta advises that motor vehicle records show the tag comes back as a 1970 Chevy station wagon registered to Wayne Williams, a black male age 23, that NCIC is negative with no *wants,* meaning that there are no arrest warrants outstanding for Williams, and that the vehicle is not stolen. Williams is clean. Gregg advises they are going to stop the station wagon. He goes 10-7, ending his transmission. The air goes dead.

The cops and I wait. Everybody in the FBI and Atlanta PD wait. I stare at *my* bridge, sneer at it as unworthy, wish that whatever happened on the Jackson Parkway Bridge had happened on my bridge so I could be right in the middle of things. We wait. FBI radio directs more units to Gregg's location. We wait. The cops and I speculate that if there had been trouble at the stop we would have heard by now. There is no trouble, probably.

FBI radio comes alive. Mexican Joe transmits in Spanish. I figure Joe had better get his spurs off the air. His transmission is cut off by a voice that identifies himself as the FBI night supervisor, and that whoever is doing all that Spanish should get off the air.

We wait. Time drags, hems and haws, and the cops and I come off the adrenalin mountain a little. We are primed to spring in any direction, but there's no direction. It's getting lighter and bridge traffic picks up as folks drive to work.

FBI radio cracks. The dispatcher talks to the police cadet under the Jackson Parkway Bridge. The cadet reports that he can't see anything floating in the Chattahoochee River.

If a body *did* go into the river, how long would it stay submerged? Would it surface, and where?

A mic is keyed on the FBI network. Gregg comes back on the radio, identifies himself, reports that the driver of the 1970 Chevy station wagon is Wayne Williams, who we now know is the registered owner of the vehicle. Williams is cooperative and friendly, says he stopped on the Jackson Parkway Bridge to dump trash into the river, that he throws trash in the river all the time. Bullshit to that, the cops and I say to each other. Gregg notes on the air that clothes are visible in plain sight in the back of the vehicle. Williams insists the clothes are his. Maybe there is something else back there with the clothes, Gregg speculates on the radio, other evidence. He wants to interview Williams in depth and requests marching orders from the FBI night duty supervisor, the same supervisor who told Mexican Joe to get off the radio.

Gregg's transmission suddenly ends. The radio goes silent.

We wait. We're jumping in our own internal juices, convinced that Wayne Williams is the serial killer because he fits the profile to a tee: *black male, roomy vehicle, suspicious clothes lying in the back of the vehicle.* The cops and I don't buy Williams's story that he dumped trash off the Jackson Parkway Bridge into the Chattahoochee River.

The night duty supervisor comes back on the air and orders Gregg to give him a *land line,* which in English means to call him so that they can have a cozy little chat out of earshot of those slugs out in the cars. Hells, bells, and grits, the two Atlanta cops and I assert. We've been cut out of the loop. Decisions are being made while we sit on an impotent bridge.

The vote in my BuCar is 3-0, unanimous in favor of hauling Williams into the Atlanta FBI office and interrogating the hell out him. We want his 1970 Chevy station wagon searched and vacuumed immediately. We want to bug and search everything in the world that Williams owns and stuff he doesn't own as well.

Meanwhile, the sun is up and this one particular bridge, the one the cops and I have been surveilling for two weeks while drinking Waffle House coffee, is worthless and a dead end. Screw this bridge. We want to haul over to Gregg's location.

This was pre-cell phones, so Gregg is now forced to find a telephone, which street agents don't have in their BuCars but which supervisors have even though supervisors don't need them. But that's another story.

Gregg Gilliland, an FOA tender and inexperienced in FBI years, has been thrust centerfold into the white heat of the most important and high-visibility investigation in the Bureau. I'm confident he is up to it. I admit a bias since Gregg is a friend as well as a colleague, but I damned well know a good agent when I see one. Besides, he's an essential player on our FBI softball team.

Gregg breaks through on the radio, says they are finished with Wayne Williams and have turned him loose. Gregg is returning to the Atlanta FBI office.

Turned him loose! Say whaaat?

The cops and I are incredulous. The Bureau is playing softball with Williams instead of jumping in his knickers. I smell a Bureau supervisor who lost his nerve. I don't know how high up the FBI food chain this stupid decision goes, but even from the distance of my BuCar, Williams looks good on these serial murders of black children. We, the two Atlanta cops and I, have already tried and convicted the bastard. We trust our law enforcement instincts.

The two-week surveillance of the bridges is finished. The cops and I say goodbye, promise to keep in touch even though we know we won't. I'm going home to Birmingham and my family, but not before I go into the Atlanta FBI office to have a talk with

Gregg about what went down and what went wrong with Wayne Williams on I-285.

I drive downtown in a mess of traffic to the FBI office adjacent to the Hyatt House Hotel, and use my special card to gain entry into the Bureau's garage. I ride up the elevator to the 10th floor. Gregg is waiting for me, gets me aside for a private talk. He tells me the first thing out of Wayne Williams's mouth when Gregg pulled him over on I-285 is, *"Is this about all those murders?"* Williams has no idea why he is stopped. For all he knows, the tail lights on his Chevy wagon were out.

Williams says he threw trash off the Jackson Parkway Bridge, that he's in the music business, a bachelor who lives with his parents. He is calm, even-tempered, enjoys talking to Gregg and the cops. He's sorry about littering, throwing trash into the Chattahoochee River, and won't do it again.

Gregg is certain he's lying. The story about throwing trash into the river is absurd. Mindful of the profile, Gregg had looked into the station wagon and saw a variety of clothes lying loosely in the back. Williams had claimed the clothes were his. Neither Gregg nor the cops on the scene believe Williams's story. Gregg and the other law enforcement on the scene want to detain Williams for further interrogation in the FBI office.

Why does Williams walk? I want to know.

The night supervisor said to turn Williams loose, Gregg said.

Cover yourself, I advise Gregg. Do it now before we drive back to Birmingham. Don't wait until we get home to file a report about what happened. File it right now, here in Atlanta. Report that you wanted to bring Williams in for questioning and were overruled by Bureau higher-ups. Gregg will then have his story firm on paper in case the night duty supervisor has clouds in his memory, hedges, or does a backstroke away from who in hell made the decision to release Williams. Gregg sits down and drafts his report in the isolation of a small interview room in the Atlanta field office.

Mexican Joe and other agents come into the office after leaving their bridges across the Chattahoochee River. They question why we didn't hold Wayne Williams. There is no clear answer from the bosses in the office. We listen on the FBI radio for any sign of a body floating down river from the Jackson Parkway Bridge.

Gregg finishes his report and has it typed. He signs it while I wait for him, hoping that a body will surface in the river so that we can pay a visit to Wayne Bertram Williams.

It's afternoon before Gregg and I break away from the office to eat breakfast for lunch at the International House of Pancakes. The media has a scent that something was up last night on the Atlanta Child murders investigation. Press inquiries are being made. Gregg and I leave our guns, handcuffs, and portable radios in our BuCars while we eat so that we won't look like cops and have to answer questions from the waitresses about what in the world went on last night on the bridges across the Chattahoochee River.

Wayne Williams drove to his house in the Atlanta area after Gregg was ordered to release him that morning on I-285. According to neighbors, he hauled boxes of stuff out of his house and cleaned the inside of his station wagon.

Two days after Williams dumped something large into the Chattahoochee River, the nude body of a black male named Nathaniel Carter surfaced downstream. During that time, the Bureau and the Atlanta PD had Williams under loose surveillance and looked into his background; he owned a German shepherd dog and had driven a surplus police vehicle at one time. He liked to listen to police radio on a scanner. He fit the remarkable profile done by John Douglas and others from the FBI profiling unit at Quantico.

When Carter's body floated up, the surveillance tightened, and Williams had an escort on his bumper every time he left his house. The FBI calls this *bumper locking* a subject, following so close that the subject knows he's under surveillance. Agents love this maneuver, which stands in contrast to the usual directive not to be *made* on a surveillance.

Williams cooperated initially, voluntarily coming into the FBI office in Atlanta, where an interrogation was not fruitful and a polygraph inconclusive. He was intelligent, articulate, enjoyed talking to agents and looking around the office.

At first there wasn't enough evidence to arrest Williams; nevertheless, a search warrant was executed at the residence he shared with his parents and on his 1970 Chevrolet station wagon. Neighbors had already reported that Williams had cleaned his car, and now hair and fiber evidence linking him to twelve of the twenty-eight murder victims was found in his car and residence.

After the hairs and fibers were matched by labs in Georgia and at FBI Headquarters, Williams was arrested on June 21, 1981, for the murder of Nathaniel Carter, almost a month to the day after Williams dumped Carter's body into the Chattahoochee River. The evidence was irrefutable.

Williams's trial began in January of 1982, on two counts involving the murders of Nathaniel Carter and Jimmy Ray Payne. The scientific evidence was overwhelming: fibers from twelve murder victims were matched to Williams's bedspread, the carpets in his bedroom, living room, and 1970 Chevy. There were also hairs from his German shepherd found on the victims. On February 27, 1982, the jury returned a verdict of guilty in both murders. Williams was sentenced to two consecutive life terms, which he is in now serving in Georgia. He continues to maintain his innocence.

In the opinions of Gregg Gilliland and other cops and agents at the scene where Williams was stopped on I-285, Williams should have been arrested or at least brought in for questioning. Gregg was not blamed for releasing Williams, and his career did not suffer. The FBI night duty supervisor was not officially criticized for his baffling decision. Winning in court can smooth over a landscape of wrinkles.

CHAPTER EIGHTEEN

WILLIAM H. WEBSTER

In February, 1978, President Carter appointed William H. Webster, judge, U. S. Court of Appeals for the 8th Circuit, to succeed Clarence Kelley as Director of the FBI. The Senate easily confirmed Webster, who had an impeccable record of integrity and fairness as a judge.

From a distance, Webster seemed a cold fish. He had a natty, Ivy League lawyer look that telegraphed he was in the wrong place, that he should be over at CIA, where he indeed ended up in 1987 after he voluntarily left the Bureau in good standing. Meanwhile, he was ours.

Webster came to Birmingham on October 5, 1981. My job was to guard him. I formed a team of agents. Warnings preceded Webster's arrival in Birmingham; the Charlotte FBI office apparently hadn't given Webster the royal treatment he felt he deserved. After he returned to the cushy seats on the 7th floor of Headquarters, Webster complained that the security around him was lax during his brief visit to Charlotte for a speech.

Webster had another complaint about his trip to Charlotte: agents put him on the wrong plane for the commercial flight back to Washington. The mistake was discovered before the plane took off. Agents rushed up the ramp and fished the Director of the FBI out of the plane. Webster was furious. Hoover would have transferred the entire Charlotte office, including the janitors, to Butte.

Webster was coming to Birmingham to make a speech at the Cumberland School of Law on the campus of Samford University. My youngest son, Deke, would get his J.D. there in 1996. Webster's visit would require an overnight stay in the city. Because of his complaints about his protection in Charlotte, I was going to cover him with a swarm of agents every minute he was in Birmingham, not give him any reason to bitch about lax security. I picked my team to guard Director Webster—mostly SWAT guys, but others, too, including women. There were no women on any FBI SWAT team nationwide. It was coming, but not yet.

It was unusually hot when Webster landed in Birmingham in a small Bureau plane in early afternoon. He wasn't taking any chances this time with a commercial flight. The FBI air force flew him to Alabama, and we were waiting for him at Hangar One, a private terminal across the runway from the main Birmingham passenger terminal.

Webster traveled to Birmingham alone. No aides or pilot fish from Headquarters were with him. Birmingham SAC Cecil Moses introduced himself to Webster. Webster then turned for other introductions, gave me a firm handshake, and I introduced him to the agents who would provide security for his visit. He was soft-spoken and congenial. The part in his dark hair was razor straight. He wasn't a barroom rowdy like Clarence Kelley. I couldn't imagine Webster as a street agent or a firearms instructor, posts where Kelley had served early in his Bureau career. Kelley was FBI; Webster was a judge.

We had been briefed before Webster's visit to Birmingham that he loved to play tennis. I scheduled a doubles tennis match for him at the Birmingham Country Club with a federal judge and several folks on the staff of the United States Attorney. No Birmingham agents wanted to play tennis with Webster. What strategy should you use in playing your boss, the Director of the FBI? Should you beat the guy senseless or just let him win?

I had a caravan of BuCars lined up to take Webster to the Birmingham Country Club for his tennis match. We moved him out of Hangar One at the Birmingham Airport and into a BuCar with the SAC and an agent driver. I drove the lead car, a Ford, followed by the vehicle holding Webster. A backup car full of agents followed. I sent a car ahead to check out the Country Club; the agents were armed with shotguns and M-16s. We were taking no chances.

We drove into Birmingham on the Airport Highway, headed for the Red Mountain Expressway, which would take us over Red Mountain to the Birmingham Country Club. It was stop-and-go traffic. Because the day was so hot, the temperature gauge in my BuCar, a Ford, slowly rose toward the red. I picked up speed to see if that would get the needle down. It didn't. We hit traffic lights and lots of stops along the Airport Highway. The temperature needle on the Ford went deep into the red. The BuCar was having a stroke. Steam began to escape from the radiator under the hood. I had to get moving.

I threw the blue light up on the dash and gunned the Ford. I busted through a red traffic light and onto the Red Mountain Expressway, a high-speed road without lights or stop signs. The BuCar with the Director of the FBI and the SAC ran the light as well, trying to keep up. So did the backup car. I jumped the accelerator and flew up the expressway. The temperature needle began to drop. I removed the blue light from the dash. The agents in the car with me were gagging, but I got Webster to his match on time.

At the Birmingham Country Club, the SAC introduced Webster to his tennis partners. He changed clothes in the Club locker room and took to the courts. He seemed to be enjoying himself. He didn't say a word to me about the wild ride from the Airport.

The SAC got me aside while Webster played tennis. *What the hell were you doing back on the highway?* I told him about the overheating engine. He laughed and shook his head.

Cecil Moses had only been SAC in Birmingham for a few weeks before Webster's visit. He was a Southerner with country origins, a good ole boy with beer belly to match, but a shrewd and insightful guy who had risen from the clerical ranks to become the head of a field office. It was not unheard of in the Bureau for clerks to become stars. Ralph Miles, the previous Birmingham SAC, had started as a clerk. Moses liked to be one of the guys, drinking and breaking bread with just about anybody. His management style was as laid back as he was, giving agents room to work their cases; however, he had the pulse of the office, knew everything that went on, and was wired at Headquarters. He liked whiskey, country music, and women. He had kids and went through several wives. One of his sons became an agent.

I occasionally peeked around the corner of the courts at the Birmingham Country Club to check on Webster and his doubles tennis match. Webster was a fit and seasoned player. He was the best athlete on the court. We kept our distance and gave the players privacy to enjoy their game.

That evening we took him to The Club for dinner, a private, pretentious watering hole for the washed of Alabama. The Club sat high above Birmingham on the crest of Red Mountain. The view of the city at night was spectacular.

While my security team grabbed fast food hamburgers off the grounds of The Club, I sat down for a lavish dinner with the Director of the FBI in front of a large window overlooking the lights of Birmingham spread out for miles in the valley below. Others present were: Cecil Moses, his chief assistant, the ASAC, the supervisors in the office, including Luther Brannon, and Tom Moore, the agent who handled legal matters for Birmingham FBI. I was the only grunt, the only street agent there. Luther and I would occasionally look at each other with an expression that said: *What the hell are we doing hanging out with the Director in this blueblood place?*

Conversation centered around the Freedom of Information Act, enacted by Congress in 1966, which opened FBI records for public view, with certain safeguards to protect confidential sources. The legislation was a monster that ate up scores of agents and clerks at FBIHQ and in the field offices trying to keep up with public demand to see Bureau files. Congress, in typical arrogant fashion, exempted itself from the requirements of the legislation that Federal agencies release information from their files. Congress shielded its own papers, while forcing the FBI to open its files to the Mob and any other scumbag criminal who wanted to zero in on who had fingered him. Safeguards protecting identities of sources were built into the legislation, but I had doubts that the protections would be effective.

Although Webster told us over dinner that he had reservations about releasing information from Bureau files, he supported the legislation in general, particularly as it applied to most other government agencies and activities, those with non-law enforcement or national security mandates. We urged Webster and Headquarters to take a hard approach when releasing anything out of any FBI file, and that any question about whether to release information be decided in favor of not releasing it. Webster agreed.

Webster was formal even in relaxed conversation. He spoke in measured language. Like his dark hair, there wasn't a word out of place. He sat erect, held forth like a judge instructing a jury. He had a patrician bearing, trim physically and mentally, low key and under control.

Over coffee, the SAC told Webster about my contribution to the arrest of Wayne Williams, the Atlanta child murders suspect, earlier in the year. Webster was familiar with the case, so I confined my remarks to what it was like to sit on the surveillance of a bridge over the Chattahoochee River in Atlanta for two weeks. I left out the part about sunbathing with coeds in Grant Field and playing on the tennis courts at Georgia Tech. I subtly stabbed the supervisor verbally who had released Wayne Williams that night on I-285.

I left the group on the terrace and collected my security team. We supplied some special equipment to Webster so he could communicate with Headquarters. After Webster ate breakfast at the hotel the next morning, we took him to the Birmingham FBI office in the 2121 Building. Not wanting to tempt fate again, I assigned an agent to an elevator in the building with instructions to lock it off and stay put. We drove Webster into the garage and walked him to the elevators. I stepped into the elevator behind Webster and looked at the panel of buttons. They were all dark. I smiled and pushed 14.

Webster gave a speech to all the employees in the office while my team took a coffee break in the back of the room. He toured the office after his speech. He was friendly and mixed easily.

I sent an agent into the hall to hold an elevator. I still wasn't going to take any chances.

We took Webster down to a waiting BuCar. An agent had stayed with the car to keep the air conditioning going. We formed a three-car caravan and took the Red Mountain Expressway again, this time at a much lower speed than the ride from the airport to the Country Club. We drove through Homewood and along Lakeshore Drive to the campus of Samford University. The Cumberland School of Law gave added luster to the academic status of Samford University. The campus was anchored to the side of a mountain and was the second largest Baptist university in the country behind Baylor.

The date was October 6, 1981. Webster was to speak at the Law School forum in the quaint Chapel on the eastern edge of the campus. Webster had one request for me: he did not want to field questions from the press after the speech; he had no objections to inquiries from anyone else. I relayed Webster's request to the officials running the event.

The Chapel filled up. TV cameras and reporters from local stations set up around the room. School officials told them Webster would only take questions from students. I eyed the crowd like you're supposed to do. I saw people I knew and I waved. I know the Secret Service would not have approved of the casual way I did things, but I had a team of professionals protecting Webster, and we enjoyed our work. We were laid back, but so what. I put agents in the audience and positioned several in the back. There was an agent at the back door and in the BuCar we used to transport Webster. I took a seat in the front row.

Webster was introduced and received a warm welcome. Approximately fifteen minutes into the speech, Birmingham FBI radio traffic advised us that a communication had just been received from FBIHQ with the flash that Anwar Sadat, President of Egypt, had just been assassinated on a reviewing stand in Cairo. Director Webster was to be advised immediately.

I wrote a note for Webster and handed it to a law school official on the platform, who gave it to Webster. He stopped speaking, read the note and announced the news. The audience gasped. I keyed my small hand-held FBI radio and asked the office whether we should take Webster to his plane. The office replied that FBIHQ had not requested the Director return to Washington immediately. It was Webster's call.

Webster made his decision on the platform. He cooly continued with his speech and then asked for questions. He was prepared and decisive. Indeed, he was *crisp,* a word he used when he became Director to describe how he wanted FBI agents to look and perform. Webster was *crisp.*

At the end of the questions, my team of agents hung back several paces as Webster walked across campus with school administrators and students to the cafeteria where he ate lunch with them in a roped off area surrounded by business-as-usual students on lunch break. We stood around at a distance and watched Webster eat. I couldn't imagine J. Edgar Hoover breaking bread with students in the middle of a school cafeteria. That was not Hoover's style. The FBI had changed.

We drove Webster back to Hangar One at the Birmingham Airport in mid-afternoon. SAC Cecil Moses rode with him. The FBI plane was waiting with an agent pilot. Webster posed for photos and thanked us for an enjoyable visit. He flew back to Washington on a clear day with unlimited visibility.

A few days later SAC Moses learned that, once back at Headquarters, Webster complained about the heavy security in Birmingham. He was aggravated because agents had tagged his every move, watching him play tennis, giving him little privacy.

I didn't get to know Webster like I had known Clarence Kelley. Which was fine with me.

CHAPTER NINETEEN

A Perfect Moment
in an Imperfect World

Birmingham was a good place to be an FBI agent and to raise a family. My career prospered. My family prospered. Our first daughter, Laura Kathryn, was born nearly nine months to the day after I returned home from two weeks on a bridge in Atlanta. I was buzzed with anticipation as I drove Pat to St. Vincent's Hospital on February 20, 1982. I had never been in the delivery room before. I remember exactly what transpired between Pat and me, she in the throes of contractions, me behind the wheel, as we raced to the hospital:

Me: "Damn, what a show this will be. I can't wait!"

Pat: "Shut up!!"

At the hospital, after the numbing effects of an epidural injection began to take over, Pat relaxed a little. We were both kind of giddy with excitement. We partied, full of cheer and happiness as the nurses periodically measured Pat's contractions. Then a nurse calmly walked into the room, checked Pat, and sprang into action. The baby was finally arriving.

Pat was wheeled into the delivery room. One of the nurses tossed me a gown and hat and told me to get a move on. I was so nervous I couldn't get the cap and gown to work. I plunged into the delivery room, and when Pat saw my hat, which made me look like Sally Fields as the Flying Nun, she burst out laughing. The delivery staff also found me quite an amusing sight.

Then everyone got down to business.

Laura Kathryn Owens was born—*without incident,* as we say in law enforcement—at precisely 5:55 p.m. that day. One of the splendid perfect days of my life.

CHAPTER TWENTY

DON'T SHOOT! WE'RE REPUBLICANS!

June, 1983. Another night roadblock in the sticks. Another rural highway, this time in Alabama instead of Mississippi. I trust the agents who are with me; we've made arrests as a team before. At the top of the food chain in the posse is Luther Brannon, a damned fine street agent turned supervisor. Luther is unflappable. I'm glad he's running this fugitive hunt.

Our backs are to Logan Martin Lake a few miles away. There are eight agents in four cars, two to a car. We're in the outback of Talladega County east of Birmingham not far from where my wife grew up with her three sisters near the city of Talladega itself. The area where we set up the roadblock is a patchwork of farm land and low hills that feel like ocean swells when you drive eighty up and down them. Mt. Cheaha, the highest point in Alabama at 2400 feet, is off to the east in the Talladega National Forest.

I'm behind the wheel and Luther is riding shotgun, and has the shotgun to prove it. Unlike many arrests where you wait and wait some more, there will be no delays tonight because the bad guy is close. Other FBI units in the county report by radio that the fugitive is heading in our direction and is about two miles away. When he's right on top of us, we'll pull across the highway, put the blue lights on the dashes and stop him.

The FBI radio adds a twist, reports there are two cars coming up the highway traveling close together. The fugitive is in the lead vehicle, followed by an accomplice. There is always some little hook to spike your adrenalin.

The guy we're looking for is a white male with bank robbery etched into his resumé of sins. He is *A & D*—armed and dangerous. There is no information at this moment to further assess the bad guy in the second vehicle. The informant who provided the information that set the roadblock trap in motion is a *reliable* source, meaning that previous information he provided to the FBI turned out to be true. We've paid him before and we'll pay him again tonight.

Four headlights appear and disappear as they surf the Talladega County hills looking like giant fireflies. They're a half mile away. Luther and I are in the lead car. I pull the BuCar across the highway. The three BuCars behind us follow suit. This time there are cars coming at Luther and me instead of a big wrecker towing a Mustang. I turn on the blue light and blue lights spring to life behind us. Luther and I bail out of the car and use the hood for cover.

The two vehicles bear down on us with blinding head beams. I squint, watch and hear the bad guys brake to a stop just feet ahead of us. It's a standoff as we stare into the lights. No one moves. I point my .38 revolver at the driver of the first car. Agents crouch on both sides of me, asses and elbows in shotguns.

FBI! Get out of the cars now! Luther shouts.

The driver door on the first car opens. The guy eases out from behind the wheel with his hands up. It's the fugitive we're looking for, no doubt at all. Luther commands him to walk around to the front of his car and stand in the beams. He complies. Agents run at him and throw him to the ground face down. They handcuff his hands behind his back, palms out, the Bureau way.

Which leaves the second car.

Open the door and get out of the car! Luther shouts.

Nothing happens. The door doesn't open. I'm tense, ready to rush the car. Shotguns are pointed at its windshield. Both front doors of the second vehicle slowly open simultaneously. A dome light illuminates the interior of the car. Two elderly ladies are hunkered down in the front seat dressed in their Sunday finery and looking horrified. Their hands are jammed in the air against the interior roof of their car. They surrender without a fight.

I walk up to the driver side with my .38 on them even though they are bluehairs. Old, well-dressed women can shoot you just as dead as a 200-pound man. Luther keeps his shotgun pointed to cover me. He and I walk up on the ladies. The driver says in a high-pitched voice:

Don't shoot! We're Republicans!

The two ladies from Talladega County had just been to a meeting of the Republican faithful to discuss politics. In their seventies, they were activists and believed in the emergence of the GOP as a force in rural Alabama. They just happened to be on a country road behind a car carrying a bad guy and ran smack dab into an FBI roadblock and a host of shotguns. They were certain that being Republicans would save them. They were right.

Agents in the Birmingham FBI office inventory evidence collected in a domestic terrorism investigation of the Aryan Nation in 1987. From L-R: G. Wray Morse, Bob Sligh (the Fox), me, Supervisor Bill Westberg, Steve Brannan, Marvin Freeman, Supervisor Luther Brannon.

CHAPTER TWENTY-ONE

AND THEN CAME MOLLY

It was not long after this escapade that Pat became pregnant again. I thought it would be nice to have another girl, but Pat wanted a boy this time. She conceived one night on vacation in Florida. Pat was wearing exceedingly becoming short shorts and had just finished exercising to a Jane Fonda tape in the living room. I owe a lot to Jane Fonda.

Molly was born April 20, 1984, at St. Vincent's Hospital, the same wonderful hospital where her sisters were born. This time I expertly donned my delivery room outfit. This time there would be no flying nun. And this time I kept my mouth shut on the drive there. And they say you can't teach an old dog ...

Everyone said Molly's blonde hair and blue eyes would transition to brown as she got older. They didn't. So Pat and I have redheaded Stacey, Laura the brunette, and Molly the blonde.

Molly was only four weeks old when we had an emergency at home. She was sleeping in a crib next to us. Suddenly, in the middle of the night, Pat sat straight up in bed: Molly wasn't breathing. We instantly reached for her. She was trying to breathe through heavily congested and blocked nasal passages. Apparently, babies have to *learn* to breathe through their mouths. Molly was struggling.

Pat bolted for the bathroom while I held Molly. Pat raced back with a syringe and suctioned mucous out of Molly's nose. I called an emergency number and an ambulance was dispatched. The EMTs examined Molly and it was decided to take her to the hospital for observation. Our next-door neighbors took Stacey and Laura and we followed the ambulance to Birmingham's Children's Hospital. Molly was held overnight there, and Pat and I sat by her bed, relieved and emotionally exhausted. Molly awoke hungry as hell.

That was not the only time Pat saved Molly's life. We were at a backyard pool party for Stacey's softball team. I was one of her coaches. Molly was four. Players and their families sat around the pool, and Molly, wearing her little orange water wings, played in the pool with other children. Then the hosts called everyone up to the porch to load up their plates and help themselves to beverages. I walked up with Stacey, and Pat rounded up Laura.

"Where's Molly?" Pat asked Laura. Laura did not know. Pat looked at the group heading towards the food table. Molly was not among them. Then she spotted Molly's orange wings on a lawn chair.

"Molly!" Laura screamed, pointing to the deep end of the pool.

Pat ran to the edge of the pool and looked down. Molly was completely submerged in the water, without her wings, arms raised to the surface, sinking. Pat fell to her knees, flattened out on the concrete, reached into the water, and with both hands yanked Molly out of the pool.

Molly started crying. "I drownded," she said.

Pat's knees were bleeding when I reached her. She was pale and breathing rapidly, and her body shook all over. She held Molly tight. Laura was crying.

When everyone headed for the house to eat, Molly had taken off her wings to go into the house to use the bathroom. When she returned a few moments later, she jumped back into the pool, forgetting that she needed to wear her wings.

The full impact did not hit our family until later. Laura, who had seen Molly nearly drown, could not talk about it for a long time. Pat replayed the incident in her mind for years after, seized with dread every time the vision intruded. It froze me where I stood.

Molly, on the other hand, makes light of the episode. She has no place for darkness in her bright universe.

CHAPTER TWENTY-TWO

FOREIGN COUNTERINTELLIGENCE

The 1980s was a busy decade for the FBI, a time that changed my Bureau life. President Reagan survived an assassination attempt outside the Hilton Hotel in Washington, D.C., on March 31, 1981. A loon named John Hinkley, acting alone, used a handgun to wound the president, as well as the president's press secretary, a Secret Service agent, and a local police officer. The Bureau kicked into gear, did what it does best, a nation-wide investigation, one that pinned down and peeled back Hinkley's life, actions, and motives. There was no conspiracy. Hinkley's insanity defense worked at his trial, and he went into a mental hospital instead of a prison. I agreed with the overwhelming feeling in the FBI that Hinkley got off easy.

President Reagan was very popular in the FBI because of his conservative, anti-communist, pro-law enforcement policies, but in January, 1982, the Reagan Justice Department did something that was not well received in the Bureau: the FBI was forced into a merger with the Drug Enforcement Administration, the DEA. DEA agents had a reputation in the Bureau for being a rowdy bunch of Lone Rangers who couldn't put a big case together. They screwed up a lot and couldn't win in court. Drug cases could be messy, street-driven affairs involving small cases on up to massive investigations such as at the importation of cocaine from South America and the bribery of judges and public officials centered around the drug trade. The DEA was understaffed, overworked, and in need of the direction and punch the FBI could give it.

My head told me that the FBI-DEA merger was a good thing for law enforcement, although my gut didn't want to work drug cases. I didn't give a damn about drug cases or working with DEA agents; I wanted to handle traditional Bureau matters like bank robberies, kidnappings, extortions, and fugitives. I got my wish. In the mid-1980s my career went in a singularly FBI direction: Foreign Counterintelligence, FCI.

The Bureau was the lead investigative agency in combating spying inside the United States, whether spying by foreign intelligence services or by disloyal America citizens. During the Cold War, this meant the FBI went against the Soviet intelligence services and their East Europe puppets, as well as the Chinese, North Koreans, Cubans, or any other hostile spy service. All operations and counter measures against spying in the U.S. had to be coordinated with the FBI. Federal agencies with intelligence mandates such as the Pentagon, the Department of State, or the CIA, whose activities were mainly directed at overseas operations out of their Langley, Virginia, headquarters, could not run domestic counterintelligence operations without Bureau oversight. The FBI ruled spy prevention in America.

By 1984 I was ready for a change. I'd spent the first years of my career in the Bureau trenches working criminal cases, the reactive investigations the Bureau is known for, especially bank stickups and hunting down federal bad guys. I'd also gotten cozy in the recruiting arena, traveling around Alabama's universities and law schools looking for talent to bring into the FBI, but I was primed to pounce on something else. My opportunity came when there was an opening on the FCI squad in the Birmingham office.

I was approached by agents on the spy squad about jumping into the middle of the Cold War to have a go at the KGB. I listened to their pitch about launching counterintelligence operations out of Birmingham, that the Soviet intelligence services, both military and civilian, thought Alabama was full of cotton and raccoons, that the FBI couldn't possible hurt the vaunted KGB from a small Bureau backwater like north Alabama. Which was one of the reasons why the Birmingham counterintelligence agents had been so successful in hopping into the back pockets of the opposition, the hostile intelligence services run by the communist countries in Europe and Asia.

Another reason for Birmingham's success in the spy trade was the caliber of agents running the investigations. Bill Westberg, the Assistant Special Agent in Charge, the ASAC, had miles of operational experience in the spy big leagues of New York City. The top agent under Westberg, and the best agent with whom I ever worked during my career, was Bob Sligh, also known as The Fox. Bob had been tagged with that nickname by a guy he'd sent to federal prison on a domestic terrorism case, a guy who recognized he'd been *outfoxed* by Sligh, but who had no hard feelings about it, only respect. Bob was like that. He was such a consummate professional that he could run circles around you and make you enjoy the ride.

Bob had once been a supervisor of East German operations in the Bureau's other FCI big leagues of Washington, D.C. He'd kicked the East Germans where it hurt, snarling some of their spy operations in the U.S. He might have risen to heights at FBIHQ if he hadn't opted for a medically-related transfer to Birmingham in order to take care of his terminally ill mother.

Bob Sligh was an Alabama native, a graduate of Georgia Tech, also had a law school JD at another school, and was a veteran of the Vietnam War with a distinguished record. He'd flown helicopters in some butt-puckering operations in southeast Asia. Like me, he'd never practiced law. Skilled with firearms, Sligh was as good mixing it up on the street in criminal cases as he was in spy games. There was nothing the guy couldn't do.

So Bob came back to his native Birmingham with his wife and two young daughters and became a street agent once again, and, along with ASAC Bill Westberg, turned Alabama into a launching pad for sending rockets up the ass of the KGB. When not trapping spies, Bob was a regular on the FBI softball team, and we coached our daughters together in softball.

Bob's sidekick and partner on the Birmingham FCI squad was George Pare, another veteran of the spy game, who once labored in the Bureau cesspool of Newark, New Jersey, before getting lucky and transferring to Birmingham. George was a native of Washington, D.C., a species I didn't know still existed. George's wife had once been in the Bureau, and they had started their careers as clerks at FBIHQ right under the nose of J. Edgar Hoover.

George became a member of a special security team of clerks who ran FBI errands for Hoover, and who were frequently in Hoover's presence at work or at Hoover's northwest D.C. home. Pare was fond of the Old Man, said that Hoover was polite and considerate of the clerks who worked closely with him.

The fourth member of the Birmingham FCI squad when I came on board in 1984 was Steve Brannan, another Vietnam veteran who'd skippered a swift boat during the war. Unlike Westberg, Sligh, Pare, or me, Steve Brannan was a devout churchgoer. He was also a practical joker, had a mischievous sense of humor and didn't shy away from an off-color joke. Brannan had an impressive resumé of counterintelligence achievements in other field offices, was transferred to his native Birmingham as part of Westberg's efforts to fashion an FCI squad of heavy hitters. Brannan and I partnered up since Sligh and Pare were inseparable. I joined Westberg's spy hunters on the condition that I would not have to give up my membership on the SWAT team. Almost all FBI agents working counterintelligence were not involved in handling investigations of criminal matters or participating in arrests or hostage release operations conducted by SWAT. This difference highlighted the *house-divided* nature of the Bureau's jurisdiction. FCI operations had a separate budget within the FBI, dealt in matters that were classified *secret* or *higher than secret.* Very hush-hush stuff.

The Birmingham FBI foreign counterintelligence squad had a Soviet in its sights. George Pare led the surveillance team and gave the orders. The Fox, Steve Brannan, and I were in plain clothes as members of the surveillance. Agents from the criminal squads in the office helped as well.

The Soviet we targeted was dirty, an IO, a known intelligence officer, KGB variety, a spy, a duck through and through. Agents are trained not to ignore what's right in front of their eyes: if it looks, walks, and quacks like a duck, it's a duck. Same with spies. KGB didn't go anywhere in America without a reason. He'd come to Birmingham to service an agent, pass a document or receive one, or gauge FBI surveillance in a backwash like Alabama, compare our coverage of him to the FBI teams that followed him in the big leagues in Washington, New York, or San Francisco. It pissed me off that he thought he could come into our backyard and pull something.

The IO flew coach from Washington National Airport to Birmingham on an unusually cold Alabama day in January. You could see your breath mingle with light snow flurries. The case agent assigned to him in the Washington Field Office, WFO, had given us the IO's flight number, the Birmingham Hotel where he had reservations, long lens surveillance photos of him in Washington, and the particulars of why the Bureau thought he was a spy. He had diplomatic cover and worked out of the Soviet Embassy in Washington. Our surveillance team picked him up as soon as he stepped off the plane at the Birmingham Airport. He was dressed in a suit and could have been any American businessman going about his work.

The IO carried his luggage off the plane, bypassed baggage claim and hailed a cab. We followed him to the large Sheraton Hotel in downtown near the FBI office. He checked into the hotel and went straight to his room. By pre-arrangement with the hotel management, we were assigned a room right next to him. An agent was in that room at all times when the IO occupied *his* room. We used the door peephole to monitor when he left. The rest of us waited in the lobby or in BuCars on the street at all the hotel exit points. The hotel supplied us with the phone numbers of all outgoing calls from his room. We also bagged the contents of the trashcans in his room when the maids emptied them. No good leads arose out of the phone records or the trash coverage. The IO was a professional, didn't do anything careless during his weekend trip to Birmingham.

After checking in, the duck wasn't in his room long before he came back out, grabbed an elevator to the lobby and immediately left the hotel. We followed. Our team took him on foot and in cars and vans. He walked up 21st Street and I leapfrogged ahead of him, used my membership card to get into the Downtown YMCA and set a long lens in the window of the fourth level of the Y near the indoor track. I took photos of the duck as he walked by alone on the street below, sharp, in-focus black and whites that I later sent to agents in WFO to add to their collection.

The duck walked for blocks in the business district, up one street and down another with no apparent destination. He looked over his shoulder, glanced from side to side, stared into shop windows at the reflection of who was walking or driving by. He tied his shoes, reversed direction several times, and once stopped dead in his tracks and did a 360. He kept walking.

I photographed him from atop the parking deck next to the closed Loveman's Department Store, a well-known Birmingham landmark. Another agent held a telephoto lens on him as he moseyed up 2nd Avenue North. He walked slow, he walked fast, window shopped, then went up 20th Street under the railroad tracks into the south side at a good pace. We followed. He walked a mile or so to the top of Red Mountain to the statue of Vulcan overlooking the city, its cast iron head facing north into town, its bare ass mooning Homewood to the south. The duck stared up at the massive Vulcan statue, the largest cast iron statue in the world. After a short while, the duck went back down the mountain on the sidewalk. He walked like he'd been born walking, ignoring the cold. He was a Russian. We followed, melted into the busy lunch hour scene of pedestrians and traffic. Damn we were good.

He took a window table at McDonald's where he could see the door, sidewalk, and street. He finished his meal, left quickly, signaled a cab, opened the cab door, talked to the driver, shut the door and walked away. An agent immediately interviewed the cabby, who said that the guy had a thick accent and wanted directions to the nearest mall.

After talking to the cabby, the duck headed across the windswept grounds of Linn Park, crossed 8th Avenue North, and took his time going into the front entrance of the Birmingham Museum of Art. With the duck out of sight, the surveillance team quickly formed a huddle outside the Museum. We put our heads together, set up the next play courtesy of Pare, the agent running things: several agents here, several there, several more with the *eye,* that is, in sight of the duck in the Museum.

I poked my head up out of the agent huddle. The duck was staring a hole through us. We flew apart like sprayed roaches. The duck hadn't been in the Museum long enough for the 25-second clock to run out. He'd walked in, done a U-turn and walked out. He'd caught us red, white, and blue handed. Had *made* every stupid one of us.

We had just reaffirmed the law of spies and roaches. When a duck goes into a building for a few seconds, does a quick U-turn and emerges into God's own sun looking for surveillance, surveillance scatters like roaches. We were the FBI's second team out in the bush of Alabama. An inviting place to run KGB operations in the future. The duck went back into the Birmingham Museum of Art. We regrouped out of sight of the Museum, sent agents into the Museum to take the *eye,* the rest laying back, waiting for the duck to come out again for the next round of games.

The duck stayed the weekend in Birmingham, then flew back to Washington. We never observed him do anything dirty like service an agent or pass information. His report about the FBI clowns in Alabama is buried somewhere in KGB archives.

✭ ✭

Much of what agents did in the counterintelligence field was buried deep in the bowels of the Bureau, never to see the light of disclosure. If you worked FCI, you had to be content to labor quietly, matching wits with hostile intelligence services, dog fights that *even fellow agents couldn't know about*—especially colleagues who investigated criminal matters and not counterintelligence. The criminal agents looked down their noses and cigars on the minority who swam in the secret sea of spies, thus pitting the rough and tumble *criminal* agents against agents in the FCI arena. I didn't care what other agents thought when I signed on for FCI in 1984. I wanted a change, but I hedged by remaining on the SWAT team. I never regretted either decision.

Bob Sligh, the Fox, told me I was ready to step into an undercover role for a go at a hostile intelligence service. He told me I was going to do something no other agent had ever done before. Bill Westberg agreed with Sligh that I could be trusted not to start World War III, and gave his approval to begin an undercover operation. FBIHQ also gave a thumbs up. I'd been working counterintelligence for a year when this opportunity jumped out of the hat. I'd never gone undercover before.

I took to counterintelligence straight off. I had the background and temperament for it. I was bookish, had an introspective side, and had saturated myself with history books and biographies since childhood. I studied the USSR and Eastern Europe in college and had built a substantial personal library. I was a Navy junkie and a member of The United States Naval Institute, which kept me well informed about what the military, especially the Navy, was up to during the Cold War. I agreed with Reagan's dramatic increase of the U.S. Navy to 600 ships, and the release from mothballs of the four Iowa class battleships. I was concerned about the submarine threat from the USSR and was eager to uncover and lynch any American who betrayed the U.S. through espionage, particularly if the treachery hurt the U.S. Navy.

I reveled in spy cases and concluded I'd spent the first fifteen years of my FBI career preparing for what I was about to do. The FBI's Washington Field Office, WFO, one of the Bureau's major players in foreign counterintelligence, was cut into my undercover operation from the beginning and would provide support whenever and wherever needed.

The target was a spy working for his country in its Washington embassy. Agents in WFO had extensive knowledge of the target's background and activities in the U.S., and were invaluable in briefing me about what sort of duck he was. FBI surveillance would be nearby whenever I left the embassy with the target. Once inside the embassy itself, however, which is considered foreign soil under international law even though the embassy is located in the U.S., I would be entirely on my own, without help should something go wrong. There was always the possibility that my real identity and occupation would be unmasked and used to exploit an incident in the press, a *provocation,* as the communists referred to it—an attempt to embarrass the United States Government and the FBI.

I carefully crafted an undercover identity by obtaining an Alabama driver's license, as well as business and credit cards in my undercover name. I kept my first name and adopted a new surname. I used an actual Birmingham business office as a front, a business whose CEO agreed to work with us after we cleared him and his secretary through a national security check. The secretary would answer a telephone the Bureau had established for the undercover operation. My business was listed in the Birmingham Telephone Directory, and I joined the Chamber of Commerce. A special telephone was set up in my residence in my undercover name, and my wife was cleared by the Bureau to answer it if I wasn't there. I told our three daughters not to answer that phone or use it under any circumstances. We told them it was FBI business. They thought that was cool and never violated the prohibition on using it (as far as I know).

My undercover identity involved posing as a Birmingham businessman in the grain storage business overseas. America ruled the universe in the technology of grain storage. We were, after all, the breadbasket of the world. I would use this undercover identity to build a personal relationship with a spy from one of the countries under Soviet domination, nations the Bureau referred to as the Eastern *Bloc.*

The target of this undercover operation was a guy whom the Bureau had identified as a *known intelligence officer,* or *IO.* He was *dirty,* a spy posing as a diplomat at his country's embassy in Washington, a spook who was in the United States to collect (steal) classified information or recruit Americans to steal it for him. He reported his U.S. contacts to his bosses in his intelligence service back home, a *Bloc* country puppet under the thumb of the KGB in Moscow.

I hoped to establish a personal relationship with this spy from Eastern Europe, regardless of how much time it took, by meeting with him in his Washington embassy as often as possible to discuss how my company could do business in his country. He would ascertain straight off from talking to me that I was a businessman who had no access to classified information, myself, but over time and many meetings, he would hope to determine whether I had friends who might have such access, friends who I would introduce to him. It could require months or even years to reach a point where he trusted me, where we were friends. During that time, I would assess his vulnerability to a recruitment pitch by the FBI, that is, *turn* him, convince him to stay in place and report the activities of his *own* intelligence service to a Bureau handler. That handler would not be me. Nor would I make the pitch. If the IO agreed to this pitch, it would not be because he was eaten up with America or loved us. He would do it because he wanted money.

The number one reason why people betray their country is money. The number two reason why people betray their country is money. Forget ideology, revenge, hate, or mothers-in-law. They might be in the mix at times, but rarely.

I told the Fox that I didn't know anything about the business of grain storage. He pointed out that the intelligence officer, IO, didn't know crap about grain storage either. It didn't matter. The IO was a duck and I was a duck. We were both in the intelligence business serving our countries, both pretending to be people we were not, lying like hell to each other.

Get to know the guy, the Fox told me. Buy him vodka, steaks, or women, men if he tilted that way, whatever. Make him your own. I pictured travel and long dinners in Washington restaurants and no limit credit cards in my undercover name. I pictured right.

Operating under my undercover identity, traveling to my first meeting with the spy from Eastern Europe at his embassy in Washington, D.C. I got off to a rocky start at the Birmingham Airport when summer thunderstorms grounded my flight. After many hours of delay, the plane took off, but I missed my connection in Atlanta. The Atlanta airport was a zoo even in good weather, crowded and disorganized. Heavy rainstorms up and down the east coast closed runways along the Atlantic seaboard, and I spent hours trying to get a flight out without success. I finally surrendered, checked into a hotel around midnight at airline expense, slept four hours and was back at the Atlanta airport at daybreak for a flight to National Airport in Washington.

Pressed for time for a morning meeting with the target of the undercover operation, I took a taxi to my hotel, checked in, changed into a business suit, doubled-checked to make sure that I didn't have any ID or articles on me that would reveal my true identity, walked to the embassy, and arrived on time for the meeting.

I pressed the buzzer at the heavy front door, hoped I didn't look like an FBI agent in the numerous security cameras. I knew that FBI surveillance was on me until the moment when I went inside the embassy. It made me self-conscious at first. Then I forgot about it. A voice from inside the embassy asked why I was there. Nervous, I said I had an appointment with so and so, and after a short delay, was buzzed into the embassy. I stepped into the lobby and was warmly greeted by the target. A four-year odyssey begins.

After numerous trips to Washington D.C. in the late 1980s I became quite comfortable working undercover as a Birmingham businessman in the grain storage business, and thoroughly enjoyed the company of a spy from Eastern Europe who was also working under diplomatic cover. The guy was an engaging companion, well-educated, spoke excellent English, even American slang—but in a thick accent, knew American country and western music well enough to name his favorite artists and songs, was humble and easy going with a good sense of humor. He liked wine, whiskey, and strong tobacco, was a former boxer who looked fit enough to go back into the ring. Above all, he loved his wife and two daughters. We compared notes on how much fun it was to raise daughters. He bragged about how well his daughters were doing in local American schools. They were fluent in English and rock and roll. He said he felt fortunate to be a diplomat stationed in the United States. Only experienced career people were selected to serve at his country's embassy in Washington. He was grateful for the assignment.

Although I was using a fake identity, I purposely stayed as close to my real identity as possible, used my real first name and the fact that I'd grown up in the coal fields of West Virginia, was a graduate of the University of Alabama, and was happily married with three daughters. I told the truth about the names of my wife and children, all to make conversation with the target flow more easily for me without too much concern for a slip of the tongue about my domestic life. Still, I had to be very careful and alert in order to avoid any reference to my real life in the FBI. Working undercover was both demanding and a kick, a bit of a thrill.

As I knew little about grain storage and the target knew less, we would muddle through talks about business, pay lip service to my company setting up shop in his country, then move on to topics that he really enjoyed, like NBA basketball and his favorite team, the Boston Celtics. He liked talking about the hair-raising quality of his country's coffee, and disdained Gorbachev's restrictions on excessive drinking of vodka at USSR embassy social functions. The target laughed at these drinking restrictions, thought they were bureaucratic bullshit.

Sometime during our conversations at the embassy, the target would request that a staff member bring in a cup of the blackest coffee I had seen. I love coffee, and I matched him cup for cup, which amused him. I was the only American who could stomach the stuff, he said.

My first meeting with him lasted around three hours, after which I took him to lunch at one of Washington's expensive restaurants, where we talked for several more hours over wine and less vigorous American coffee. As the meetings with him piled up, one every six weeks or so, we would leave his embassy and eat at different restaurants in the city, where I always picked up the check. I also took him to an NBA game in Washington one night, and even lined up tickets to the Boston Celtics, courtesy of the Boston FBI office. The tickets were never used, however, because the target could not get away from Washington due to work demands.

I always assumed my visits to his embassy were recorded by his embassy, possibly filmed as well. We sat alone in easy chairs or couches in a large, rectangular room. He chain-smoked cigarettes. I initially feared I would freeze up in conversation, be too conscious of the eavesdropping, but I wasn't, primarily because the target and I were comfortable with each other.

Only once in four years did he invite anyone from the embassy to join us. The guy he invited was also a duck, a spy under diplomatic cover, who only stayed a short while before leaving. This new guy was all business with no sense of humor, a stereotypical, hardass communist. When he left the room, the target rolled his eyes and gave me a look that said, *Yeah, I know. He's an asshole.*

It was after my third visit to Washington to see the target that my confidence grew to the point of cockiness. I was dead certain I could do this undercover stuff as good as anyone in the Bureau.

As was my routine after a long visit of talk and coffee at his embassy, followed by a leisurely lunch and drinks, I returned to my hotel for a lengthy session of putting my thoughts down on paper for later dictation into a report when I got back to the Birmingham FBI office. I wrote everything I could remember about what the target and I had discussed, and whether he said anything that would hint he might be so discontented with his life he would switch sides and work for us. There were indications we might turn him, hints based on his often-stated desire to better his family, particularly to send his daughters to the best American universities, the Ivy League maybe. The target's tour in the U.S. would be up in a few years and he would rotate back to his country for a long stay before ever coming back to America, if at all. It was my assessment that this guy was worth the undercover effort for as long as it took to woo him.

I finished writing the notes from memory of my third visit with the target. I had pages of notes, and in fact was damned proud of myself. Exhilarated but exhausted, I tried to wind down from the stress of working undercover. I leaned back in an easy chair and enjoyed the view of Washington, content with what a wonderful agent I was. By going into a foreign embassy in an undercover capacity to conduct an operation against a known intelligence officer from a hostile intelligence service, I'd done something that no other agent had ever done. Damn I was special.

I lit up an expensive cigar I had purchased with my undercover credit card, the same high-grade cigar that I had given to the target as a present over lunch, for which he was most grateful. I couldn't have been more content as I relaxed in my hotel room. I was ready to change into casual clothes and treat myself to a fine meal at a Washington restaurant.

I took off my battle uniform, my white shirt with French cuffs and silver cufflinks that showcased the initials of my undercover name. I had thought of everything, even down to my cufflinks. Attention to detail was the mark of a good undercover operation. I hung the dress shirt next to the regimental-striped tie I had worn that day. Then, something on the shirt caught my eye. I looked closer: a laundry stamp! I froze and stared in disbelief. My real name was stamped in bold black letters on my shirttail. My REAL NAME!

I deflated like I had just taken a called third strike. Of all the knock-down, stupid things I'd done in my life, that laundry stamp topped the list. Super spy my ass. What a fraud I was.

Rightly punctured, I convalesced over an order-in hamburger in my room. I did not tell the Fox about the laundry stamp.

I met regularly with the target over a four-year period. He always seemed relaxed and to enjoy my company. We developed a friendship and an easy relationship. Although he issued a general invitation to me to meet his wife and children at his Washington apartment, he never got specific about a date. It was always going to be sometime in the future. We had many lunches and a few dinners together, drove around in his American car and my undercover Lincoln Continental, which the FBI had confiscated in a drug case, talked about everything from baseball to the history of his country and how the communists had taken over at the end of WWII. Although he praised America endlessly and the opportunities for individual advancement here, he never was critical of the stranglehold the communist party and the Soviets had on his country. He seemed resigned to a lesser standard of living under communism. He readily pointed out, though, that as a member of the communist party himself and a diplomat serving his country, he had advantages many others in his country did not enjoy. He considered himself fortunate to be stationed at the embassy in America and to have many special privileges when he was back home. He had a nice apartment in his nation's capitol.

My reports to FBIHQ and to WFO stressed my belief that the Bureau should pitch the target. The carrot would be money of course, plenty of money, and a secure future for the target and his family in America after he remained in place for a while and reported to the FBI on the worldwide activities of his intelligence service, particularly its operations inside the U.S. That secure future for the target would include whatever leverage and juice the Bureau could bring to get his daughters into top U.S. universities.

FBIHQ agreed with my assessment that we should pitch the target and authorized us to proceed, in cooperation with WFO. A complicated scenario was hatched whereby another agent would make the pitch. This took time, months in fact, and was initiated in the fourth year of the undercover operation.

Meanwhile, when I wasn't meeting with the target in Washington, I went about my normal agent duties in Birmingham, which included SWAT operations and numerous counterintelligence matters. More significantly, I expanded the undercover operation to include meetings with known intelligence officers, IOs, ducks, in the American embassy of the USSR, as well as another Eastern Europe Bloc nation, utilizing the same fake identity of a Birmingham businessman specializing in grain storage technology. I traveled to New York City for a meeting with an IO at the trade mission of a Bloc country. After meetings with these IOs, spies, I concluded they were not candidates for a pitch by the FBI and advised as much to FBIHQ, WFO, and the New York FBI. The IOs were hard line, fat cat communists unlikely to change sides. My recommendations were accepted and no pitches were developed.

During my four-year undercover (UC) operation against the KGB and other hostile intelligence services during the Cold War, I met at the FBI Academy with a supervisor and an analyst from Headquarters who were charged with overseeing my UC activities. The meeting took place in a room that agents dubbed *The Cone of Silence*—a phrase from the old TV comedy series featuring secret agent Maxwell Smart—because the Bureau's sound wizards had made it secure from hostile penetration. In other words, you could say whatever the hell you wanted without fear of being overheard by our enemies. During that meeting in the *safe* room at the Academy, I was dismayed to learn how little the HQ supervisor and analyst knew about my UC operation, what little thought they had given to its potential, or how far to take the case. My field office, plus agents in the Washington Field Office and in New York, had invested years of work into my UC operation. The analyst did not even recognize the name of the foreign intelligence officer who was the target of the case. What the blazes were these people doing with their time?

During the late 1980s, while I was rocking and rolling with another spy matter, I sent urgent memos to FBI Headquarters concerning my suspicions about a novel and unprecedented operation being run covertly in America by the KGB. An agent in another field office, working independently, reached the same conclusion and sounded the alarm at FBIHQ as I had done. I met with the other agent and compared notes. We sent a joint communication asking HQ to pay attention and order all FBI field offices to initiate their own investigations. We were concerned about how widespread the KGB covert operation might be. We also asked FBIHQ to query the CIA for anything it might have in its files or be able to contribute. Instead, Headquarters let our probe die slowly from neglect and lack of support from the top down.

Agents rarely expect vigorous or inspired leadership from FBIHQ in solving cases, providing insights or intelligence. The best that field offices can hope for is that HQ will not get in the way or spike our investigations.

Using my own growing experience working undercover, I recruited a Birmingham businessman to work undercover in an operation against the GRU, the military intelligence service of the USSR, in its Washington office. The operation showed great promise but fell flat. WFO again cooperated and provided support, and we were puzzled as to why the operation had failed.

It was about the time of this failure with Soviet military intelligence that my undercover operation against the original target dried up as well. The Bureau was nearly ready to make the pitch to the target when he became harder and harder for me to contact. My telephone calls to him were returned late or not at all. The switchboard operator at his embassy would tell me that he was usually *out* or *unavailable*. When I did talk to him, he agreed to meet me at his embassy but not go out to a restaurant or anywhere else, citing pressing business. He was as friendly as ever, relaxed and polite, but clearly, something was wrong. His tour at his embassy in the U.S. was nearing its completion. After a while, we shut down the complicated scenario to pitch him.

Coinciding with the demise of my undercover operations, the USSR imploded and changed its name back to Russia, embracing free elections. The Eastern European countries, the Bloc, had already shed the domination of the Soviets and had led the charge to freedom and democracy. These monumental changes ended the Cold War. Our previous adversaries became our friends, some of them allies, including their intelligence services. The FBI opened offices in American embassies all over Europe, even Moscow.

I pushed the failure of my undercover operations to the back of my mind and moved on to other Bureau pursuits. I stopped brooding about what had gone wrong. I never worked undercover again. I resurfaced for good.

PART FOUR

CHAPTER TWENTY-THREE

HEADLIGHTS

April, 1986. The Birmingham FBI SWAT team descended on northeast Alabama near the border with Tennessee to arrest two bad guys after a drug buy by an undercover agent, UCA. It was pushing midnight. My fellow SWAT team members and I fanned out in the woods and tall grass to surround the site where the drug buy would occur along rural Highway 34 on Grant Mountain. This operation had been carefully planned by some damned fine FBI agents. We got into position well ahead of time so we could observe the undercover agent sell 4 kilos of cocaine to two Alabama rednecks who were brothers. All that was left was to execute the arrests after the buy was made.

The undercover agent himself looked like a criminal. I wanted to arrest him the first time I saw him. He was an agent who had been imported from another FBI office, a guy none of the drug dealers in Alabama could possibly know. You would have never made him as an FBI agent with his shaggy dark beard and rundown appearance.

My SWAT partner was Chuck Pierce, a talented and savvy FOA with movie star looks and the athletic build to go with it. He was good with firearms and defensive tactics, one of the few FOAs on the SWAT team. Chuck and I were friends as well as colleagues, and I had full faith in his ability and judgment, even though he had not been in the Bureau a long time. He was fast and played right field on our FBI softball team.

Chuck and I picked a spot in tall grass near the highway. We got comfortable, kept our heads low because it was time for the arrest to go down. I snuggled against a shotgun for comfort, parked my 9mm Smith and Wesson semi-automatic on my right hip in a black SWAT holster. Chuck was armed with the same. The two bad guys were supposed to drive down the road in their pickup past our location to meet with the UCA a few hundred yards away. They were known to carry weapons. The rest of the SWAT team was spread out nearby, ready to pounce.

A vehicle came toward us down Highway 34 on the narrow two-lane, its engine sounding like a pickup. Chuck and I got as low as we could to avoid its headlights. I had an urge to push the safety button on the shotgun to red so it was ready to fire, but I restrained myself because it was too early. There would be plenty of time to ready the shotgun. The vehicle was close and I was certain it was the truck we were waiting for. The bad guys were supposed to drive on by us a short distance, then turn left onto a dirt road where the UCA waited.

I could barely see the headlights of the vehicle as it slowed, then stopped on the highway, engine idling. A door opened and quickly closed. The vehicle then drove slowly down the road and turned onto the dirt road, if my ears were right. What the Chivas Regal was going on? I heard footsteps coming from the highway, coming from where the truck had stopped, coming directly toward us. I hunkered down even more.

Remember when you played hide-and-seek as a child and you closed your eyes, certain that the kid who was *it* couldn't see you if you had *your* eyes shut? Well, I closed my eyes on this drug bust in north Alabama as the footsteps got closer to the spot in the tall grass where Chuck and I were hiding. I stifled an urge to pop the shotgun safety. I didn't dare move. Whoever walked away from that truck was right on top of us.

Who in the hell had come up on our hiding place and into the middle of a drug bust? I knew. I lifted my head and looked.

A guy stood a few feet from Chuck and me, staring down at us. Chuck raised up. The three of us froze.

"Ya'll with that other group?" the guy said, casual as could be. He was a thin, wiry bastard. Probably drank away all of his drug sale profits.

I was about to say something, probably something stupid like, *Who wants to know?*

There wasn't time. The guy bolted away at full speed, cutting a new path through the tall grass. Chuck and I were up and running with our weapons and gave chase. Chuck was out of the blocks ahead of me, shouting *FBI! Stop!* I shouted something, but I don't remember what. The guy changed directions, a mistake that gave Chuck and me a better angle at him. The party was now headed back toward Highway 34. I stepped into a deep hole and something popped in my right knee. I fell behind. I sprinted, dreamlike, running but not getting anywhere. My right knee was numb, off on some mission of its own. Chuck tackled the guy smack dab in the middle of Highway 34.

By the time I got there, Chuck and the guy were going at it on the hardtop, fists, arms, knees and feet flying. I dove into the middle of it, still gripping my shotgun. This was not the way they teach arrest techniques at the FBI Academy. Although it all became a violent blur, I remember getting an opening and slamming the stock of the shotgun into the guy's head, hard enough to crack the stock. I popped him several times. The blows didn't faze him. He kept kicking and raising hell. It didn't occur too me that I might have killed all three of us if the shotgun had gone off.

Chuck and I finally got the upper hand and planted our knees in the guy's back. I dropped the shotgun sometime during the melee. I couldn't get my handcuffs out because my hands were full holding the guy down. An engine blared down the highway. My eyes were scorched by bright headlights. We were on a stage in the middle of Highway 34. There was a roar like a train bearing down on us. I looked into two pools of headlights that grew larger. I lost my grip on the guy.

The roar of a pick-up truck blasted like an explosion. I fought to regain control of the guy, who bucked like a horse. Brakes sounded like a dying animal, engine squealing at high pitch, headlights in my face so close I could have licked them.

The engine screamed, the truck flew into reverse, then stopped, revving like a plane preparing for takeoff at the end of a runway. Both my hands were on the back of the bad guy's head, holding him down. The headlights bore down on us at high speed. Chuck raised up, drew his 9mm and fired at the truck. The headlights came at my face and I dug a hole into the back of the bad guy. The truck swerved at the last second, drove close by and disappeared down the highway. I raised up and caught a glimpse of the truck's taillights in the distance.

We arrested the driver of the truck the next day. By *we*, I mean Bureau agents, not me. I was in Birmingham limping on a knee with a torn miniscus. My hands and elbows looked like they'd gone through a shredder. The hardtop had eaten me. It ate Chuck and the bad guy, too. The three of us were scraped and dented from wrestling and carrying on in the middle of a road on Grant Mountain. Chuck and I mended. The bad guy mended in jail.

Chuck had fired one round that went into the grill of the truck, missing the driver. When you fire your weapon in the FBI, you could spend the rest of your career explaining why you did so. Chuck was careful to emphasize in the endless paperwork that followed that he fired at the driver and not at the grille of the truck. The Bureau deadly force policy is firm: you only fire your weapon in self-defense or in defense of others. If you use deadly force in the FBI, you shoot to kill. Agents do not fire to disable a person or to disable a vehicle in life-threatening situations. You fire to kill. Where a vehicle is involved, you shoot the driver, not the vehicle.

FBIHQ accepted Chuck's explanation. He had rightly fired at the driver in an effort to stop the driver from running over two agents attempting to arrest a subject. The incident was declared a *good shoot.* Deadly force was justified. The driver of the truck and his brother, who Chuck and I arrested in the road, were slapped with assault of federal officers in addition to the drug charges. Chuck and I testified against them at their trial.

I particularly remember the trial because my youngest son, Deke, then 15, sat in the courtroom to watch me being questioned by the Assistant United States Attorney, a law school classmate, and by the defense attorney, a casual acquaintance. It was all so civilized in contrast to what had gone on that night on Highway 34 on Grant Mountain.

My son watched the trial with real interest, not only because I testified, but also because he was considering a career as an attorney. He later went to law school at Cumberland School of Law in Birmingham and into a successful practice in Jacksonville, North Carolina.

I had an operation to repair the torn miniscus in my right knee. I never did talk privately with the driver of the truck. I did talk to his brother, the guy who Chuck and I arrested in the middle of the highway. I told the dude his brother could have killed all three of us driving the truck the way he did. Why did his brother do that? I asked.

Fuck off! he told me.

I dreamed about headlights after that night on Grant Mountain. Many dreams.

The dream always began with two headlights racing toward me. The two lights fused into one that came straight at my face. I was lying down and couldn't move or get out of the way. There was a roar in my ears in the dream. I was blinded by a light as fierce as the sun.

Each time my wife woke me from the dream, I was holding onto her, yelling. The Bureau had two psychologists on staff at Headquarters. They were a married couple. Hiring the two psychologists was an invention of the 1980s, a gentler, more understanding Bureau. They were there for *us,* Headquarters assured agents. Requesting help would not be held against us or hinder our careers. We didn't trust Headquarters.

Seeking official help for emotional or mental problems was not something most street agents would do, and I was no exception. I feared the stigma of asking the psychologists for counseling. It would go into my personnel file at Headquarters and I would never be trusted again. My capacity to make life or death judgments on the street would not be trusted. At least that was my opinion.

Chuck and I were ordered to attend a post-traumatic stress conference with the two psychologists at the FBI Academy at Quantico, Virginia. It was standard procedure for all agents involved in shooting incidents or other mayhem to attend those get-togethers. I did not go. My undercover work in counterintelligence took precedence, I stressed.

Months later, early in 1987, I was again ordered to the conference by Headquarters. I didn't go. The undercover assignment again kept me in Birmingham. Chuck went. He sat in a circle of agents for a week, talked, listened, and watched in sympathy as other agents broke down and cried. The agents had either shot someone or had been shot at themselves. One of the sessions was attended by an agent who had fired through the windshield of a speeding car, missed the driver and had nearly been run over.

When Chuck came back to Birmingham from attending the post-traumatic stress meeting, he asked me how I was doing. I said I was fine, which had become my standard reply. He said he was *fine,* too. We were both *fine.* Maybe he was; I had no reason to believe otherwise. I never told him about my recurring dream. I was an intensely private person and kept most things to myself. I had the love and support of my family, which was, is, all that I wanted or needed.

Chuck later went on to pass the difficult physical, mental, and psychological tests for membership on the Bureau's prestigious national Hostage Rescue Team, based at Quantico. I never received a third summons to attend a post-traumatic stress conference, although I did receive a telephone call from one of the psychologists, the husband, who wanted to know how I was doing. I told him I was *fine.*

He asked me for details about what had happened that night on Highway 34. He seemed genuinely interested, so I told him. I speculated that the bad guy who got out of the truck and surprised Chuck and me could not have seen us from the road, and that he was probably on his way to scout the scene of the drug buy and possibly ambush the buyer, the undercover FBI agent. We had SWAT members all around the area, I told the psychologist, but we weren't expecting what had happened. We were taken by surprise.

The psychologist listened to me and was sympathetic. He invited me to call him or his wife if something was bothering me as a result of the incident, or anything else at the Bureau or in my private life.

I thanked him. I did not mention the dream to him. I figured the dream would eventually go away and no amount of talking would make it go. I was right.

I repressed an impulse to tell him I had been afraid of birds my whole life.

Birmingham SWAT team leader and friend, Starley Carr, left, watches as I fire a rifle during training, circa 1986. Carr was an excellent marksman, unflappable under pressure. He was a true leader.

CHAPTER TWENTY-FOUR

AREA CODE 215

February 2, 1987. I was driving my BuCar north on I-59 between Tuscaloosa and Birmingham in mid-afternoon. The drive was an easy 45-mile haul, interstate all the way. I played the good time radio in the BuCar, listened to an FM rock station out of Tuscaloosa. Later, I'd change to a Birmingham station as I closed in on the city.

I had just left the campus of the University of Alabama, where I'd attended a conference and represented the FBI as well as the 1st and Ten Club of Alabama, a non-profit organization dedicated to helping football players at the university secure employment in the professions of their choice after they graduated. Most college football players, even at tradition-rich Alabama, did not play pro-football, and the mandate of the Club was to advise players about interview techniques when they applied for jobs, as well as to give them tips concerning how to dress and present a professional image. The Club also circulated the resumés of the players to the 150 members of the Club, all of whom were successful business and professional men. I was the only FBI agent in the Club.

I reemphasized the qualifications for becoming an FBI agent, and of the Bureau's need for agents with good communication skills. It helped to have a degree in law or accounting, or a fluency in a foreign language, especially Spanish, but the most important attribute was the ability to speak and write well, because that was what agents did. We interviewed.

I was proud of the fact that the University of Alabama was one of the top schools in the nation in supplying agents to the FBI. Two members of my law school class of 1969 had joined me in the Bureau.

I enjoyed the ride between Tuscaloosa and Birmingham along I-59. It was almost an unbroken line of pine forests and hardwoods that did not thin until the outskirts of Bessemer, south of Birmingham. My FBI work frequently took me to Tuscaloosa. I was approaching the rest stop on I-59 north of Tuscaloosa, when the FBI radio operator, call letters 200, came on the air from his location deep inside the Bureau's fourteenth floor office in the 2121 Building in Birmingham. The operator loudly called out my credential numbers: 3674.

I picked up the microphone of the dash and identified myself as 3674. The radio operator told me to call a certain number in area code 215 *as soon as possible.* I did not recognize the phone number. It was not that of my younger brother, Bob, who lived with his family in West Chester, Pennsylvania in area code 215. My brother taught physical education and coached football at East High School in West Chester. He had five sons.

"An emergency?" I asked. The woman said *as soon as possible,* the radio said back to me. Something was up in Area Code 215. It had to be my brother, another one of his jokes.

My brother liked to play tricks on me. When we were young, he would let the air out of my bicycle tires or hide the mouthpiece of my trombone. He said only sissies played trombones. I told him he was adopted. I put poison ivy in his bed sheets.

I figured Bob was up to something with the message to call a number in area code 215. He had telephoned the FBI office before and asked to speak to me, not revealing that he was my brother. When told that I was out of the office, he'd say things to the secretary: *The FBI should tear me away from my daily racquetball game and return his call.* Or, *who was fighting crime and the communists while Jack Owens was out of the office running laps?* I would tell my brother or any other caller that I was on a mission for God when I was out of the office, which is street agent for *none of your damn business what I was doing, this is the FBI.*

I closed in on Birmingham on I-59 between 70 and 80 mph. I drove fast, like FBI agents everywhere. It was our birthright. If stopped, I put the emergency blue light on the dash, showed my credentials to the state trooper and said that I was *working.* I might not even have to show my credentials because I knew many of the troopers along the interstates. If stopped, we would chat about the upcoming Alabama Police Olympics in the summer, or how the Crimson Tide was going to fare in the fall. We would talk off the side of the highway, the trooper and I, his blue light going atop his car, my blue light going on the dash.

I ate up the miles along I-59, crossed into Jefferson County, not far outside Bessemer. I headed straight toward Birmingham, up the industrial valley past the mostly dormant steel mills in Fairfield that no longer pasted the city with foul air.

I topped a hill and drove the BuCar into downtown Birmingham. Bank towers dominated the skyline in front of me. Red Mountain loomed on my right, dividing the city from the suburbs.

I took the 22nd Street exit, turned into the alley behind the 2121 Building a block from the interstate exit, and drove up the garage ramp to the Bureau's sealed third floor parking area. I took the elevator up to the fourteenth floor, walked to the door reserved for office employees, punched key pad numbers to enter the kingdom, and went in.

I thought about how to get even with my brother. I considered asking the squad supervisor to call the telephone number in Area Code 215 and say I couldn't come to the phone just then because I was having a sex change operation.

Bob Sligh, the Fox, who taught me the joys and bumps of the spy game, said hello as I walked into the squad area. The Fox knew I'd been to Tuscaloosa, and inquired about the quality of the chippies on the Quad at the University of Alabama. You could find some of the most beautiful women in the world there, if looking at beautiful women was of interest to you. If not, you could go to Auburn.

The other agents on the squad took turns at me, as we always did to each other every day. Steve Brannan, a Vietnam veteran like the Fox, had his choirboy face lit from end to end. Steve's humor was usually at someone else's expense. You had to be on your toes around him, be prepared to dish it right back at him. Steve was a mischief maker, even looked like Dennis the Menace. I looked at the wall over my desk and saw why Brannan was laughing. He had drawn mustaches on the glass of the framed photos of my children while I was in Tuscaloosa.

I laughed and made no move to erase the mustaches off my kids.

I sat down at my gray metal desk next to Steve. In front of me were mementoes my daughters had made for me when they were in elementary school. There was a clay pirate's hat, an airplane, and a cup in one corner of the desk. Two seashells and a jar of sand from a family beach trip were in another corner. The hammer and sickle dominated flag of the USSR stood at attention just off the edge of my ink blotter. The red Soviet flag was always a conversation piece when visitors came through the office.

I dialed the telephone number in Area Code 215 that I did not recognize, ready to shadow box with my brother. I waited through a number of rings.

"Hello." It was a woman's voice I couldn't place. I decided to play it straight until I could see what my brother was up to. I identified myself and said that someone at that number had placed a call to me not long ago.

"Hold on," she said.

When my brother came on the line, I was going to tell him that the District Attorney in West Chester had just phoned in a report that Bob Owens had been seen in a number of gay bars.

"Mr. Owens?" Another woman this time, older. "Yes."

The women said that she was a nurse at Chester County Hospital in West Chester. I knew it well. I had lived in West Chester during my teens because my father taught and coached Football at West Chester State Teachers College, and my mother was a third grade teacher at nearby Chadds Ford Elementary. I had been rushed there twice with broken collarbones from junior high football, the left side both times. Bob too. He broke his left collarbone trying to run a quarterback sneak into the end zone in a high school game.

Chester County Hospital was also where EMTs had brought the battered body of Danny, Bob's sixteen year old son, who had been struck down on his bike by a hit-and-run drunk driver six months ago. Danny was pronounced dead at the hospital.

The nurse said that she was very sorry to have to tell me this, but that my brother had died of a heart attack an hour ago. I couldn't speak. I knew from her tone that the nurse was not kidding. I pictured Bob bent over my stretched out body on a football field during a night game. He had come out of the stands to beat the trainers to me. He had knelt over my face and asked if I was all right.

I had to say something to the nurse: "My brother is dead?"

The rest of the squad heard this and froze. We were frozen in time like that—I can still see us—as the nurse told me that Bob was refereeing a basketball game when he suddenly dropped to the floor. They were not able to save him.

✷ ✷

Bob was thirty-eight years old, covered with inner strength and outer strength and a head full of blond hair, seemingly in perfect health, a former professional baseball player, a member of the Pennsylvania Sports Hall of Fame, and a loving husband and father. I had seen him carry two of his youngest sons up a long flight of steps to the top of a water slide last summer as I carried my young daughters alongside him. He looked fit. He looked indestructible.

I thanked the nurse, told her I knew it hadn't been easy for her to tell me. I hung up, stared at the wall photographs of my children smiling through mustaches drawn in black ink. It would be months before I could bring myself to wipe the glass clean.

Three days later, after a packed church service that included my eulogy, we took Bob in a long procession of cars to a rural Pennsylvania spot near the Brandywine River. My parents never got over Bob's death. You could see it in my mother's face from then on. She aged and she smiled less. My father had long periods when he did not speak. He would go off to be by himself. He and Bob were wonderfully close, tightly bonded in appearance, thought and action, a love born of a shared worship of baseball and nurtured by the clipped cadence of man talk. They were men's men.

Sometimes I whisper to myself, *Damn you Bob, you've gone and left me without a brother. That was a thoughtless thing to do.* He'd have said the same of me. I miss him.

CHAPTER TWENTY-FIVE

PRISON HYMN

In November 1987 I sat with my partner in an FBI car and watched the Atlanta Federal Prison burn. It was freezing cold; we ran the engine to keep the heater going, idling away the night.

The animals had taken over the zoo. A thousand Cuban inmates had overrun the maximum security prison in Atlanta, setting fire to everything in sight. They took one hundred hostages, some of them women. Although the Bureau had rushed scores of SWAT teams to the scene from nearby field offices, there still weren't enough of us to storm the prison and rescue the hostages. I feared for the women.

The Cubans were straight out of Castro's prisons and mental wards. They were admitted into the United States in 1980 after the Cuban leader duped Federal authorities into accepting them. It was a decision that President Carter came to regret.

It was hours until sunrise and the BuCar was low on gas. Our orders were to stay put. We couldn't drive off the prison grounds to gas up. A holstered Smith and Wesson 9mm semi-automatic cut a rut into my right side. I had fourteen rounds in the clip, topped by one round in the chamber. The weapon became more uncomfortable the longer I sat.

The good time FM radio was going strong, a tonic for staying awake with top 40 tunes. I was tired, hungry, and mad at the radio announcer, who told me what I already knew, that there was a mess at the Atlanta Federal Prison. I burrowed deeper into my green army surplus coat, prepared for the worst.

My partner, Don Wright, and I were parked in a gray Chrysler at the northwest corner of the high and intimidating prison wall. Flames danced hundreds of feet into the air and obliterated the stars. It looked like the entire prison was in flames. Would the inferno force the Cubans to make a run for it? I looked around and did not see any other FBI faces. Don Wright was as solid as they come, unflappable and thoroughly professional. I had been through other Bureau wars with him, knew that he wouldn't wilt under pressure or lack of sleep. To pass the time, I asked him about his days as a running back for the Golden Eagles of the University of Southern Mississippi. His body was a mess from playing college football, he said, particularly his hip. He was going to have to replace his hip.

There were sirens in the Atlanta distance. I discounted the National Guard because they don't announce themselves. Fire trucks weren't coming either. They had been held back when the riot and fire started earlier in the afternoon because of the possibility that the prisoners had guns. It was too risky for the firemen. The prison burned. The sirens faded, mischief elsewhere in the city.

Don and I were experienced members of the ten-man Birmingham FBI Special Weapons and Tactics team, SWAT. We were told to pack for two days. With the sun at our backs, we had driven east out of Birmingham on I-20 toward Atlanta. It was a 150-mile ride with only one stop: an exquisite buffet dinner at Shoney's Restaurant in Anniston, Alabama. The lemon icebox pie at Shoney's was wonderful.

Now, in the middle of the night, I was hungry again. Worse, there was no coffee. Atlanta FBI SWAT were bad hosts. They should have been going car to car delivering sandwiches and hot beverages. I suspected that they were warm and cozy somewhere, leaving us to face the Latins.

Birmingham SWAT was always tangled up with the Atlanta guys in one way or another, dating back to 1973 when the FBI formed SWAT teams in the field offices. The alphabet and geography threw Atlanta and Birmingham together for the initial two weeks of training at the FBI Academy in Virginia. There were SWAT teams from five offices at each training session. The Birmingham team was made up of runners, fast and agile. Atlanta was big, ugly, and foul mouthed.

Training began each day at 5:30 a.m. in the gym for what the Bureau called *Lions and Tigers*. We faced off every morning against the brutes from Atlanta, the rest of the Academy asleep in the dorms. Teams won by throwing the other teams off the mats onto the hard wood gym floor. I have always taken pride in the fact that I was usually the next to last Birmingham agent to land on my ass on the floor. Starley Carr, Abner, was always the last Birmingham agent to be hurled off the mats by Atlanta. Starley was our superb SWAT team leader. He never raised his voice, had a cool temperament under fire, and liked to do home repairs. He showed up for work with paint speckled on his Clark Kent horn-rimmed glasses. When the going got tough, I hid behind Starley.

The prison fire was tall and loud that first night. Every now and then there was a crack or pop coming from the blaze. It sounded like ammunition or explosives going off. I grew tired of the FM station. I reached for the dial, stopped, gave Don a courtesy look, sought his approval to change stations. He nodded through half-closed eyes, drowsy, half asleep like me, probably dreaming of a new hip.

Don was behind the wheel and periodically turned off the engine to conserve fuel in the Chrysler. We mainlined the FM and Bureau radios and sucked juice directly out of the battery.

The clock slowly spit out the minutes. Atlanta was on Eastern time, Birmingham on Central. I mentally made the adjustment and kept my watch on Central. The initial euphoria that we might storm the walls to rescue the hostages had given way to hours of sitting in the front seat of a car, waiting, then waiting some more. Adrenalin gave way to fatigue. It was going to be a long night.

The most dangerous time for captives is at the beginning, when they are first taken. Every hour increases their chances of survival. I wondered how they were faring, particularly the women. Don and I speculated that the Cubans would settle old scores with the guards, then turn on each other and fight over the women.

The breadth and intensity of the fire grew by the hour. The heat actually helped warm the Chrysler while the engine and heater were off. With the prison grounds illuminated by fire and spotlights, Don and I couldn't relieve ourselves out on the grass. We waited. Did anyone even remember we were out there?

I stared at the imposing entrance to the ancient Atlanta prison building, the front door. The fire hadn't reached there, or to the big bird cage, one of the main cell blocks behind the entrance. The high, thick stone walls had a Gothic feel, like a prison should look. Nothing cute about it, not at all the way the feds were currently building prisons. The new prisons, or correctional facilities as they were called, looked like motels surrounded by playful fences. The Atlanta Federal Prison did not look playful. It had a far-away flavor, something surrounded by water and alligators maybe, a prison on an isolated island that would change your appearance or swallow you whole.

We waited. The hours dragged. We drooped. You know the lyrics: *the darkest hour is just before dawn.* Don and I fell asleep.

We awoke several hours later. It was daylight. I bolted upright and looked around.

FBI SWAT teams were rolling into the prison grounds, joining us on the front lines. They eventually came from as far away as Los Angeles, Detroit, New York, and Washington, or WFO in Bureau slang. Border Patrol sent their SWAT teams, as did the Bureau of Prisons. It became a SWAT carnival.

Don and I were hungry. I fantasized about lemon icebox pies.

A convoy of civilian trucks pulled onto the prison grounds. The Salvation Army and the Red Cross arrived. Crews began setting up tents and kitchens, forming a long pedestrian thoroughfare I nicknamed *Broadway.* The weather remained damp and freezing.

In the coming days, we stopped living in BuCars and moved inside one of the prison satellite buildings for shifts of twelve hours on and twelve off. Birmingham SWAT teamed up with Detroit SWAT to cover 24 hours.

The media set up across the street from the prison grounds, hundreds of reporters with cameras and microphones. They milled around, watched the FBI eat while the prison smoldered and turned to ash. There was a smell of burned furniture, linens, clothes, and hell knows what else. The most prevalent odor was rubber. Small pieces of paper floated around the sky like confused snow. The Cubans could be burning their prison records, hoping for a fresh start.

I looked at my Birmingham teammates, then at other SWAT teams. I took stock. Birmingham was out of uniform. More to the point, Birmingham had no uniforms. We were wearing ten different versions of SWAT apparel, a pickup team at the Super Bowl. We were in a sea of Ninja Turtles outfitted in the prescribed dress: tailored black BDU pants and shirts, pockets everywhere, black holsters tied to their legs like gunfighters, and black helmets. They looked beautiful.

Birmingham SWAT was an outback team on a low budget. We wore white, yellow, and gray socks under our boots, with black, tan, or green camo pants, topped with blue baseball caps. Our heavy coats were green, army surplus. We lacked black. Some of our caps had FBI in white letters on the front, some didn't.

We went on like that for days, waited for the decision to go over the high walls with ladders and put down the riot. We actually climbed the ladders once, were poised to start a war with the Cubans when the *stand down* order came over the radio. We climbed back down the ladders and retreated to the food and beverage tents along *Broadway.*

FBI negotiators were hard at work negotiating in Spanish for the release of the hostages. We waited and rehearsed our assignments once we went in for real. Each SWAT team had a different assignment: Birmingham SWAT was to swarm over the walls and go straight for the Chapel deep inside the prison, where some of the hostages were kept under Cuban guard, according to Bureau intelligence. SWAT members were given authority to use deadly force on any inmate who tried to stop us or harm the hostages.

Birmingham worked the midnight to noon shift, which meant that we were officially armed and primed to rush the prison walls at any second during those hours. In reality, we slept on cots for hours in the night waiting for nothing to happen. Detroit SWAT replaced us for the noon to midnight shift.

Ashley Curry, the sniper on Birmingham SWAT, along with team leader Starley Carr, was an avid sportsman, family man, and a hell of a marksman. Ashley had grave misgivings about eating prison food of any kind, warning us not to eat anything in the prison cafeteria, which was available to SWAT teams to supplement food provided along *Broadway* by the Red Cross and the Salvation Army. Ashley had heard stories about what inmates did to food in prison kitchens. Inmates spit and peed in the food, or worse, Ashley reminded us. The rest of the team paid no attention to Ashley and frequently ate in the prison cafeteria, while he never varied from eating food along *Broadway*. After days of this routine, Ashley complimented one of the Red Cross food servers, and asked where they obtained most of their food. The server replied that much of it was prepared by non-rioting inmates from supplies in the prison cafeteria. Ashley gagged.

I got antsy and curious one night and slipped away from the Birmingham team for a closer look at the Cubans. The FBI had set up forward observation posts inside the prison where we could observe the inmates without being seen. I wanted to see for myself what the Cubans were up to. I buried my cold hands in the green army surplus coat and headed for the front entrance to the prison.

I was challenged by FBI sentries straight off. Only SWAT leaders were allowed through, the Ninjas told me. I identified myself as the leader of the Birmingham team; they let me pass.

Once inside the prison itself, the smell of fire was everywhere. Not knowing the layout, I slowly began a sojourn through layers of FBI elite, the rich and famous from Headquarters, the personal representatives and underlings of Director William Webster. The Hostage Rescue Team, HRT, the Bureau's first round draft choices, were everywhere. If we had to storm the walls, the HRT would plan it and lead us in. In my makeshift uniform, the HRT dudes looked at me as though I was there to deliver pizza.

There were ordnance wizards from the FBI lab and other technical notables in the event that we had to blast our way in to rescue the hostages. I slipped past crazed prison CEOs trying to explain to anyone who would listen how the Cubans had gotten loose in the first place.

I peeked into the room where the Bureau hostage negotiators had their heads together speaking Spanish into a bank of phones, bargaining with the Cubans for the release of the hostages. I kept walking, heading into the innards of the prison, the smell of the big fire pervasive and pungent.

I had no idea where I was. The prison was big.

"Cubans?" I asked a Ninja.

He dropped his eyes to my ratty green coat, hesitated, shot a thumb over his shoulder toward the stairwell. I thanked him and fled.

I walked up a flight of stairs to the next level, climbed a metal ladder, then another, I forgot how far, 'til I reached a landing, headed against Ninja traffic coming down a dimly lit hallway. Several walls of blankets hung from ropes to seal off light. I quickly stepped through the blankets into the near darkness on the other side. The lights had been turned off. I let my eyes adjust.

Several Ninjas stood guard. They eyed me.

"Cubans?" I said.

"Come on," one of the Ninjas said. He guided me ahead with a pinpoint flashlight. I knew I was close because of the smell. The toilets in the cell blocks were not working. The FBI had turned off the water, and the Bureau was negotiating with the Cubans to turn the water back on.

My guide turned off his flashlight, motioning for me to go ahead. I pushed back another row of hanging blankets and went on alone. There was a shaft of light coming up from the floor ahead in a crawl space. I eased forward on my knees, inched along the tunnel-like opening. I heard loud music and Spanish voices. The sounds of a festival. A celebration. The shaft of light com-

ing up out of the floor looked like rays from a slide projector. I
smelled cigarettes and piss.

I eased up to the grate in the floor and looked down. I was in
the ceiling of one of the big bird cages, a massive cell block. Below
was Mardi Gras and the bleacher seats at Wrigley Field combined.
Hundreds of Cuban inmates partied in prison whites, short sleeve
T-shirts and cuffed pants, sporting their colorful tattoos and freedom. They looked warm and happy. I envied them.

Tier after tier of cell doors were wide open. Dozens of radios
and cassettes were going at once, a cacophony of vocals and bands,
a mix of rock, Latin, and jazz. Percussion, bongos, castanets, and
sassy brass bled through to the rafters where I watched out of
sight. I tapped my fingers to the music. I looked for the hostages.
I couldn't spot a one. Inmates played one-wall handball with a
yellow tennis ball. The music wailed. I watched and listened for
several minutes.

Then something changed. The mood altered. An orchestra,
barely audible at first, slowly emerged through the din of music.
I strained to hear. The montage of competing sounds began to
subside. Cassettes and radios went silent. The full orchestra grew
in volume. The inmates went quiet and listened. I listened with
them. The music was beautiful. Violins floated above the cells,
brass, woodwinds in harmony, amplified from a speaker somewhere, absorbed by the ceiling where I hid. The hymn *Fairest Lord
Jesus* filled the big bird cage. I felt my heart rise.

I'd never heard a full orchestral treatment of this old song,
only choir renditions, especially in the little Methodist church in
Number 6 Hollow in the coal mining camp of Jenkinjones, West
Virginia, when I was a wee lad. The words of the hymn came back
to me: *Fairest Lord Jesus, Ruler of all nature.* Cubans barely stirred,
their ears cocked. *O thou of God and man the Son; Thee will I cherish, Thee will I honor.*

The orchestra was the only sound in the cell block. I mentally clicked off the lyrics, hummed along: *Thou, my soul's glory,
joy, and crown.*

The orchestra finished. Radios and cassettes fired up again and the air stank of tobacco, urine, and shit. The big cage came back to life.

I inched backwards on my knees, out of the crawl space, stood, adjusted to the dark, and groped ahead to a blanket. I pushed it aside and stepped into Federal control again.

"Hear that?" I asked one of the Ninjas.

"Hear what?" he replied.

"The orchestra … you know, *Fairest Lord Jesus.*"

"What are you talking about?" the Ninja asked in a Yankee accent.

"Down there." I pointed toward the shaft of light behind the hanging blanket. "The Cubans got quiet for the orchestra. You didn't hear the hymn?

"I didn't hear any orchestra." The Ninja squinted at me. "Where you from?"

"Alabama. Birmingham SWAT."

"I see," he said, raising a condescending eye. Probably thought I drove a NASCAR special over to watch the fire.

"Never mind," I said. I made my way back through the strata of FBI authority and out of the prison. I asked repeatedly in the coming days, but no one else heard the orchestra. No one experienced the hymn.

The siege of the Atlanta Federal Prison lasted eleven days. The Cubans finally gave up and released their one hundred captives. None of the hostages was harmed. The Cubans surrendered without incident and walked into the arms of the Ninjas.

On the day the hostages were released, one of the long TV lenses caught the Birmingham SWAT team just outside the main entrance to the prison as the hostages came out to a joyous reunion with their families. My wife, watching back home, thought Birmingham SWAT was part of the prison maintenance crew until she spotted my face.

We were on site for two weeks, doing what we'd been trained to do in SWAT, our mission. Afterwards, there was a move by some of the SWAT teams to get extra compensation for the long hours in Atlanta in addition to the regular overtime pay built into our salaries. I thought that this was wrong. So did every other member of the Birmingham team. We did not demand extra money. We did what we had been trained to do. We did not need or deserve any special treatment or compensation.

The Birmingham SWAT team rehearsing its assignment to storm the chapel in the Atlanta Federal Prison to rescue hostages, November, 1987. The FBI national Hostage Rescue Team and field office SWAT teams were each given different areas on Prison grounds to storm to rescue the hostages. I am in the foreground armed with the standard SWAT issue 9mm semi-automatic pistol. The rescue was not necessary because the rioting inmates surrendered without incident.

CHAPTER TWENTY-SIX

WILLIAM S. SESSIONS

In November 1987, William S. Sessions took over the reins of the FBI. Sessions, chief judge for the Western District of Texas, was selected by President Reagan to succeed William Webster to run the Bureau.

Sessions was a mouse. He did things in the dark, then hid during the day. Under his watch, the FBI turned into a collection of special interest groups, each promoting its own agenda, pushing for advantage, shouting discrimination to get its way. Every time Sessions went behind closed doors to meet with one of those pressure groups, the group won, the FBI lost. For agents who worked the streets, his two favorite words were *settlement* and *concession.* We tagged him Director ConSessions.

Under Director William Sessions, when African-American agents and Hispanic agents and women agents fell short of getting all the things that *all agents have wanted forever*, they formed ranks and brought suit or threatened to bring suit, and Sessions caved. They pressured him and he gave them what they wanted. Nobody in the FBI had ever formed interest groups *within* the Bureau with such real authority before Sessions became Director: the FBI *was* the interest group—the *only* interest group.

The way we were used to doing things, if we didn't like the squads to which we were assigned, we bitched. If we didn't like the cases we were given, if they were not big enough or important enough, we bitched. We wanted the spotlight to shine on us, to showcase our investigative talents. We wanted to be in on all the arrests, especially the ones of notoriety. We maneuvered to be on the surveillance teams where lives were at stake, to be in the middle of the storm and put bad guys in jail. We wanted to catch spies and work cases that smothered foreign-directed operations and espionage, that uncovered Americans who betrayed their country. We wanted all these things, whether we were Hispanic agents from Texas, or the sons or daughters of coal miners from McDowell County, West Virginia.

Street agents demanded to be on field office SWAT teams, or members of the national Hostage Rescue Team. We raised hell if we weren't selected to be hostage negotiators or one of the field profilers who worked with the big guys at Quantico. We asserted our right to be in our offices of preference right away without years of waiting—and no time in New York either, or some other purgatory—send me to Birmingham. It was my right as an FBI agent in be in Birmingham.

Street agents clamored to be pilots or physical fitness coordinators. We *must* have one of the new BuCars every time the fleet was expanded. Damn we were special.

We demanded all of the above whether we were white women from Oregon or black men from Baltimore. When street agents raised their hands and joined the management program, they complained that they were in the wrong division at Headquarters, or were not promoted fast enough, or were sent out to supervise a field office they didn't want, or were passed over for SAC or ASAC. Universal whining at every level.

When the agent special interest groups closed ranks and threatened suit, they got what they wanted. The vast sea of white male agents resented it, charging reverse discrimination, and complained that no one spoke for them. Which was nonsense. The Bureau had always been run by white males. But there was divisive bitterness anyway, on all sides.

Many of the Bureau's Hispanic agents were hired because of their high degree of fluency in Spanish. They were told when they were hired that their language skills would be utilized in their careers. Regardless, Hispanic agents brought suit complaining about working in cities where there were large Spanish speaking communities, what they derided as the *Taco Circuit*. The Bureau had told them from the recruiting stage on through their hiring that they might at least start their careers utilizing their Spanish language skills. Later, if they wanted to go into management, they could raise their hands like everyone else.

During the Cold War, when the Bureau was in the thick of it against the KGB and the Kremlin's puppets in Eastern Europe, there was talk in the FBI's counterintelligence community about establishing a separate career path for agents working those matters. They would spend their years in the murk of the spy business, theoretically not being bothered with the work that agents were doing in hundreds of types of criminal violations. Counterintelligence agents were not to go shoulder to shoulder with their unwashed brethren working bank robberies or kidnappings.

The agents with law degrees who served as legal advisors in every field office, the Chief Division Counsel, CDC, a full time assignment, demanded to be at the salary level set aside for supervisors, the GS 14 level. They wanted supervisor pay without having to be supervisors. They eventually won. Although I had been through law school, I ran in horror from any attempt to sew me into a legal jacket. I would have never agreed to it, although I did see the justice in awarding the title of ACDC to the number two legal advisor in every office.

J. Edgar Hoover refused to hire minorities and women as agents but Patrick Gray changed it. There were many in the FBI in the field and at Headquarters who immediately welcomed diversification. I was one of them. Succeeding Directors have been committed to it, distancing the FBI from the hiring practices of Hoover. The white old boy network retired. By the time I retired in 1999, the FBI was fully inclusive in its hiring and promotions.

One of the agents whom I recruited in the 1980s, an African-American male, rose to an influential position at FBIHQ, and eventually became my boss in the recruitment and hiring of agents, support staff, and Honors Interns. In addition, the agent who ran the Montgomery, Alabama, FBI office in the 1990s, Carmen Adams, was an attorney I recruited in Birmingham. She became the ASAC in New Orleans, later SAC in Birmingham after I retired.

Janice Windham, the supervisor who headed foreign counterintelligence and anti-terrorism operations in north Alabama in the 1990s, was an agent whom I recruited out of a teaching career in Birmingham. She became my immediate boss and was an effective and innovative leader. It was not easy for her to supervise me, or to command a squad that included Bob Sligh, the Fox. I had no qualms about serving under Janice.

Windham and the Fox spotted a talented Hispanic FOA in Birmingham, Roel Carranza, and recruited him off criminal matters and into counterintelligence. Carranza flourished, becoming an expert on Chinese matters, and made cases on his own initiative. He later went to Headquarters as a supervisor.

In the arena of FBI firearms instructors, traditionally a male bastion with few women, Tuscaloosa agent Vicki Davis became one of the most respected firearms experts in Alabama. She helped me on the range right up to the time I retired. She was also a good recruiter, bringing talented people into the FBI out of the University of Alabama.

None of those agents needed Sessions or any other Director to give them a leg up or special treatment in order to have successful Bureau careers. There were no barriers placed in front of them, no cause to form a class and sue the FBI. They made it because they were talented.

Where discrimination *did* exist in the Bureau, Sessions should have cut it off at its head. He should have uncovered the agents responsible for bias and punished them. Made examples of them. He should have dealt on an individual basis with every allegation made by Hispanic, black, or female agents, or any other minority, provide immediate redress, correct it and move on. Instead, Sessions rolled over for class action suits or threats of suits. He demeaned women and minorities by appearing to give them preferential treatment; they didn't need it. They weren't suffering institutional discrimination. They were experiencing the frustrations inherent in the culture of the FBI, traditional agent gripes, whether in the field or at Headquarters. Sessions came to Birmingham in 1990 to tour our expanded and remodeled office. He was warm, generous with his time, posed for endless photographs, met our families, and congratulated us. I'd heard that he was a likable guy in person, even though he wasn't a strong leader. I enjoyed his company. However, at home with my family, I complained about Sessions to my wife, Pat, within earshot of my children. When Sessions posed for a photograph with my family and me in the office, my youngest daughter, Molly, in grade school at the time, asked in a sweet little voice whether Sessions was the guy I didn't like. I'm sure Sessions heard what Molly said, but he smiled and never let on. Pat and I were mortified. It is still a story we laugh about.

Although Sessions was a weak FBI Director, he was strong about not giving up his job. He refused to resign in the fall of 1992, after he was caught using federal money to improve his home, similar to what Clarence Kelley had done. Sessions had also set up Bureau-funded plane rides for his wife, as well as a parking place in the garage of FBIHQ for her shopping trips in downtown Washington.

President Clinton fired Sessions on July 19, 1993.

"Daddy, is this the man you don't like?" Visit by FBI Director William Sessions to the Birmingham Office in 1990. L-R: Director Sessions, me, my daughters Laura and Molly, wife Patricia, and daughter Stacey. The quote is from Molly. Sessions heard Molly and reacted with grace and humor.

CHAPTER TWENTY-SEVEN

LINCOLN AND GRANT

Spring, 1989. I was alone in a parked BuCar reading an old edition of Carl Sandburg's *Lincoln, The War Years, Vol 1*. I had the other three volumes at home in my library. I was a member of an arrest team on a low-grade thief, a bisexual guy with a boyfriend who lived in an upscale apartment complex in the southern suburbs of Birmingham. We were waiting for the fugitive to show at his friend's place.

There were four FBI cars on scene, one agent per car. I was not the case agent and was along for the ride, parked out of sight of the apartment. Although I was a member of the Birmingham SWAT team, the arrest business that day was not a SWAT operation. This was going to be a lazy Southern arrest. Magnolias were nearby.

We had set up early in the morning in a perimeter around the apartment complex, the usual effort to blend into the city and not be seen. The case agent had the *eye*, a direct view of the apartment door we were watching. After picking a spot that was a bit back, I parked the BuCar, content to be alone. I couldn't actually see the apartment door. I opened up the hard cover book in my lap and found my place. My head came up occasionally to check things out.

I quickly lost myself in Grant's mood at Shiloh in April, 1862. One night in a drenching rain, Grant tried to grab some sleep under a tree behind Union lines. His foot throbbed from when he'd been thrown from his horse. The incident gave thrust to rumors that Grant was drinking heavily again and couldn't sit a horse. Miserable in the rain, unable to sleep, he sought refuge inside a nearby log cabin where surgeons were spending the night amputating limbs without anesthesia. After an hour of listening to the cries of agony from the wounded and dying, Grant left and went back to the comfort of the storm.

His dirty blue uniform sour and itching from the rain, Grant thought about how to drive the enemy the next day, a Sabbath, drive them 'til there was nothing left of the enemy but carnage. His answer to upheavals was to throw in more fresh troops. He had them, the Confederates didn't. The Confederates wanted war, Grant gave them war.

Someone said something over the FBI radio in my serene BuCar. We were having radio trouble in the Birmingham FBI. We always had radio trouble. The radio techs blamed Babe Ruth's trade to the Yankees, pyorrhea, or communists. Our Bureau car radios were big suckers mounted in the trunks. Inside the BuCar, the transmissions blared forth without warning to scare the stew out of you, then cut off in mid-sentence. FBI radios were an invasion of privacy.

I adjusted my book on Lincoln, Sandburg's prose, rested it against the steering wheel. People drove out of the apartment complex going to work in the rush hour traffic.

Lincoln wrote this in a proclamation after Grant's victory at Shiloh: "It has pleased Almighty God to vouchsafe signal victories to the land and naval forces engaged in suppressing an internal rebellion …" If I could write like that, I wouldn't be sitting alone in an FBI car surrounded by radios that didn't work.

I was writing a novel about the assassination of President Kennedy. I kept a legal pad on the front seat of the BuCar to write ideas while speeding up and down Alabama's highways. I also kept a notebook of words I wanted to remember, either for spelling or because I liked the way they looked on a page or rolled off my tongue: *sanguine, clairvoyance, decrepitude,* and *coalesce, aficionado, machinations, mimicry,* and *chicanery. Buggery* was an interesting word, and I was hoping to use it in one of my speeches to the Rotary Club or a Baptist women's group.

I came out of my reverie and looked around the apartment complex. All was well, so I dove back into Sandburg's book. The rumors in the North about Grant's drinking continued after his victory at Shiloh. Too many Union homes were draped in black from the loss of sons and fathers who'd been driven by Grant into the mouths of Confederate cannons. Needless slaughter it was said. Grant was a butcher. Lincoln listened to his party's professionals, members of his Cabinet, and the Republicans who ran Congress, listened to them complain at a White House meeting about the butcher and drunk General Ulysses S. Grant. Grant should be replaced, they said.

Lincoln listened, did not interrupt. When everyone in the room had had their say, when the vehemence against Grant was played out, Lincoln unfolded his long legs and brought the meeting to a close. "I can't spare this man. He fights."

There was a knock on my car window. I looked up out of the book. The case agent was staring at me.

"You didn't see my signal to move in?" he asked.

I tried to think of something. I was asleep? I was cleaning my gun? Fiddling with the Bureau radio maybe? I drew a blank. The case agent grinned and walked back to his BuCar. The fugitive was already sitting in the back seat, under arrest.

Hemorrhoids. Concubine. Oodles. Dalliance.

I and fellow members of the Birmingham FBI SWAT team assist in the clearing of the Atlanta Federal Prison after the release of one hundred unharmed hostages and the peaceful surrender of one thousand rioting inmates in November, 1987. L-R: Agents Ashley Curry, Bill Temple, me, Starley Carr.

CHAPTER TWENTY-EIGHT

ASSASSINATION OF A FEDERAL JUDGE

Part One: December 16, 1989

My home telephone rang. It was Luther Brannon calling from the office. Judge Vance had been assassinated by a bomb. Federal Appellate Judge Robert Vance was a friend of mine. Luther said someone had mailed a bomb to Judge Vance's home in Mountain Brook, which, as everyone in Alabama knew, was a highly wealthy suburb of Birmingham, the richest community in the state. The bomb blew up in Vance's kitchen.

My wife and I were dressed for the annual FBI Christmas party at a downtown hotel, with the babysitter on the way. Luther told me to report immediately to the office for a meeting before joining other agents at Vance's home. The FBI Christmas party was canceled.

I changed out of my party clothes, a dark suit, white shirt and red Santa tie. Only the FBI, IBM, and the National Republican Party would wear suits to a Christmas party. I put on a light sweater and black SWAT pants, BDU's, with all the pockets, gathered my 9mm semi-automatic and SWAT bag full of equipment. This could be like the Atlanta Prison riot of '87, where we were told to pack for two days and were gone for two weeks. I left all the *un*-arrangements to my wife and headed to the office.

I thought of Judge Robert Vance. He was charming and could put you at ease. He didn't take himself too seriously. I had interviewed him frequently on Bureau business. He appreciated irony and wit and was a compelling conversationalist. We had always hit it off and had an easy rapport. We talked about everything from history and politics and law enforcement to the turmoil of the civil rights movement in Birmingham.

A native Alabamian who'd been born in Talladega where my wife grew up, Vance had seen and lived a lot of Alabama history. A liberal and national Democrat in a sea of states' rights Southern conservatives, Vance was a beacon of reason and moderation in contrast to the reactionary right wing politics of such Alabama politicians as George Wallace. Vance had supported John Kennedy and had been a delegate to the 1960 Democratic National Convention in Los Angeles that nominated JFK. Vance and I spoke the same political language.

Like me, the Judge was a graduate of the University of Alabama School of Law, a Crimson Tide fan through and through. He headed the Alabama Democratic Party for years and stood up to Wallace and the Klan. He was tough and had no patience with unprepared attorneys.

I liked Robert Vance. Who would kill him?

He was a federal appellate judge for the 11th Circuit and did not do trial work. He read briefs and listened to quiet arguments by appeals lawyers, and did not come face to face with bad guys. He mostly handed down opinions as one in a panel of judges. He was removed from the tension and rancor of a courtroom where lawyers went at each other and the accused stared a hole through the judge when he handed down the sentence. The prisons are full of dirtbags who are steaming at judges.

Whoever killed Judge Vance didn't do it at the Federal Court House in Birmingham where the federal judges have their offices, where the U.S. Marshals have things buttoned up, where I had recently helped a marshal with some security precautions in case one of the judges was taken hostage in his own courtroom or chambers. The bomb came to Judge Vance's home. A personal thing. I wanted to find who did it.

The FBI was on a war footing by the time I got to the office. The mood was grim, icy. Every agent in Birmingham was activated, plus agents from all over north Alabama. Before we're finished, there will be agents from all over the country working the case. If you killed a federal judge in America, the weight of federal law enforcement would crush you like a bug.

I felt a rush of adrenalin. There was always a belief at the outset of a major case that we would catch the thug who did it straight off, that an arrest was imminent. We'd go all night and all day and all night 'til we got him.

Allen Whitaker, the Birmingham SAC, brought the meeting to order. I collected the gist of what Whitaker had to say, then half-listened as he droned on, biding my time 'til I could go to the scene of the assassination.

The judge's body was still in the kitchen where he died. That afternoon, he'd picked up a package delivered to his mailbox by a postal carrier, a mailbox about a hundred yards from his house at the beginning of his driveway. He had walked down to get the mail through a tree-shrouded lawn typical of Mountain Brook estates. He picked up mail full of Christmas cards and a package that looked like it might be a gift, and brought all the mail into the kitchen. When he opened the package, it blew up in his face. His wife was in the kitchen with him and survived, though badly wounded. She somehow made it to a neighbor's house before collapsing.

The bomb was full of nails. Judge Vance died instantly. The nails exploded into his wife as well. She was in surgery in a Birmingham hospital. She would be interviewed as soon as possible. SAC Whitaker pointed to a female agent and told her to conduct the interview. The agent left for the hospital.

The ATF arrived, Alcohol, Tobacco, and Firearms, along with Postal Inspectors because the bomb was delivered by mail. We all knew up front that this case would be a turf battle between federal law enforcement, and probably intra-FBI as well, as Bureau field offices fought to control the investigation. Careers would be made. Careers would be unmade. The Director of the FBI, the Attorney General of the United States, and perhaps even the President would be watching, looking over our shoulders. We would have to contend hourly with FBI Headquarters, which would second and third guess every move. Having to deal with those slugs at HQ was the worst aspect of any big case. Some empty suit in Washington who had never worked a bombing in his career would tell us how to work a bombing. I'd never worked a bombing assassination either, but never mind.

There would be no holiday season, Whitaker was quick to point out. Annual leave was cancelled until morale improved. Whitaker enjoyed passing on information like that. He had the countenance of an undertaker. Several years later, after being told over the telephone that my mother was dying, I requested emergency leave to rush to her side. Whitaker's response was to ask me whether I had someone to cover for me in an upcoming meeting.

I decided to make a break for it. It didn't take me long to drive the four miles or so to Judge Vance's home in Mountain Brook. His antebellum mansion sat on a hill at 2824 Shook Road. I pictured the Judge walking back up the hill carrying a package that had come in the mail. The winding driveway was full of Mountain Brook PD units and unmarked BuCars. I pulled over on the grass and killed the engine, walked the rest of the way up to the garage. I was greeted by several cops and agents. I huddled with Bill Fleming, an experienced FBI agent who worked a variety of criminal cases. Bill was the profiler in the office, and I expected he would be doing a profile of the bomber, working with the Bureau's best profilers at the FBI Academy.

Fleming was a persistent and dogged investigator, tireless, just the guy you want on a major case. He later went on to national recognition as the agent who put together the case that convicted the Klan-linked killers of four young black girls in the 1963 bombing of the Sixteenth Street Baptist Church in Birmingham. A Southerner and Civil War buff who carved flawless wooden ducks, Fleming looked more like a professor than an FBI agent. He and I had spent hours dissecting Civil War battles and the attack-and-die attitude of Confederate soldiers, as well as the humor and brilliance of Lincoln.

Although Bill and I had distant relatives who fought for the Confederacy, I also had kin who remained loyal to the Union, mountain folks who had broken with Virginia and helped to carve out the new state of West Virginia. I was a Union man, had Lincoln in my veins. My respect went to Grant and Sherman, Lincoln's hammers. I agreed with Grant that the Confederate cause was an unholy rebellion.

Fleming knew that Robert Vance was my friend. "Don't go into the house," he said.

I thanked him, walked through the well-lit garage past tools and rows of storage shelves. Inside the house, I headed straight for the kitchen. The door to the kitchen was open, more cops were inside. One of them was videoing the scene, speaking softly over the video. The kitchen was surprisingly small for a big house. I stepped into the kitchen and stopped. Debris was everywhere from bomb damage. There were nail holes in the ceiling and walls, but no apparent flame or charred areas. The Vance kitchen telephone was ringing loudly. No one answered it.

Judge Vance was lying on his right side against the wall at the far end of the kitchen. I had the odd sensation I was invading his privacy, that I shouldn't be standing in *his* house with him lying there. The cops spoke in hushed tones. Maybe they felt the same, that we were not where we should be.

I stared at Judge Vance. He was missing his heavy rimmed glasses. I'd never seen him without his glasses. His altered appearance fed my imagination that it was not really him lying there. His full head of gray hair looked like the wind had ruffled it, but not enough to cover the part on his left side. His face was speckled with red dots that looked like freckles. A thin jacket covered his upper body, the jacket he had worn to get the mail. It had been a mild Alabama December day and you wouldn't need a heavy jacket.

The violence was below his waist, a massive wound that was partially hidden with a yellow towel. The kitchen phone rang again. No one answered it. Cops walked in and out of the room. I stood there and thought about Robert Vance. He'd lost a brother, as I had. He loved the English, as I did. He found comfort in the Anglican rituals of the Episcopal Church. So did I. We both had sons.

I stood in his kitchen transfixed by the sight of him, feeling at that moment more as a friend than an agent, doing nothing to help. He might have said, *Hell Jack. Now isn't this a damn fix?* Judge Robert S. Vance was a remarkable man.

His wife, Helen, was equally remarkable. She survived the bomb explosion in the kitchen and told what happened. *There had been people in and out of the house all day. Friends, children, things to do before Christmas. She'd been in touch with her son, Robert Jr., and his wife, Joyce, both attorneys in Birmingham. Her other son, Charles, was in school at Duke University and would be home for the holidays.*

Judge Vance brought the mail into the kitchen, including a heavy package about shoe box size, wrapped in brown paper and white twine. The package was covered in stamps. The return address on the package was that of a colleague and friend in Newnan, Georgia, another judge from the 11th Circuit Court of Appeals, headquartered in Atlanta. Vance set the package down on the kitchen table. He stood, leafed through the other mail, mostly letters and Christmas cards, maybe a bill or two.

The TV was on in the kitchen and there was something in the microwave. The judge stood over the table while he looked through the mail. She sat at the table across from him. They made small talk, things about Christmas and family matters.

The judge picked up the package, held it waist high, stood, looked down at it. He gripped one end of the package with his left hand and unwrapped the other end with his right. He opened it.

A violent explosion knocked her to the floor. The blast was deafening. Stunned, she laid on the floor and tried to clear her head. She was numb and there was a roar in her ears.

She got to her feet and stumbled over to him. He was lying in the corner of the kitchen. She knelt over him, spoke to him. He didn't respond. He was bleeding, she was bleeding. She got up somehow and dialed an emergency number. She couldn't hear, didn't know whether anyone was on the other end on the line. The roar in her ears continued.

She dropped the phone and made her way to the car. In a haze, she drove down the driveway to the street and over to the home of a neighbor.

Somewhere, in the recesses of her memory, there was the image of a wife placing a yellow towel over the massive wound on her husband's lower body.

I left the Vance residence late the night he was killed, and went back to the office. There were meetings. More meetings. We were tired. Most of us made a night of it. We starting digging in the files for the crazies, the professional haters, people who'd made threats against state or federal judges, cops, or agents. We queried files about inmates who were particularly vocal in their anger at anyone in the criminal justice system. We also pulled files on international terrorist groups and individuals.

With the sun coming up on a clear day, I requested to be present to witness the autopsy of Judge Vance scheduled for that afternoon. Permission was granted by my supervisor. The Fox and a female agent were assigned as witnesses, also.

I had never seen an autopsy in person, only on film. I did not waver as to whether I could get through it, especially as I knew the victim. I was certain that I could. I felt compelled to go. It was a gesture of my respect and admiration for Robert Vance. I wanted to see him through it.

After hours of paper work and endless coffee, I headed to Cooper Green hospital on the south side of Birmingham for the autopsy. It took place in an isolated area on the first level of the hospital.

The pathologist needed over five hours to complete his work. There was a lot of evidence on the Judge's body. Nails and pieces of pipe from the bomb.

The Judge was a big man. Six feet tall and over 200 pounds. His face was serene, his eyes closed. He seemed asleep. At peace.

Standing there a few feet from him, I wondered what his last thought had been. Knowing his sense of humor, I imagined him opening the package and realizing for a tiny instant that there was a bomb inside, and thinking to himself: *Damn, I've really screwed up this time.*

That is how I remember him.

Part Two

Walter Leroy Moody, Jr., age 56, killed Judge Robert Vance with a steel pipe bomb five and one-half inches in length and one and one-half inches in diameter. The pipe was sealed at each end with threaded end caps, and was packed with Hercules Red Dot double-base smokeless powder. There was an improvised detonator constructed out of the barrel of a ballpoint pen filled with CCI brand primer. The initiator was designed and electrically triggered to explode, detonating the main explosive charge when the top lid of the box was opened. Eighty nails were secured to the pipe.

To make the crime appear to be racially motivated and thus focus the FBI investigation on white hate groups, Moody mailed a nearly identical pipe bomb to the office of African-American attorney, Robert Robinson, in Savannah, Georgia, where it blew up, killing him. Not finished, Moody mailed pipe bombs to a National Association for the Advancement of Colored People, NAACP, office in Jacksonville, Florida, and to the Federal Courthouse in Atlanta, Georgia. Both bombs were defused, providing law enforcement with a good look at the components of the bombs and how they were put together, their *signature*.

Continuing with his plans, Moody mailed threat letters with racial overtones to NAACP offices in Atlanta and Jacksonville, plus to three judges on the 11th Circuit Court of Appeals. The letters were from a group that Moody made up, a group he called Americans For A Competent Federal Judicial System. The group took credit for the pipe bombings.

Initially, the FBI had over three hundred suspects in the case, but as one suspect after another was eliminated, the Bureau kept coming back to Moody, who lived in Rex, Georgia, a suburb of Atlanta. He had made a pipe bomb in 1972 almost exactly like the four bombs mailed in 1989 in the Vance case. The ATF liked Moody for the Vance murder right away. The ATF was right. Their files were full of particulars about how Moody had put together his bomb in 1972.

Six months after he killed Judge Vance and attorney Robinson, Moody was the prime suspect. The Bureau's profilers from Quantico said that the bomber was an intelligent middle-aged white male with legal training. Moody fit that profile. He had attended law school but did not have a degree. He lived by posing as a literary agent and ran a scam from his home in Rex, bilking amateur writers out of money with the promise to read their work and find them a publisher. All federal investigative efforts, including wire taps, listening devices, searches and surveillances, came down on Moody. After he was arrested, agents bugged his prison cell, where he talked in his sleep and said incriminating things to a fellow inmate when awake.

Moody was convicted in federal court, where he received seven life sentences plus four hundred years in August, 1991. As federal and state authorities had planned all along, Moody was then tried for murder in Alabama where he was convicted and sentenced to die in the electric chair. Considering the slow pace of appeals, one of these years he'll be put to death.

My contribution to the investigation of the Vance assassination was to interview many of Judge Vance's closest friends, including colleagues on the Federal bench, attorneys, prosecutors, buddies from the military, and people he knew by virtue of his many and varied interests. I also spent time over the months with his wife, Helen, his son, Robert Jr., and daughter-in-law Joyce, trying to get a complete background of Judge Vance to determine whether his murder might be personal and not related to his 11th Circuit rulings. I never developed any suspects.

On my own initiative, I contacted a psychic whom I had used in other investigations. She felt that Vance's murderer was in Birmingham and led me to several suspects. I checked them out and eliminated them.

I was assigned to gather information and intelligence related to the possibility that the Klan, whether from Alabama or elsewhere, was responsible for the murder, or whether other white supremacist individuals or groups might be involved. I interviewed Don Black, head of the Klan in Alabama, who had told me to get lost in previous attempts to talk to him over the years, but who wanted to talk in the Vance case because he didn't want any part of the murder of a federal Judge. Black told me emphatically the Klan was not involved. I believed him but took a hard look at the Klan anyway. They were not involved.

I also spent time with an informant I had developed, a drug runner with ties to national and international terrorist groups. He told me he had no idea who had killed Judge Vance and hadn't heard anything in his circles about who was responsible. He nosed around for months at my direction and never came up with a thing. Dozens of agents were working other angles and possibilities. We all kept eliminating suspects.

The investigation shifted full square to Enterprise, Alabama, where a junk dealer named Robert Wayne O'Farrell felt the full weight of federal heat for weeks. Agents traced the old manual typewriter, used to type the threat letters and address labels for the mail-bombs, to O'Farrell. The typewriter had distinctive characteristics for the numbers 2, 3, 5, 7, and 8, and the capital letters for A, M, S, and W. O'Farrell denied any involvement. Agents searched his house and business, but could not locate the typewriter. It was O'Farrell's wife who eventually got him off the hook when she viewed a line-up and identified Moody's second wife as the person to whom she had sold the manual typewriter in 1989. Moody's wife was not involved in the bombings and eventually divorced him.

I left Enterprise to go to Atlanta, where I guarded a female witness who had been threatened by Moody. I stood at a window in an apartment from midnight to eight watching her apartment for a week. I was alone and had to keep the lights off, couldn't read or play a TV or radio, which made it hard to stay awake. It was one of the longest weeks I ever experienced in the FBI.

In early April, 1990, right after the guard duty assignment, I headed one of the teams that monitored Moody's telephone conversations at his residence. We did the monitoring twenty-four hours a day from a room in the Atlanta FBI office in the Martin Luther King Building. The coverage was called a Title III in Bureau language, and was done with court approval.

Agents planted listening devices all over Moody's life, bugging the hell out of his home and cars, following him everywhere, including a motorcycle trip he took down I-75 into Florida with his wife. The New York FBI office supplied its biker team of agents for that one. They were decked out in black leather and beards. We didn't know whether to have a beer with them or shoot them. Moody suspected we were on to him and was guarded in his conversations and travels. He made a ritual of making love to his wife every night for our benefit.

The Atlanta FBI took over much of the case. The chief federal prosecutor was Louis Freeh, a former agent and future Director of the FBI appointed by President Clinton in 1993.

I always enjoyed rappelling down a practice tower. The photo was taken during SWAT team training in east Alabama in the early 1990's. Alas, I never got to rappel on an actual FBI operation.

CHAPTER TWENTY-NINE

LOUIS J. FREEH

President Clinton appointed Louis Freeh to succeed the fired William Sessions on July 20, 1993. Freeh formally took over on September 1, 1993. He was to serve until the eve of the September 11th attacks in 2001. I spent as much time with Freeh as I had with Clarence Kelley.

I first heard about Freeh when he was the United States Attorney who successfully prosecuted Walter Leroy Moody for the pipe bomb murder of Federal Appeals Judge Robert Vance. Freeh was a good prosecutor, quickly gaining command of the mountain of evidence that agents had provided him in the Vance case, and smoothly digesting the Bureauese in all the reports, the language of agents, and formulated a strategy that strangled Moody's defense.

Freeh's dark blue blazer and gray slacks were wrinkled, his shoes scuffed and unpolished. His indifferent attire was in marked contrast to every one of his predecessors, Directors of the FBI from Hoover through Sessions, who were spit and polish, natty dressers, looking the part. Freeh didn't look the part in terms of clothes. However, he was in terrific physical condition and took pride in his level of fitness. He looked like one of us, like he belonged with street agents, which he had been at one time.

Freeh had been a street agent in 1975, and had worked organized crime investigations in New York City. He was a good agent. He left New York to become a supervisor at FBIHQ. After the Moody trial, Freeh went on to serve as a U.S. District Judge in New York before coming back to the Bureau as Director.

Freeh visited field offices, as all the Directors had done since Hoover. When he came to Birmingham in the mid-1990s, I was assigned to escort him around the three floors of the Birmingham FBI office in the 2121 Building. I was told to keep Freeh on schedule when he went around the Birmingham office holding meetings. Freeh was calm and unhurried in the meetings, stoic yet friendly. He spoke with conviction, was businesslike without being formal. He was steady, had unblinking eye contact when he wasn't busy writing on a legal pad. I would have trusted him on an arrest.

I was seated in the audience and Director Louis Freeh stood next to me in the aisle of the auditorium at the FBI Academy in Virginia. It was typical of Freeh to come off the stage to speak to us. He was informal, comfortable, at ease with being in command of the FBI. I looked closely at him from my cushioned seat in an audience of the Bureau's physical fitness instructors. Freeh talked about the importance of agents being fit; about the need for the Bureau to set the example for the rest of law enforcement in terms of handling stress and maintaining control of a subject during an arrest; the importance of being prepared for confrontations on the street that we know are coming, but not when. Freeh had all of us breathing with him, one heartbeat, a team ready to play on any field he chose. His message was our gospel: exercise, strength, flexibility, endurance.

Freeh's hair was wet and cut severely short. He'd just come from a five-mile run with one of the new agent classes in training at the Academy. We, his audience, had just completed a week's in-service at the Academy, honing our knowledge of fitness and nutrition, how to make it work for FBI agents. Freeh was preaching to the choir.

The in-service had been organized and run by Bob Rogers, my close friend and colleague from our FOA days together in

Denver. After being transferred to San Diego following my transfer to Birmingham, Bob had established an impressive record as a street agent in California before accepting a promotion to the physical training unit at the FBI Academy. Bob and I had stayed in touch over the years. I respected him and coveted our friendship. He was the best motivational speaker in the Bureau. He looked exactly what he was: FBI, Notre Dame, Marine Corps.

Freeh's visit to Birmingham went without a hitch. The Bureau car did not overheat. I met with him twice at Headquarters in my role as a member of the Special Agent Advisory Committee, the Director's link with street agents from around the country. There were twelve of us from six national regions. Freeh listened to our gripes and recommendations several times a year. We met with him in his office on the seventh floor of FBI Headquarters, the J. Edgar Hoover building on Pennsylvania Avenue.

Prior to walking into the Director's office for our session with Freeh, we met for several days with the heads of the various divisions at Headquarters. We filled them in on what the field needed and wanted. If they had the authority to change Bureau policy without Freeh's signature, they would, and we would not bring up the issue with Freeh. Many of our concerns were settled at a lower level. We saved the larger issues for the director.

Freeh usually met with the Advisory Committee alone in his office, without script or advisors present. He didn't make speeches about how good things were or pound his chest.

Freeh was effective in these sessions with the Advisory Committee. If he didn't know something, he said so, then pledged to find out and get back to us, and he would.

Freeh was genuinely committed to hiring more women and minorities as agents. I'm convinced of this from being with him and listening to him in person, watching his body language and measuring the tone of his voice. However, he blew it when it came to hiring African-American women. He wouldn't listen to the field about how to recruit black women; instead, he listened to his advisors at Headquarters, who were dead wrong.

I give Freeh high marks for trimming a load of fat out of FBIHQ as soon as he became Director. He transferred supervisors to the field offices where the real work of the FBI was done. Freeh brought a street agent's perspective to the deadwood at Headquarters. He took out his knife and went at it. He also trimmed the staff at the FBI Academy at Quantico.

Freeh presided over major terrorism cases in the 1990s, including one that he inherited, the February 26, 1993 massive bomb that exploded in the underground parking garage of the World Trade Center (WTC) in New York City. The blast killed six people and injured more than a thousand. The Bureau joined with the ATF and NYPD to investigate, code-naming the case TRADEBOMB. Early findings showed that the explosion had come from inside a van, and after exhaustive and meticulous digging through rubble that was five stories deep in the garage, agents found the small metal plate containing the vehicle identification number (VIN) from the van. The VIN was traced to a Ryder Truck Company vehicle in Alabama, a lead that landed on my squad in the Birmingham office.

A Birmingham agent talked to Ryder Truck officials who identified a Ford Econoline van that was rented in Jersey City, New Jersey, by a twenty-five year old Palestinian named Mohammed Salameh. The Ryder Truck information led to the arrests and convictions of fanatic Muslims under the leadership of Sheik Omar Abdel Rahman, who preached out of a mosque in Jersey City. The FBI, ATF, and NYPD did excellent work in what would later be known after 9/11 as the first WTC bombing. Freeh gave the field agents the support they needed to operate informants and run with the leads. That massive effort paled in light of the Bureau's investigation into the events of 9/11, where 3000 people died in New York and Washington.

Freeh directed the FBI and ATF roles in solving other notorious bombing matters, the destruction of the Murrah Federal Building in Oklahoma City on April 19, 1995, and the arrest of Unibomber Ted Kaczynski in rural Montana on April 3, 1996, ending a serial bomber investigation that dated to 1976.

I shared the opinions of other agents when we talked over coffee at the office or out on surveillances, that the FBI should continue to be the lead agency and aggressively investigate domestic and international terrorism. I garnered personal and professional satisfaction in the '70s and '80s from successfully working cases against the Klan, neo-Nazis, and other white supremacist groups like the Aryan Nation. The '90s brought the same thugs to the forefront of Bureau investigations under the umbrella of militias, survivalists, and religious sects. The events at Ruby Ridge and Waco were examples.

The Freeman matter in Montana in 1996, involving more right wing crazies, took a personal turn for me when my son Duane worked against the Freemen as a member of the FBI's Special Surveillance Group, SSG. The Freemen were a collection of haters and right-wingers who proclaimed that they were immune from paying taxes or obeying federal laws. An 81-day armed standoff between the FBI and the Freemen at a Montana ranch ended peacefully, resulting in convictions for financial fraud and threats to kill a judge. Director Freeh monitored the case closely, kept FBIHQ in constant touch with agents on the scene. When it ended, my son moved on to other Bureau pursuits.

I admired Freeh's devotion to his large family. He had photographs of them on the walls of his office, and he brought his family to official FBI functions at Headquarters. Freeh seemed to have successfully balanced his professional life with his domestic life—something I tried to accomplish, but not always successfully because of my own mistakes. Office gossip had it that the Director of the FBI went home every night to a list of chores and things to do.

I admit to partiality about Bureau directors. As a street agent cocooned in the Bureau's culture for over thirty years, I was most comfortable with Bureau men at the helm of the FBI after Hoover died. I wasn't accepting of Patrick Gray, William Webster, or William Sessions. They were not one of *us*. I received Clarence

Kelley and Louis Freeh with open arms, gave them the benefit right off because of whom they had been, former street agents, and in Kelley's case, an SAC in Birmingham. Kelley and Freeh knew what an FD 302 was, and how to work a neighborhood after a bank robbery, or develop sources for nailing car thieves and burrowing into the Mob.

I realize that my bias in favor of promoting from within the ranks to the top spot of the Bureau may not always be politically possible. Directors can serve up to 10 years at the pleasure of the President. The President needs to have someone he can trust at the FBI. Which will probably not be an on-board agent.

Freeh and President Clinton got along well at first, then their relationship soured; perhaps the puritanical Freeh could not abide the loose sexual morals of Bill Clinton. Their relationship cooled and them became frosty, in spite of the fact that Clinton authorized the largest increase in the number of FBI agents in Bureau history. Clinton also approved the biggest operating budgets in FBI annals. No matter. Freeh and Clinton did not get along.

I don't want the FBI to become like the CIA, with a revolving door at the top and problems of low morale, plagued by a shrinking mandate and, since the end of the Cold War, an identity crisis. The Bureau is focused and comfortable with its mandate. It doesn't suffer from maladies that eat at the CIA. FBI Headquarters will always be Headquarters.

Right after I retired, Louis Freeh made participation in the agents' twice-yearly physical fitness test voluntary. It was no longer required, as it had been since 1983. As a result, participation in the test fell off dramatically. I was astonished that Freeh, the most physically fit director in history, would flush fitness down the toilet. Someone must have gotten to him. I smell a lawyer, someone out of the chief counsel's office at FBIHQ maybe, a Headquarters animal shrinking from a challenge or a possible law suit about the *job-relatedness* of physical fitness to what agents do. Headquarters wilted, and Freeh went along.

Directors of the FBI are like federal judges. You think you know them until they hand down their next ruling.

CHAPTER THIRTY

COLIN POWELL

It took a year of planning to get General Colin Powell, Chairman of the Joint Chiefs of Staff, to come to the University of Alabama to make a speech to the football team, but in March 1993, as president of the 1st and Ten Club of Alabama, I was in the middle of preparations and doings to bring him to Tuscaloosa.

The 1st and Ten Club had been founded by Coach Paul "Bear" Bryant's ex–players at Alabama to provide career counseling for graduating players. The Club had 150 members and was not limited to former Alabama athletes. I joined in 1984.

One of the Club members planning Powell's visit was a bank president and the highest ranking Army Reserve officer in the state of Alabama. He guided me through the Pentagon labyrinth. I did not speak to General Powell himself prior to his visit. I dealt with his subordinates—lots of them. Every chance I got I used the Bureau name for leverage and grease, worming my way into the bowels of the Pentagon. I don't know how, but some of the generals may have gotten the impression I was the agent in charge of FBI operations in Alabama. It was not, however, the clout of the Bureau or the luster of Alabama's football tradition that landed Powell: his wife was from Birmingham and she wanted to visit.

It was a Friday. The preparations for Powell's visit were complete. The General and Mrs. Powell landed in Birmingham, where she went to see family and friends. The Alabama Army Reserve

General handled the Birmingham end of the trip. I readied things at the University in Tuscaloosa.

We had backup plans for the backup plans. A year of thinking of things we hadn't thought of or that could go wrong. We were ready. Powell's visit to Birmingham was accomplished without a flaw. An Army helicopter flew the general out of Birmingham to a cleared landing area behind the football complex in Tuscaloosa. The weather forecast called for light rain later in the afternoon, with the possibility of snow flurries in the mix.

The venue for Powell's speech was the lavish football offices and facilities on the southern edge of the University campus. We selected a large room normally reserved for team meetings. The dignitaries took their seats. The football team was assembled, having done its job for the long-awaited visit by winning the national championship in 1992, defeating the University of Miami 34-13 in the Sugar Bowl to claim the title.

Also present to hear the general speak was head football coach Gene Stallings and his assistants, the President of the University of Alabama, prominent alumni, Army VIPs, an Alabama Congressman, businessmen, and over one hundred members of the 1st and Ten Club. The spacious, carpeted room was jammed.

We stood when General Powell walked in. As president of the Club, I served as Master of Ceremonies. I introduced the guests. Outside, dark clouds rolled in and the temperature dropped. The wind picked up. I introduced former Alabama and Green Bay quarterback, Bart Starr. He eloquently introduced General Powell. I sat in the front row next to Starr.

Powell gave a wonderful speech, emphasizing his humble upbringing in New York City. He was inspiring, especially, I imagined, for the black players. We all were in awe of him.

At the end of his talk he leaned on the podium, clasping his large hands. He took questions, answered each one with confidence and humor, in full control of the room. He smiled and ducked the question about whether he would run for president in 1994.

We ushered Powell outside the building for the short walk to the indoor football practice field where the photographs would be taken. I hadn't looked out for a while and was surprised when we stepped into the weather. Snow was falling and the temperature had dropped dramatically. You could see your breath. Low dark clouds were full of mischief. It was mid-afternoon and nearly dark. Almost an inch of snow had accumulated since Powell had come into the football offices to make his speech.

Powell talked easily with the football players and guests as we walked the 100 yards to the indoor practice field. He laughed about snow in Alabama in March. Flakes accumulated on his graying hair and green uniform. The snow was heavy and wet, ideal for snowballs. The University had a cameraman atop the indoor tower used to film scrimmages. Powell posed with the players, joking with them while cameras clicked. People took photos with their own cameras. The air was thick with snow, the ground accumulation building. We lined up dignitaries with him, posing one group after another. Powell was relaxed and patient.

An Alabama state trooper took me aside and said that roads and interstates were getting dicey, the skies closing, that we shouldn't wait too much longer to fly the general back to Birmingham to pick up his wife for the return flight to Washington. Weathermen were revising upwards their forecast for snow.

Alabama shuts down every two years or so when it snows an inch. Panic grips the Heart of Dixie. People rush to the Piggly Wiggly for bread, Bud Light, and Jesus Saves candles, abandon their vehicles in the parking lot, then hide in their homes waiting for the power to go out. The cops close the highways and shut down the electric chair in Kilby.

The snow silently piled up on the campus spring grass, and wind whipped American flags and the nets of the varsity tennis courts. Visibility was low. I could not see the top of Denny Chimes on the campus Quad. I huddled with the Alabama Army Reserve General. He cursed the weather under his breath and made the arrangements to chopper Powell out of Tuscaloosa in a hurry.

I rejoined the members of the 1st and Ten Club for our photo with Powell. He seemed unconcerned about what was happening outside. He was gracious and gave us all the time we needed to set up the photos. I stood near him and thought about the preparations of the last year: all the phone calls to the Pentagon, all the meetings. We had everything covered, no detail had been left unattended. The day had gone without a rattle, the precise scheduling had been smoothly accomplished. The only thing that could gum it up, we joked, would be a snowstorm in Alabama in March.

It snowed 14 inches that day.

General Powell left Tuscaloosa in a helicopter. He and Mrs. Powell flew out of the Birmingham Airport back to Washington without a hitch. I fought my way back to Birmingham in a BuCar on what was left of I-20/59. I could barely see the road. Cars were in ditches or left by the highway. I pulled into my garage five minutes before they closed the highways.

Snug in my kitchen, I hugged my wife and three daughters. The power went out. I built a fire in the fireplace and settled in with my family for the duration. Alabama sank into a stupor.

The power was off for four days. We took photographs of the snow. The kids drank all the Dr. Pepper and Diet Cokes. The family drained cans of black-eyed peas and devoured bread from the Piggly Wiggly. My wife and I ate all the Scotch.

CHAPTER THIRTY-ONE

TALLADEGA UPRISING

On November 22, 1994, a man carrying a TEC-9 semi-auto-matic assault weapon calmly walked into the headquarters of the Metropolitan Police in the District of Columbia and opened fire, killing FBI agents Martha Dixon Martinez, age 35, and Michael John Miller, 41, and police officer Sgt. Henry Joseph Daly, 51. The gunman, eaten up with anger, was the subject of a joint cold case investigation by the D.C. police and the FBI. Police returned fire and killed the gunman.

When she died, Martinez had been married for two months to George Martinez, an FBI agent. She was ready to start a family. She wanted children.

I knew her as Martha Dixon. We had served together at the uprising of 121 Cuban inmate detainees housed in Alpha Unit, Federal Correctional Institute, Talladega, Alabama. The trouble at the prison started at 10:00 a.m. on Wednesday, August 21, 1991. The Bureau titled it TALPEP: MAJOR CASE 39.

It was my twenty-second year as an FBI agent. This time the prison riot was not in Atlanta, as in 1987, when one thousand Cuban inmates took a hundred hostages that required two weeks to peacefully resolve. However, the Talladega uprising did include some of the same Cuban inmates who had rioted in Atlanta. Instead of expelling them from the U.S. back to their native Cuba, federal authorities had transferred the Atlanta rioters to other American prisons. That bonehead decision was finally being reversed, and the Cubans had been told that they were headed back to Cuba. They didn't want to go, and rioted in Talladega to remain in the U.S. They had control of one building on the prison grounds. They preferred American prisons to going back into Castro's firing squads, and had nothing to lose by killing the hostages or us.

The FBI had called the riot in Atlanta an *insurrection*. The Talladega takeover by some of the same Cubans had been labeled an *uprising*. The difference was nothing more than semantics out of FBI Headquarters.

I stood next to Martha Dixon when the leader of the FBI's Hostage Rescue Team, HRT, led us in prayer right before we stormed the prison to rescue the hostages nine days after the riot started. HRT and SWAT teams from Atlanta, Birmingham, and Knoxville were about to implement what the Bureau called a *tactical rescue operation*. It was 4:00 a.m., Friday, August 30, 1991.

Martha Dixon was a member of Knoxville SWAT. She was the first and only woman to be selected for the Knoxville team. I talked to Martha before the rescue began. She was under transfer to the Washington Field Office, WFO. She had worked hard and effectively to gain membership on SWAT, and was going to compete for a place on the WFO team when she settled in there. She was excited about moving to WFO, where there were big league cases and criminals. She loved Knoxville and her fellow agents, but looked forward to the challenge of working in Washington. I told Martha I was confident she would be selected for WFO SWAT.

I shared something with Martha beyond SWAT. We both had worked foreign counterintelligence. We talked about the sting still left in the KGB even though the Cold War was over.

Martha was an excellent shooter. I'd seen her shoot. Administratively, Birmingham was in the same SWAT region with Knoxville and Atlanta. The teams were frequently together for training and live cases. The Knoxville team was also known for its ability to track criminals through rough terrain, particularly in the mountains of east Tennessee. Martha stayed right with them in the woods.

Martha was physically and mentally strong, a dedicated and smart agent. She wasn't intimidated by the male culture of SWAT. She could do everything the men did, and had held her own nicely when the Knoxville team joined Atlanta SWAT for training and competition with the Marines at Camp LeJeune, North Carolina. I liked and respected Martha. We all did.

Martha put on her black helmet and strapped it tight. I put on mine and stood next to her. The room at the Talladega prison was full of HRT and the three SWAT teams. There were a hundred of us. Tension and confidence filled the air. For comic relief, we had been watching the movie *Naked Gun*. We were about to take on 121 Cuban inmates who were armed with spears, knives, machetes, and metal shafts. We were bringing guns to a knife fight. I liked our odds.

My youngest son, Deke, a place kicker on the East Carolina University football team, was scheduled to play at the University of Illinois the next day. I didn't make the game.

We raised our heads after the prayer. It was still dark outside. I saw one hundred FBI Ninja Turtles dressed in black from heads to boots. Martha was simply another Ninja. You couldn't tell there was a woman under her helmet. There was another female agent on the Atlanta SWAT team, also well respected.

The Bureau's technical wizards had secretly planted listening devices in Alpha Unit right after the Cubans took the hostages. We could hear what the inmates were saying and planning. They were ready to kill one of the nine hostages, a prison guard. They'd drawn his name out of a hat.

There had been ten hostages, comprising six Bureau of Prison employees, BOP, and four from the Immigration and Naturalization Service, INS. There were seven men and three women. One of the women had been released earlier in the week for medical reasons. There was really nothing wrong with her. She'd faked illness and had talked her way out.

One of the women hostages, an INS employee, was a strong leader. She posed as being on the side of the Cubans, supporting their right to remain in the U.S. She helped stage the illness of the woman who was released. All the hostages showed poise and courage.

We had rehearsed the forced entry into Alpha Unit in an identical building on prison grounds out of sight of the Cubans. The building had been emptied of prisoners so that we could practice. Every midnight, we'd gone in the other unit to rehearse the entry plan formulated by HRT.

With tension mounting and the minutes ticking down until we executed the entry, Allen Whitaker, the SAC in Birmingham, came into the room. He took me and Starley Carr, our SWAT team leader, aside. Instead of voicing his support and confidence in us, Whitaker pointed to Bill Sievers, a member of the Birmingham team, and wanted to know why Sievers was making the entry since he had missed the practice sessions for the operation. Starley and I looked at each other as if to say, *can you believe this asshole?* Here we are, ready to jump off, and Whitaker shows up to disrupt morale. We told Whitaker that we had thoroughly briefed Sievers, an experienced SWAT guy, and that he was ready to go. We crowded in on Whitaker and told him that Sievers *was* going with us. The usually easy-going Carr glared down at the shorter SAC, who backed off and retreated out of the room. Sievers expressed his gratitude. We thought that we were rid of the Birmingham SAC, but we were wrong.

We got the word that President Bush had given the order to proceed. We poured out of the room just before dawn and quietly climbed into a long line of vans out of sight of Alpha Unit where the Cubans were mostly asleep. On signal from HRT, we sped right up to the prison doors, jumped out and went to our positions. There were loud cheers from hundreds of FBI and BOP personnel watching from vantages around the prison grounds. The explosive guys planted devices to blow open the doors to Alpha Unit. I crouched down in the grass and leaned against the building with my Birmingham teammates. Martha Dixon was with the Knoxville team just ahead of us. I covered up as best I could. We anticipated that the Cubans would throw everything they had down on our heads from the roof.

The explosion severely shook the building. It jarred me away from the wall. A mile from the prison in a house along Renfro Road, my wife's parents were awakened by the concussion and noise of the explosion. They knew that something was up at the prison. They knew that I was there.

The explosion was so powerful that I thought part of the building had been blown away. Our bomb guys had overdone it a tad on the thick, barricaded front doors. The concussion blew Fred Evans, one of the Knoxville SWAT members, over the hood of a van. Fred was unhurt, and later retired from the FBI to do magic tricks. His brother, Frank Evans, was a supervisor in the Birmingham FBI, and was watching from several hundred yards away in the command post. My squad of foreign counterintelligence gurus was also in the command post. Bob Sligh, the Fox, and George Pare, were working the intelligence angle, while Steve Brannan was there as a hostage negotiator.

HRT and the SWAT teams stormed into the prison immediately after the doors were blown. It was dark inside. Each team, each agent, had a precise assignment. Birmingham SWAT got inside quickly and went straight to the second tier of cells. The Cubans retreated back into their cells when they saw us. They did not put up a fight. Flash bangs, deafening grenades that shocked rather than killed, were thrown throughout the prison to contain the inmates. Everything worked as planned. The operation was a ballet, choreographed to perfection thanks to HRT. Carried out exactly as rehearsed. I didn't see Martha Dixon during the entry and operation. Knoxville had another assignment.

After the doors blew, a team from HRT went directly for the nine hostages, who were all together in the TV room on side B of Alpha Unit. HRT pointed their weapons and forced the Cubans away from the door where the hostages were kept. The door was breached by HRT, and the agents quickly collected the hostages and whisked them out of the building and away from the immediate area. The hostages were unharmed and in good spirits. They'd lost weight eating a diet of soup made from ketchup, mustard, water, and tabasco sauce. One of the hostages, an INS agent, later became a close friend of mine. We worked cases together afterwards.

HRT and SWAT kept guns on the Cubans to cover dozens of BOP personnel as they stripped the Cubans naked and conducted body cavity searches on them for weapons and drugs. After the searches, the nude Cubans were herded single file out of the Alpha Unit, where they were spread-eagled face down in the grass as the sun came up. Unlike what had occurred after the Atlanta prison riot, the Cubans were shipped out the next day to Cuba. Some of them surely faced grave punishment and prison time under Castro.

With the successful conclusion of the operation to save the hostages, the FBI stood down and gave control of the prison back to BOP. The SWAT teams relaxed and posed for photos in front of Alpha Unit. HRT, in a show of arrogance and misguided secrecy about their operational techniques, attempted to confiscate all the film of the SWAT teams smiling in victory. Birmingham SWAT said *up yours* to HRT and kept our film. The SWAT teams intermingled, elbow to elbow with each other and with the HRT Ninjas, a celebration of triumph. Martha Dixon was not far from me in one of the photos.

Re-enter Birmingham SAC Allen Whitaker.

After the photos and back slapping, my SWAT teammates and I stored our weapons in a room at the prison where we had been headquartered, as did the other SWAT teams. We all headed to the prison cafeteria for food and coffee. While seated and enjoying ourselves, letting the tension go away over jokes and fellowship, Whitaker appeared and wanted to know where our weapons were. We told him. He ordered us to go immediately back to the room to guard our weapons. *Guard them from whom?* we wanted to know. Unsmiling, without a word of *congratulations, nice going,* or *well done,* Whitaker repeated his order to leave the cafeteria immediately and guard our weapons. We complied, while the other SWAT teams looked on in disbelief at the dandy and strutting SAC. I felt like flinging Whitaker naked into the midst of the Cubans for transportation to one of Castro's shit holes.

Not a shot had been fired during the tactical rescue operation at Talladega Prison. No one was hurt. No hostages, no Cuban inmate, no FBI agent was injured in any way. The operation was flawless.

I said goodbye to Martha Dixon. We went back to our respective offices. HRT returned to its home base at the FBI Academy, Quantico, Virginia.

The agents who made the entry at Talladega Prison were praised by President Bush. We were grateful to the President for having the balls to authorize the operation. We were lauded by William Sessions, Director of the FBI, and by William Barr, acting Attorney General. We were applauded by the national press, cheered by our fellow agents, and honored at a formal ceremony in Washington in the Great Hall at the Department of Justice.

The Birmingham FBI honored its SWAT team over coffee and cookies in the office. SAC Whitaker presided. He went on and on about what wonderful leadership had been provided at Talladega by those swell folks at FBI Headquarters. Headquarters hung the moon, and probably Whitaker's underwear as well. In his speech, Whitaker barely mentioned the contribution of the local men and women who worked for him. When he sat down, supervisor Frank Evans, whose brother had been blown over the hood of a van during the entry at Talladega, took the microphone and praised everyone in the office in an emotional and genuine expression of gratitude. Evans' leadership stood in marked contrast to the tone deaf and clueless Whitaker.

My life returned to normal. I worked counterintelligence and anti-terrorism, enjoyed the hell out of them and being on the SWAT team. My undercover role had evaporated because of the treason of an FBI agent or the end of the Cold War or the decline in movie attendance, whatever; however, there were many other things that engaged my interest and enthusiasm.

Martha Dixon was transferred to WFO in 1992, where she met an agent she would marry. She delayed competing for a position on the WFO SWAT team in order to take an assignment on a task force that handled the arrests of dangerous local criminals. She worked closely with the D.C. police. She was with them and another agent when she died.

I don't think about the HRT or SWAT or the ballet of rescuing hostages when I think about the uprising at Talladega Prison. I think about Martha Dixon Martinez.

FBI SWAT teams immediately after the successful nighttime rescue of nine hostages at the Talladega Federal Prison Uprising, August, 1991. Kneeling on the far left is Knoxville SWAT team member Martha Dixon Martinez, the first woman to serve on the Knoxville team. Martha was killed in the line of duty in Washington, D.C., in November, 1994. She was a stellar agent and my friend. I am kneeling, sixth from the left, teammate Ashley Curry is seventh. Standing, R-L: Birmingham SWAT Starley Carr, Harold Schmidle (3rd), Ben Cumbie, Gerald Kelly, Marshall Ridlehoover, Jeff MacDonald.

CHAPTER THIRTY-TWO

DOGCATCHERS

It was a splendid spring Birmingham afternoon. Bill Sievers and I were dressed down for combat and speed, wearing casual clothes and light windbreakers to cover our black German 9mm semi-automatics with one round in the chambers and clips topped off with 14 rounds. We were hunting a federal fugitive. Bill was the case agent. It was his show. The temperature was low enough so that our windbreakers didn't look out of place.

Sievers, if you recall, was the SWAT team member whom the supercilious Birmingham SAC, Allen Whitaker, had tried to prevent from being on the assault team that freed the nine hostages at the Talladega Prison uprising. Whitaker was still around, but most agents paid little attention to him. He was as irrelevant now as he had been at Talladega.

Sievers had prematurely white hair. He was in his fifties, as I was. We were buddies, fellow members of the SWAT team, and he occasionally asked me to assist him on apprehensions. We'd both been agents for over twenty years. He was in charge of the Fugitive Task Force, coordinating the mesh of agents with local law enforcement in hunting down the city's worst thugs. Bill wore glasses and looked like a college professor or a desk officer at the Department of State. Appearances were deceiving. Sievers was a relentless and skillful investigator, a wise street mariner with good instincts. I enjoyed his company.

The winds blew a variety of directions in the Bureau. Although I chased spies and Bill chased common criminals, we could join together on cases if we wished, pooling our knowledge and skills.

Bill had a tip, a lead, that the fugitive was living in a black neighborhood in the western section of Birmingham. We drove out of the locked-up, camera-surveilled FBI garage on the third level of the 2121 Building, went down the circular, rough surface ramp of the garage out into the alley. We took 3rd Avenue west from downtown and into the low rent neighborhoods that spread north and south from 3rd Avenue. We drove by Rickwood Field, the oldest baseball park in America. The park was a relic, and had been the home of the Birmingham Barons for decades, a minor league team for the Chicago White Sox. However, the Barons had moved to a pristine stadium in Hoover, a suburb. Rickwood's green paint was now peeling. The city maintained the park for public festivities and high school sporting events. Hollywood filmed at Rickwood to capture the ambiance of early baseball days. I loved the place.

Bill drove the BuCar since he was the case agent, and we headed into a low income neighborhood. We circled a two-block area several times, looked, got a feel for the area, tried not to heat up the place. I studied a mug shot of the fugitive, a black male in his thirties, memorized his face, figured that the first good look I would get of him would be the back of his head as he ran away. He was a rabbit, had a history of outrunning law enforcement during capture attempts.

Bill pulled over to the curb to get our bearings.

A city dogcatcher truck drove slowly by us, a driver and a helper in the cab. The truck had a covered cage in back full of barking dogs.

Bill spotted our fugitive standing on a porch down the street. He hadn't been there the first time that we circled. The guy looked at us, suspicious. He did not appear to have a weapon.

Bill eased the heavy BuCar away from the curb and drove slowly down the block toward the fugitive. The city dogcatcher truck was just ahead of us, barely moving.

The fugitive kept his eyes on us, turned toward his front door like he was going to bolt. I figured that he'd cut through the house, hit the alley in back and be gone. I shifted in my seat, hoped that the guy would rabbit. I wanted to chase him, a pursuit just for the pure fun of running down a bad guy. I was in my fifties, had two bad knees, was maybe twice the age of the fugitive. Who the hell was I kidding?

We pulled over to the curb in front of the fugitive. The dog catchers stopped in the middle of the street just ahead.

The fugitive drilled us with his eyes. I'd seen that look, a look of fright, a look figuring your odds of escape, seeing prison walking toward you in Bureau suits. The guy tensed, making up his mind about two white dudes driving a big dark car through a black neighborhood.

I casually opened the car door, ready to come out of the blocks. I eased out of the seat and stood on the curb, looked down the street, caught the rabbit in my peripheral vision, did not look directly at him.

Bill cut the engine so the FBI radio wouldn't come on and give us away. He got out and stood by the car, non-threatening, the hood between him and our prey. I was closer to the rabbit and would have first go.

"You own a dog?" Bill asked the rabbit out of the blue.

The question caught me by surprise. Bill and I had not discussed ploys in grabbing this guy. I waited to see how it played.

"What?" The rabbit cocked his head. Bill had frozen him with the dog bit. The rabbit seemed puzzled, looked at the dog-catchers stopped in the middle of the street, then at us.

Bill casually walked around the hood. I forced a smile, stewed in my juices waiting for the starter's gun to go off. The rabbit came toward us to the edge of the porch. Bill and I walked closer, stayed several arms' lengths from each other.

"Own a dog?" Bill repeated. He nodded in the direction of the dogcatchers.

We reached the steps leading up to the front porch where the fugitive stared down at us.

"No," the rabbit said. He appeared curious, ready to talk. I kept my arms at my side to prevent the windbreaker from hiking up and exposing my gun.

Bill and I stepped up onto the porch, even with the guy. I was on his left side, Bill his right. We knew the sucker was right-handed.

"Why you wanna know?" the rabbit asked. We grabbed the rabbit's arms and held him.

"FBI. You're under arrest," Bill said. I felt the guy's biceps tense. He was strong, but he didn't pull away or resist.

"Shit!" he said, shaking his head. *Damn.*

We brought the rabbit's arms behind his back, palms out, and handcuffed him, right hand first, the Bureau way.

I looked at Bill. He grinned, rolling his eyes to convey: *Can you believe this dumb shit fell for that?* The dogcatchers drove away. We never got to thank them.

CHAPTER THIRTY-THREE

BEER FOR BREAKFAST

I had been an agent for twenty-five years in the fall of 1994. I'd beaten the arrest drums 'til my arms were weary, collaring all manner of varmint from bank robbers to terrorists to uglies on bikes. The Cold War had provided its own blanket of thrills, pitting the Bureau against hostile intelligence services in the USSR, East Europe and China. Working undercover, I had matched wits, strong coffee, and fine whiskey with spies from the other side, all of us pretending to be who we weren't. They were worthy adversaries, the Kremlin guys and their European sidekicks, and I enjoyed the hell out of the game. Then it ended.

The Berlin Wall came down in 1989. Chunks and pieces of it were sold as souvenirs around the world. The USSR self-destructed not long after, parts of it flying off in different directions like spit in the wind, 'til what was left became the UFFR: the Union of Fewer and Fewer Republics. The FBI opened an office in Moscow. The Cold War shrank to the size of Cuba.

Russian police humbly came to the FBI to beg insights and advice about the conflicts between freedom and law enforcement. How were cops supposed to behave in a democracy? The Russians didn't know what to do in this new age. They had problems at home, they said, problems they'd never had to deal with before. They could no longer round up people and have them disappear. People had rights. Democracy had brought organized crime, defense attorneys, unruly teenagers, drugs, and loud music. Russia was no longer recognizable, the cops said. They wished things were like the old days, when everyone got drunk and did what they were told.

The Bureau began conducting seminars at the FBI Academy for police from all over the old communist world. The visitors from the East were lectured on such alien topics as the requirements for warrants, probable cause for arrests, searches and seizures, judicial approval for wire taps, the world of civil rights, habeas corpus, restraints on deadly force, curtailment of cruel and unusual punishment, and the presumption of innocence.

FBI Headquarters sent Russian police around America to observe how the guys in blue conducted themselves. Two Russian cops came to Birmingham in the fall of 1994. I was assigned to escort them around the city and introduce them to local police departments.

First, I took them to breakfast. I wanted them to experience a real American meal as could only be found in the South. I drove them into the Birmingham suburbs to the Ranch House, a mom and pop barbecue joint run by a family descended from Greek immigrants. What could be more American than Greeks running a barbecue restaurant in the Heart of Dixie?

The Russians asked me to order.

I told the blond pony-tailed waitress wearing an Alabama Crimson Tide sweat shirt to bring scrambled eggs, sausage, ham, gravy and biscuits, with tomatoes on the side. Grits came without asking. There was plenty of jam and jelly on the table, and honey if you wanted. We took hot coffee right away. Neither Russian required sugar and cream. Coffee was black in law enforcement, whether in Minsk, Russia, or Bramwell, West Virginia.

The two Russian cops were most pleasant. Their English was good. They lived in Moscow and had families, wives who stayed at home with the kids. We discussed the problems and expense of raising children, particularly getting them through college. The Russians said that schools, doctors, medicine, retirement, and everything else had been guaranteed by the state in the old Soviet Union, that you were taken care of from birth to coffin by Communism. You didn't have to be creative or energetic, just show up. A philosophy of *We pretend to work, they pretend to pay us.*

No more, not in the new Russian Federation. Cops would have to earn money to pay for the things they needed for their families. They shook their heads. Police didn't make much money in Russia. Everyone, it seemed, made more than cops, including the old women in scarfed heads who brushed the brick sidewalks clear of snow. Cops weren't much better off than laid-off soldiers in the unraveling Red Army. Still, both cops planned to stay in law enforcement. Where else could they get a job that came with a car and unlimited petrol, they said, even though Moscow police vehicles had indifferent heaters and temperamental transmissions. Plus, there were special food and clothes markets reserved for cops, bureaucrats, and politicians. Some things did not change, they pointed out, whether communism or capitalism.

The two Russians were amazed by the variety in the U.S. All those brands of toothpaste. And toilet paper. And deodorant. The choices were baffling and intimidating. How could you decide? There were food shortages in parts of Russia, particularly in some of the cities. Farmers hoarded their produce, kept what they grew to feed their families. Roads and railways were primitive, making it hard to get harvests to market. Things were bad. Moscow was the place to live. The politicians were there. You could buy American jeans in Moscow if you had the money. They said that being police in Moscow was damn fine thing.

The two cops didn't like American football, but were polite about it. They said that Russians were the best weight lifters in the world. The Bulgarians were good too, but they cheated on steroids. Plus, Bulgarian wine was wretched like their Bulgarian cigarettes. Russian smokes were not much better. America made the best cigarettes.

The waitress brought our food. She spread it around our large round table.

The cops had a question. *Did this American restaurant serve beer?* The waitress nodded.

I spent the rest of an invigorating Alabama morning eating breakfast with two Russian cops. The table was covered with empty long neck Budweisers, standing mute like smokestacks in the old USSR. We traded pins, patches, and artifacts. They gave me a wool hat with the Red Army insignia, and a handsome silver pocket watch etched with hammer, sickle, and dagger. I gave them Bureau sweatshirts and blue raid jackets with FBI stamped in large gold letters on the back. We promised to write and send photos of our families. We pledged not to let bosses stand in the way of good police work, and to continue the quest for the perfect donut.

The melting of the Cold War was damn fine thing.

CHAPTER THIRTY-FOUR

LOSING THE RECRUITING WARS

Alethea Pittman wanted to be an FBI agent. She thought she had done everything required by the Bureau to meet the qualifications, having finished her education, a J.D. from the University of Alabama School of Law, my alma mater. She was just what the Bureau was looking for, she had been told by FBI press releases and recruiting literature. The FBI wanted people with law degrees. Diploma in hand, Alethea was ready to be sworn in and collect her badge.

No, I told her, we could not hire her when she graduated, *we* being the Bureau and me as well, since I was the agent recruiter who had hand picked Alethea and other eager faces in her law class at Alabama during her first year of study. I kept in contact with her during the next two years, came to know her as she performed in sterling fashion in the trenches and drudgery of reading law. She was clear headed, sensible, smart, eloquent, and a patriot. All the reasons why the Bureau should not hire her. Alethea was also African-American.

I told Director Louis Freeh about Alethea Pittman, that she had achieved undergraduate honors in her studies and had earned a Master of Public Administration with honors on her way to finishing law school. I pointed out that she was selected by us, his Bureau, from thousands of applicants to work for a summer as an Honors Intern at FBIHQ between semesters at law school. She was an outstanding intern selection, had performed well during her summer at HQ. We should hire Alethea Pittman, I said to Louis Freeh as one member of the Special Agent Advisory Committee.

Freeh listened and wrote. I talked and looked at the top of his head as he bent over a yellow pad and wrote longhand in the fishhook style of lefties. "We're losing them," I told Freeh. "Losing black women of the quality of Alethea Pittman if we don't hire them right out of law school before they're snatched up by high-paying firms. Our recent policy of requiring law graduates to practice law for three years before they'll qualify to be agents is not working and will not work. It's a misguided policy and should be scrapped."

Freeh looked up at me, didn't smile, and returned to his legal pad, writing in pencil.

"How would you fix it?" Freeh asked.

I told him. The reason why there were only 114 black females out of over 11,000 agents in the FBI was that we were looking for them in all the wrong places, to paraphrase the Nashville hit. What had been good enough for decades was no longer Bureau policy under Freeh. We were our own worst enemy. The Bureau had always hired lawyers as soon as they finished law school; indeed, that had been my path to a badge. But the FBI turned away from the law schools in its hiring beginning in 1994, told the new JD's to come back as successful lawyers around age thirty.

American law schools were blessed with a treasure of black women. Many of the brightest African-American women went into the legal profession. By looking away from them at the time of their graduation, the Bureau was turning its back on the most talented and savvy pool of African-American women in the country. We had forfeited the game, left the field without a fight.

The FBI must recruit black women while they're single and can relocate, when the Bureau's starting salary in the mid-forties is inviting, when the mystique of the FBI is still alluring—not after they had proven their worth in a law firm, had fat bank accounts and children at the table, and not when their husbands were wedded to careers and could not be uprooted to follow their wives to far off FBI field offices.

But do we need more lawyers? Freeh wanted to know. He was a lawyer, I was a lawyer. We eyed each other.

"No," I said. "But the FBI does need the kinds of people who finish law school. They're survivors, intelligent, tenacious, and can go without sleep. Lawyers usually possess the two skills the Bureau requires of its agents, the ability to speak and write well."

Freeh thanked me for my recommendations but did not commit to implementing my suggestions.

The Special Agent Advisory Committee finished its session with Freeh and we left. I believed that my arguments had been persuasive with him and that changes would be forthcoming. I was wrong.

The Bureau went on to hire thousands of new agents in the 1990s. The vast majority of the new hires were white males, many of them from police departments and the military, the FBI's traditional breeding grounds, men who walked in the front door without the Bureau having to spend a dime recruiting them. They stayed forever and made good agents, but did not alter the FBI's image as a white man's club.

I had one more opportunity to meet in person with Freeh. He visited the Birmingham FBI office in December 1998, nine months before I retired. I again pointed out to him the FBI's abysmal record in hiring black women. This seemed to be news to him. I mentioned Alethea Pittman and other African-American women who we should hire. Freeh wrote on his legal pad. I told him he could heal this wound. He wrote more, then left Birmingham and went back to the seventh floor at FBIHQ.

Nothing changed. I wrote reports and memos to Headquarters. Still nothing changed.

In 1994, I had been chosen by Louis Freeh as one of thirty-two agents Bureau-wide to bring the next generation of agents into the FBI. I left the counterintelligence squad and became the Bureau's chief recruiter of females and minorities in the state of Alabama, an assignment that lasted for five years until I retired. I was honored to be selected and looked forward to the opportunity to leave my personal stamp on the future of the FBI by recruiting the best people I could find.

My optimism turned to frustration when Freeh and his people at FBIHQ implemented policies that hurt our recruiting in law schools, particularly of black females. Other FBI recruiters shared my dismay. While the Bureau's record of hiring black males was fairly good, with nearly six hundred aboard, and white females, with approximately two thousand in the agent ranks, we were not getting black females. Neither Freeh nor his underlings at HQ would budge. Their misguided polices stayed in place.

Alethea Pittman finished law school and was accepted into the executive program for an MBA at the University of Alabama. She was off and running and I lost track of her after I retired. My guess is that she will be very successful and will not reapply to the FBI. It's the Bureau's loss.

In 1999, the year I retired, the FBI did not hire one black female agent. Freeh must shoulder the blame.

PART FIVE

CHAPTER THIRTY-FIVE

HITTING THE WALL

I never once hit the *wall* in a foot race. I've run a marathon and dozens of 10Ks. I ran track in high school and college, and never felt that I couldn't go farther. I always stayed in the race. I ran for decades until my knees cried "We give!" and gave out.

I hit the FBI wall on Monday morning, May 24th, 1999. Yeah, I remember the actual date. I walked into my office on the 15th floor of the 2121 Building at 7 a.m. I'd just finished breakfast at Ted's Restaurant on 4th Avenue South, a block off the exit ramp of I-65 south. I had diner friends at Ted's who sat near me in booth #10, waitress friends, and Greek friends who owned and operated the place. I had my usual breakfast of high rise Southern biscuits and jam and three cups of coffee. I was in Ted's every morning at 6:00 for forty-five minutes, then drove the maroon Bureau Dodge the short distance to the office.

I sat at my desk and looked out over the valley at blocks of downtown Birmingham, with Red Mountain rising up to stop the city from spilling into the suburbs where I lived. Below my window was the Downtown Library with its flat roof. The 1st Avenue viaduct stretched over the deserted grounds of the rust-colored funnels of Sloss Furnace, now cool to the touch. Birmingham was no longer layered with smoke from making steel. The miles of mills and furnaces were mostly gone, a few remaining in Fairfield off to the west. Birmingham was now a medical research and hospital-dense place, touched on the south by the air-conditioned glass offices of white collar prosperity. New businesses and shopping centers flowed south like lava over the valleys and ridges that fronted Double Oak Mountain at the end of the Appalachian chain.

When I reported to Birmingham in 1970, the University of Alabama at Birmingham had one main building and a security force of old men who checked doors at night to see that they were locked. Now, the UAB police department was one of the largest in the state, serving a campus area that covered a square mile of facilities and medical buildings that consumed the south side of town.

I looked at my appointments for the next two weeks. I would be giving the semi-annual Fitness Indicator Test, FIT, to agents on three upcoming days. I was the physical fitness coordinator in the office, an assignment I had held since 1983. The FIT was mandatory (until Freeh killed it in 2001). I'd already sent out the memo telling agents when and where to report for the test. They would be tested in pushups, situps, and a mile and a half run. I was numb from administering the test so many times over the years. I was not looking forward to it.

A sidelight of my fitness duties had led me to participate in the International Police Olympics in Sydney, Australia, in October, 1988, along with 6000 sworn police officers from around the world. There were competitions in dozens of athletic events and firearms proficiency.

My wife Pat and I went to Sydney for a week so that I could compete in the 1500 meter run and wrestle in my weight and age class. As it turned out, I should have wrestled the runners and run against the wrestlers.

The opening ceremony for the Olympics was held in a downtown Sydney soccer stadium, where we all marched in before a large crowd. The Alabama contingent was made up of local and state law enforcement, and two FBI agents. Tom Wiseman, the other agent and former head of the Birmingham SWAT team, came home with a dozen gold medals in firearms events.

The Alabama group stood next to Australian customs officers during the opening ceremony. I turned and asked one of the Aussies, "Who's minding the borders? "

"Who gives a shit, mate," came back the reply.

My 1999 calendar was chockablock with campus visits and career day appearances. I had a speech at the University of Alabama's main campus in Tuscaloosa at the end of the week. I was going to talk to a group of Russian language students, tell them they'd chosen a neat and special area of study. Some were going to Russia on exchange programs and would be there for a year or more. I'd recruited two women from Russian studies in the mid-1990s for the FBI's summer employment Honors Internship in Washington. Both students had lived in Russia. Both wanted to be agents. They were smart, talented, and athletic. I was certain they would be agents some day. As it turned out, one of them did, and is stationed in the Washington Field Office, WFO. I used to love making speeches at the University of Alabama, but not so much anymore.

My mind drifted to a novel I was writing about a twelve-year-old girl who was psychic and haunted by disturbing visions. I'd written four novels during the past decade, but had not been able to sell them. My literary agent was confident that the one about the girl would sell. I yearned to write full time.

Next week was firearms training at the Jefferson County Sheriff's ranges north of Birmingham. I was not enthusiastic about firing another whole day. I'd been firing various weapons for thirty years, could fire the Bureau's firearms courses in my sleep, and approached weapons training as just another part of the job. I considered not going to the ranges. In fact, I had resigned from the SWAT team in 1992 because of the press of foreign counterintelligence and anti-terrorism investigations. I was no longer in on the big arrests, which didn't bug me; I'd done enough arrests, big or otherwise.

Questions hovered ceaselessly: What would I do otherwise in the FBI? What did I want to do? I didn't know. Nothing came to mind. In the past, whenever I'd have a direction I wanted to go as an agent—competing for a place on the original SWAT team, hunting and arresting fugitives, public appearances for Crime Resistance, speeches for recruiting, pushing to make an undercover assignment work in foreign counterintelligence—I would bear down and make it happen. But not now.

When the Soviet Union dissolved in December 1991, the FBI reassigned hundreds of agents from counterintelligence to violent crime investigations, reflecting the realities of the 1990s in terms of the cooperation between federal and local law enforcement. The good guys were going after street thugs and gangs, as *well* as drug dealers who operated worldwide and the corrupt officials they bribed. The Bureau also tore into white-collar mischief involving fraud in the health care industry, banks, S&Ls, and securities, focusing on big time corporate thieves, racketeers, and organized crime.

While I recognized the need for the FBI to expend its resources on these important investigations, I was not eaten up with working them. I was more interested in having an impact on the Bureau's future by recruiting the best young people I could find. With hiring winding down, where could I turn?

The Gulf War, Operation Desert Storm, had been fought and won. When it ended, the FBI continued to work domestic and international terrorism cases, while I moved into recruiting agents. I had an interesting experience with one agent in particular. At one point I had to interview Iraqi nationals to solicit their cooperation and knowledge about operations being conducted by the Iraqi government in America, and to find out if they had been pressed into service by Iraqi intelligence to spy in the U.S. I didn't uncover any wrongdoing during these many interviews and was generally well received. Some Iraqi males, however, were arrogant and condescending toward women; they thought women were inferior to men in every way. To counteract this, I frequently took a female agent with me to the interviews. It aggravated the hell out of these dudes to have to answer questions from a woman.

The men would keep their eyes on me most of the time, and wouldn't even look at the woman agent asking the questions. I thoroughly enjoyed their discomfort, as did the female agent with me. The Bureau wanted visiting Iraqis to know that the FBI knew who they were and where to find them.

The FBI also interviewed American citizens of Iraqi descent, seeking any knowledge they might have as to what was going on in Iraq. In spite of national criticism from some quarters that these interviews were violating the privacy rights of Americans, I found Iraqi-Americans to be patriotic, cooperative and understanding as to why the Bureau had contacted them.

By the late 1990s, I had been away from terrorism investigations a long time and was not interested in getting back into that arena. For me, it was another example of having been there and done that and not wanting to retrace my steps. I had no enthusiasm for responding to bank robberies, setting traps for kidnappers, or looking down holes for spies. I was the youngest agent in the office when I was transferred to Birmingham in 1970. Now I was one of the oldest. I was nearly 55, nudging against the mandatory retirement age of 57.

The FBI was worshiping at the feet of the computer gods, planning for the near future when every agent would have a laptop and be plugged into the internet and into FBI files. We were going electronic, from email to e-this or e-that, requiring agents to type into a computer all their investigative work, and to store on disk everything they did. How the hell were agents going to be out on the street when they spent so much time in front of screens, hunched over, their ties brushing against the keys?

Young agents viewed letters and stamped mail as relics from another age, akin to sending smoke signals into the sky. I figured lightening would strike FBIHQ one day, kill the master computer and erase all of our files, or some hacker would send all of our files to China or the Mafia.

I had served as Master of Ceremonies at the retirement parties for both Luther Brannon and Leon Sizemore. I spoke at the retirement ceremony for Starley Carr. Luther became a private investigator, and Leon and Starley were making good money in business. Bob Sligh, the Fox, eventually retired in Memphis and took a lucrative job there. FBI agents were always in demand after they retired.

Ed Tickel, my close friend and roommate in New Agents Class #17, 1969, was now a convicted felon. Early in his street agent career, during my first years in Birmingham, Tickel gained notoriety in the FBI as well as the respect of J. Edgar Hoover, when he killed a thug in Florida with a shotgun during an arrest. Hoover granted Tickel's request to work in the FBI laboratory, where Ed became one of the Bureau's top lock specialists, an artist at cracking safes or picking locks for covert entries on some of the FBI's most secret operations. Then he went over a cliff.

In April 1980, Tickel was caught after hours with his hands in the safe of the FBI Federal Credit Union at HQ. He made up one stupid story after another as to why he was on his hands and knees in front of a safe he had picked; he eventually failed a polygraph. It also came out that Tickel was involved in stealing FBI radios for friends. He was acquitted in federal court on the Credit Union theft, but was found guilty of transporting stolen property across state lines in another matter, plus tax evasion and obstruction of justice. He also pled guilty to stealing the FBI radios. His eight-year federal prison sentence ran concurrently with state convictions for theft and a second-degree sex offense.

I was in Montgomery on counterintelligence business and had some spare time, so I visited the minimum security federal prison at Maxwell Air Force Base in Montgomery, the facility where many of Nixon's Watergate cronies had done time, and where Tickel was incarcerated. The inmates rake leaves and tend the golf course and tennis courts. It's easy time in a warm climate. I wanted to talk to Tickel, renew our friendship, talk about everything but why he was in prison instead of out drinking with me or driving his hot Chevy. But I chickened out. I didn't have the guts to even say hello. I thought it might not look right if I talked to him. Which was silly. Plus, I was angry that he'd ruined his life.

I ran out of town with my head between my legs. I still have not talked to him these many years later.

I sat in my cushioned chair in a corner office on the 15th floor with a splendid view of Birmingham on Monday, May 24th, 1999, and took stock. My closest friends were no longer agents. I could no longer work with them, which had taken some of the spark out of the job for me. I was a dinosaur; I had gone the way of typewriters. Computers did not fascinate me except as a convenient vehicle for writing and storing my manuscripts. Keyboards made my eyes glaze over, the same haze that had formed over my eyes in 1969 when I considered practicing law. I'd opted for the FBI then. Now, Bureau technology was flying by me. I no longer wanted to be in the race.

I had hit the wall.

I walked out of my office, went down to the 14th floor to the office of the Special Agent in Charge, the SAC, with the unlikely name of Joe Lewis. Lewis was the first black agent to head the Birmingham FBI office. He replaced the jackass Allen Whitaker as Birmingham SAC. Whitaker had been transferred to FBIHQ where he could practice making rooms light up by walking out of them. Before going to HQ, one of the last pieces of nonsense that Whitaker inflicted on the Birmingham FBI was a decree that agents could no longer take their BuCars home overnight. There was no reason for this other than Whitaker's need to show us that he was all-powerful. One result of this decision was to deprive the SWAT team of the ability to respond quickly to a crisis. We had to drive to the office in our own vehicles and get an official car before going to the scene of an emergency. Agents began to carpool to and from work while our BuCars sat useless in the garage.

Unlike Whitaker, Joe Lewis was an actual human being, a sensible guy who kept an open door policy and left you alone. SAC Joe Lewis had once served in the Detroit Office with Birmingham FBI supervisor, James Brown. One night in Detroit, a local cop stopped Lewis and Brown for a traffic offense on their way home after a day in the FBI office. The white cop asked the two black guys in the car who they were? They replied: *James Brown and Joe*

Lewis. The cop considered placing them under arrest for being smartasses. Which turned into a big laugh after Brown and Lewis showed the cop their FBI credentials.

Anyway, I was in Joe Lewis's office and he cordially invited me to sit down. After some pleasantries, I informed him I was retiring from the FBI to write novels and magazine articles and short stories and chapters about my life as an agent. I wasn't mad at him or at anyone else. I wasn't disillusioned. I wasn't resigning in a tiff. There were no hard feelings, only soft ones. I loved the FBI, had loved it since the moment when I walked into New Agents Class #17 and raised my hand to take the oath. The Bureau had been my life and my sustenance—my oxygen; I had needed it to breathe. I no longer did.

Lewis was gracious, said complimentary things about me and about my accomplishments as an agent. I thanked him and left his office. Resigning from the FBI at the time that I did was the second best decision I ever made. Joining the FBI was the first.

CHAPTER THIRTY-SIX

RETIREMENT

Although I thoroughly enjoyed attending the retirement dinners of other agents, and had served as Master of Ceremonies for the departures of close friends, I wanted no part of a retirement dinner for myself. I didn't want the fuss or to put my friends to the trouble of planning and bringing off one of those evenings. Instead, I acquiesced to a retirement breakfast in the office a week before my last day. I wanted to go out the way I came in, on Bureau soil.

I was surrounded by my family and FBI people in the Birmingham office the day of my retirement breakfast in late August, 1999. Luther Brannon and other retired agents were there. They reported to the reception room to sign in before being escorted to the large meeting room on the 15th floor where the ceremony would take place. A week later, when I officially left, I too would need an escort to get back into the office. I'd be a non-Bureau person.

Leon Sizemore and Starley Carr were retired and prospering in new careers and couldn't attend the breakfast. They called me to assert that I wouldn't be any better at retirement than I was at being an agent. Leon reminded me of the day back in the 1970s when I had responded to a bank robbery to interview the tellers. I showed my FBI credentials to one of the bank employees, who looked at them and laughed. I examined my creds to see what the hell was so funny: Leon had taped a cutout of Mickey Mouse over my official FBI photograph.

I got him back. One day I switched his suit jacket coat with that of a shorter agent. It was easy to do since all of our coats in the office were dark and were hung on a rack when we were working at our desks. When Leon headed out of the office in a hurry to respond to a case, he strained to force himself into his coat in the elevator on the way down to the FBI garage. The sleeves were half way up his arms. The coat didn't even cover his gun.

After I announced my retirement, I received letters and phone calls from members of my agent training class, NAC #17. My classmates were spread out all over the country, all doing well. There were 7 of us still in the FBI out of a class of 51. The rest had retired. NAC #17 had not lost an agent in the line of duty.

Director Louis Freeh sent a letter stating what a great guy I was, and thanks for my 30 years as an agent. Headquarters presented a handsome dark wooden frame encasing my credentials, badge, and four gold service keys from my 10th, 20th, 25th, and 30th anniversaries in the Bureau. The following words were etched in gold letters in the left corner: *Presented to Special Agent Jack Allen Owens, Jr., 1969-Upon his retirement-1999. For loyal and devoted service to the Federal Bureau of Investigation, Badge # 5362.*

An agent in New York drew a caricature of me, which I appreciated because he gave me hair. I was going bald. I had too much testosterone was all. In addition to my face, the agent artist drew a small figure doing push-ups in recognition of my position as the coordinator of physical fitness in Birmingham.

FBIHQ mailed a heavy piece of polished wood that stood 8 inches tall with a two-inch base. My name was inlaid in gold, along with the Bureau seal and the following quotation from Phillip Brooks in gold letters: *Do not pray for tasks equal to your powers; pray for powers equal to your tasks. Then the doing of your work shall be no miracle, but you shall be a miracle.* This award was for my participation in the successful entry into the Talladega Prison in 1991 to rescue 9 hostages. I was surprised and flattered to receive it.

My close friend, Bob Rolen, stood and said nice things about me, reviewed my career from then to now. Bob was the technical wizard in the office, one of the most competent and savvy agents in the Bureau. He was frequently sent on classified assignments all over the U.S. and the world. Bob was the guy you would want on your side if you suspected that your wife had bugged your phone or your office, or if you wanted to bug your wife's phone or office. Later, I served as Master of Ceremonies at his retirement.

When Bob sat down, it was time for the roasts, the usual format for FBI retirements.

Agents took turns coming at me about going bald and being old and drooling and wandering aimlessly around the office looking for a typewriter that no longer existed. They skewered me on refusing to use email. Sherolynne Coachman, a lovely lady with whom I'd worked in recruiting, was away on business but left a thick softcover book containing nearly 400 emails that I'd never read or acknowledged. I could have been fired years ago and didn't know it.

One of the speakers, Lonnie Davis, was an agent I'd recruited out of the University of Alabama in the early '80s. He was fluent in German, a handy language during the Cold War. Lonnie was the office polygrapher and had a law degree. He spoke to the audience about an incident that had occurred one Christmas Eve morning a few years back, when he and I had driven the backwash dirt roads southwest of Birmingham looking for an address to do an interview; there was no arrest involved. We searched for hours until we located a house deep in the woods. The Bureau car had taken a pounding on the potholed roads. As Lonnie related to the audience, he was driving and stayed in the car, engine running. I got out of the car and knocked on the front door of the house and waited. The Bureau car was deep in mud. Lonnie shifted into gear to move the car to firmer ground. The tires spun, kicking mud up on the porch and all over my suit. The mud got in my hair and on my shoes. Lonnie and I started laughing. Thankfully, no one answered the door. We had the wrong house anyway. At the end of his remarks, Lonnie presented me with a check in the amount of $5 for dry cleaning my suit. I still have the check.

It was my turn to speak. The room became quiet. Traffic noise from nearby I-59/20 came through the windows. Trucks heading for Atlanta or Tuscaloosa. The day was bright and cloud-less, the way it had been when I was sworn in three decades earlier in Washington.

I'd given hundreds of speeches. This one was different. My throat closed. I had to force my voice. My eyes watered. I had contradictory feelings. I was pulled in two directions. I wanted to leave the FBI and I didn't want to leave. I still had more than a two-year cushion before mandatory retirement.

It doesn't seem like three decades, I began in a halting voice. I fought for composure. My shirt collar tightened. I turned to humor to save myself. I pointed out that the article in the Birmingham News about my retirement had been placed oppo-site the obituaries, and that there were many at FBIHQ who were under the impression I'd retired years ago.

My family sat in the front row. My son, Duane, a support employee in the Charlotte FBI office, had driven from North Carolina. My wife Pat, and daughters Stacey, Laura, and Molly smiled up at me. I blinked a few times to clear my eyes and gave myself a second to rein in my emotions. I glanced out at north Birmingham with its housing projects and mills. The police lot for impounded and recovered stolen cars was just out of sight. I'd been there many times. The FBI stored its recovered cars there too, the stolen vehicles taken across state lines. The office squad working drug cases had a lineup of sexy vehicles that had been forfeited to the government by drug dealers brought to justice. I had selected a forfeited black Lincoln Continental to use as part of my cover during the Cold War. I drove it to Washington to add luster to my fake identity as a successful businessman. I had a great time on that case.

I turned back to my family and the audience.

I started with my wife, thanked her for her tolerance and understanding in being a Bureau widow when I disappeared on cases or prison riots, and a writing widow when I stared at blank pages for hours. I told my daughters how proud I was of them, and that we would have to find a store that sold pencils and notebooks since I could no longer get into the FBI supply room. I praised my son for the splendid record he'd already achieved in the FBI. He had flourished in the Special Surveillance Group in Utah and was now in an important office position in Charlotte. He and I spoke the Bureau brogue.

I knew everyone in the audience. I liked and respected every damn one of them. They all had special stories and meaning for me, agents with whom I'd split biscuits after all-night surveillances, endless coffee and beers, the coffee always black because there was no sugar or cream in law enforcement. There were men and women in the room who had covered my back on arrests, who had tossed handcuffs to me when I couldn't reach for my own because my hands were full of some bad guy.

There were people with special talents, an agent who had played in the Super Bowl, and one who could pick a lock or tap a phone quicker than I could order a new round from the bar. Collect a group of agents from any field office in the country, any city, and ask them if there was someone present who could tune a piano. I guarantee you hands will go up.

The photography specialist in the office snapped photos of the speakers and audience. I had recruited him into the FBI from a security job at a local hospital many years before.

I finished my speech with some corny and gushing words. I couldn't help it. Finally, as the agent responsible for advice about physical fitness and nutrition, I invited the audience to join me in eating donuts.

To my great sadness, my parents were deceased by the time I retired from the FBI. My mother, Mary Helen, passed in January, 1991, and my father, Jack, five years later, in September, 1996. They were extremely proud that I was an FBI agent. They reveled in my successes and forgave my excesses. I owe them a great deal.

My parents were of *The Greatest Generation*, to borrow Tom Brokaw's book title My father was direct and uncomplicated. A World War II veteran and patriot, he lived by straightforward achievement. He mined coal in the summers to put himself through college, played football and baseball, and secretly married my mother when they were nineteen. My father's legacy to

245

me was his mantra: Never, never, never quit. Outwork everyone around you and do not second-guess yourself. Never assume anything, and don't complain. He also gave me a high forehead.

My mother taught me the grace and beauty of language, the rapture of reading books and good writing. I was slow to accept her counsel and surely disappointed her. She never gave up on me, though. She did not live to see my work published, but she *did* live to help teach all her grandchildren how to read and to hear them call her Bobshi, which is Polish for grandmother. She was not Polish, but what the heck.

I love music and dancing because of my parents. Growing up we danced and sang at home and in public—which did not necessarily play well in church, because my brother and I would deliberately sing off-key. Loudly. If my brother and my parents were still here, I would treat them to a ride in my 1997 Miata five-speed convertible. The most fun you can have sitting down.

A week after my retirement breakfast, on August 31, 1999, my official last day as an FBI agent, I said my thousandth good-bye and walked back into my now empty office for the final time. I stood at the window with a spectacular view of Birmingham and looked down on the library with its modern architecture. I loved its coffee table books of black and white photography, especially shots of barbershops in the 1940s by Wright Morris, or Sam Shaw's pictures of Marilyn Monroe looking into a makeup mirror under soft lights in the early 1950s. I also enjoyed the girls of Penthouse, but that's another story.

With a final look around, I walked away from my office and down the hall to the bank of elevators. Bureau business was percolating on four different floors. Agents and clerks huddled by the coffee pots and desktop computer screens, appliances that did not exist in the FBI when I entered on duty. The National Crime Information Center computer was busy one floor below, telling cops and agents whether the license plate on the vehicle they'd just pulled over was registered to *that* car.

My old congregation, the counterintelligence and terrorism squad, was in a meeting with the supervisor two floors below. My former teammates on SWAT operations were probably planning another practice session on the firearms ranges, another session of rappelling and firing semi-automatic weapons. All of the agents were younger than I. Cops looked a hell of a lot younger too. I was 54 years old. I would miss the adrenalin and the finest people in the world.

For me, it was time to go. I was certain of that. I had no regrets. I wanted to chase other dreams. It had been a damn fine ride.

INDEX

Photographs are indicated by *ph* following the page number.

1st and Ten Club, 165, 209–212
9/11, 206

A
Abner. *see* Carr, Starley (Abner)
Adams, Carmen, 184
affairs, extramarital, 59–60
aggression, ordered by Hoover, 15
AIM (American Indian Movement),
   84–85
Alabama Crimson Tide, 2, 13, 33,
   36, 67, 167, 192, 226
alcohol, Russians and, 150, 227–228
American University, 9
Americans For A Competent Federal
   Judicial System, 198
Army deserters. *see* deserters
arrests
   absence from, due to reading, 189
   FOAs and, 40–41
   Fridays and, 33–34
   of fugitive, alone, 87–89, 93–97
   procedures for, 58–59
   statistics, 58, 93
   see also individual names
Aryan Nation, 134, 207
ATF (Alcohol, Tobacco, and Firearms), 193, 199

Atlanta
   daily routine in, 112–113
   murders, 109–119, 125
   prison riot, 171–180, 190,
     213–214
Australia, 234
autopsy (Vance), 197

B
background investigation, initial, 7
badge, receiving, 12
bank robbery, Birmingham, 66–68
Barr, William, 219
Berlin Wall, 225
Bernius, Bill, 48*ph*
BIA (Bureau of Indian Affairs), 84
birds, fear of, 163
Birmingham
   arrival in, 55–56
   move to, 52–53
   transfer to, 51–53
Birmingham Country Club,
   122–124
Black, Don, 200
bomb, mail, 193–194, 196, 198
BOP (Bureau of Prisons), 215, 218
Brannan, Steve, 134*ph*, 142, 143,
   168, 217

Brannon, Bill, 103, 105, 106
Brannon, Luther
  absence of, 64, 69, 88
  photo of, 134*ph*
  retired, 237–238, 241
  transfer to Birmingham of, 57–58
  Vance and, 191
  Webster and, 124
  working with, 2–5, 59, 131–133
breakfast
  with fugitive, 96
  with Russians, 225–228
Brignola, Danny (nephew), 169
Broadway, 174, 176
Brokaw, Tom, 245
Brooks, Philip, 242
Brown, James, 239–240
Brown, William, 11, 15, 27, 42*ph*
brown lunch bags, 15–16
Bryant, Paul "Bear", 29, 100*ph*, 105, 209
Bunch, Bob, 40
burglary, furniture, 7–8
Bush, George, 216, 219
Butte, Montana, as punishment, 29
Byrne, Mike, 48*ph*

C
Carr, Starley (Abner)
  absence of, 64, 88
  elevator incident and, 56
  Hoover's death and, 76
  introduction to, 55
  photo of, 164*ph*, 190*ph*, 220*ph*
  retired, 238, 241
  SWAT and, 84, 173, 176, 216
  working with, 57–58, 59, 68–70
Carranza, Roel, 184
cars
  overheating of, 123, 205
  rules regarding, 39
  Whitaker and, 239
Carter, Jimmy, 110, 121

Carter, Nathaniel, 118–119
CDC (Chief Division Counel), 183
Chattahoochee River, 109–111, 114, 115, 125
CIA, 78, 121, 140, 155, 208
cigarettes, stolen, 50–51
Civil War, 194–195
Clinton, Bill, 185, 201, 203, 208
Coachman, Sherolynne, 243
code of conduct, 74
coffee, 246
  allowance of, 82
  black, 150, 226, 245
  reliance on, 1, 111
  rule against, 36–37
Cohrs, Bob, 21–24, 25–26, 42
Cold War
  counterintelligence and, 140–141, 154, 183, 244
  end of, 155, 219, 225–228
  German language and, 243
  Navy and, 146
  post, 208, 214
Coleman, John, 101–103, 105, 106–107
Coler, Jack, 85
communication with press, 74
Communism, 75, 77, 105, 139, 153, 226–227
complaints, 181–185, 205
computers, 237, 239, 246
Concord College, 9
confrontations with supervisors, 41, 92
Congress, 61, 74, 75, 78, 124–125
Coolidge, Calvin, 75
counterintelligence. *see* FCI (Foreign Counterintelligence)
court cases, evidence for, 73–74
credentials
  loss of, 38–39
  practical joke and, 241–242
Crime Records Division, 75, 79

Crime Resistance program, 101–108
Crime Resistance Team, 100*ph*
criminal v. counterintelligence
    agents, 146
Cuban prisoners, 213–214, 217–218
Cumberland School of Law, 122,
    126–127, 161
Cumbie, Ben, 220*ph*
Curry, Ashley, 176, 190*ph*, 220*ph*

D
Daly, Henry Joseph, 213
Davis, Lonnie, 243
Davis, Vicki, 184
deadly force, use of, 160–161
Democratic party, 192
Denver, arrival in, 31–32
Department of State, 140
deserters
    arrests of, 33–34
    arrests of, alone, 92–93
    mothers and, 68–70
    tracking of, 31
discrimination, 181–185
divorce, 60
Dixon, Martha, 213–219, 220*ph*
dogcatchers, 221–224
Douglas, John, 109, 118
dream, recurring, 161–163
drowning, near, of Molly, 136–137
drug bust, gone bad, 157–163
Drug Enforcement Agency, 139–140

E
Eastern *Bloc*, 147–148, 154, 155
elevator incidents, 56, 81, 125–126
escape, by prisoner, 38–39
Evans, Frank, 217, 219
Evans, Fred, 217
evidence, for court cases, 73–74
exercise
    allowance of, 82
    importance of, 204

    restrictions on, 37
    see also physical fitness

F
family
    absence from, 14, 34
    move with, 53
    problems, 59–60
    travel to visit, 108
    see also individual names
Farmer, Dale, 48*ph*
FBI offices, uniformity of, 56–57
FBIHQ (FBI Headquarters in Wash-
    ington)
    undercover assignment and,
        154–155
    v. field offices, 71, 76
FCI (Foreign Counterintelligence),
    140–156
female agents. *see* women (agents)
field assignments, receipt of, 28–29
fight, during softball game, 44, 48
firearms training, 18–24, 25–26,
    54*ph*, 235
FIT (Fitness Indicator Test), 234
Fleming, Bill, 194
FOA (First Office Agents), 28
    arrests and, 40–41
    in Denver, 35–36
food, prison, 176
Freedom of Information Act,
    124–125
Freeh, Louis
    background of, 203–204
    as Director, 204–208
    family and, 207
    letter from, 242
    physical fitness and, 204, 234
    as prosecutor, 201
    terrorism and, 206
    women and minorities and, 205,
        229–232
Freeman, Marvin, 134*ph*

Freemen, 207
Friday arrests, 33–34
fugitive (unnamed)
  arrest of, 132, 221–224
  credentials loss and, 36–39
  see also individual names
fugitive squad
  in Birmingham, 57–58
  in Denver, 31, 35

G
Gandy, Helen, 72, 78
Gilbert, Muriel, 106
Gilbert, William, 105
Gilliland, Gregg, 110–119
Glover, John, 111–112
GOP, 133
graduation, 29–30, 42*ph*
Grant, Ulysses S., 187–189, 195
Gray, L. Patrick, 81–83, 207
Grayson, Stacey, *see* Owens, Stacey
GRU, 155
GTR (Government Travel Request),
  33
Gulf War, 236
guns, inexperience with, 18
  see also firearms training

H
Hammond, 64–65
Hayes, Ken, 48*ph*
headlight, broken, 94–95, 97, 99
heckling, 26, 44
Held, Richard, 85
Hinkley, John, 139
Hogan's Alley, 25–26
Hoover, J. Edgar
  absence of, 27–28
  on agents, 14
  appointment letter from, 7
  during basic training, 15–16
  changes since death of, 103, 127
  communication and, 74

Communism and, 75
death of, 75–77, 207
disappointment of, 15–16
FBI credentials and, 32–33
handshake tradition, 29
homosexuality and, 77–78
isolation of, 71
King and, 77
Pare and, 142
photos autographed by, 72
posthumous reputation of, 77–79
recordkeeping and, 61, 73
Sizemore and, 72–73
Tolson and, 78–79
Webster compared to, 121, 127
women and minorities and, 75,
  183
Zeiss, George and, 25
horseshoes, 20
hostages
  rescue of, 217–218
  taken in prison, 171, 173–174
  in Talladega, 215–216
house divided, definition, 142
HRT (Hostage Rescue Team), 162,
  176–177, 180, 215–218
hymn during prison riot, 178–179

I
injury sustained during chase,
  159–160
INS (Immigration and Naturalization Service), 215, 218
International Police Olympics,
  234–235
IO (intelligence officer), Soviet,
  143–145
Iraqi nationals, 236–237

J
Jefferson County Jail, 98–99
job satisfaction, waning, 102
Johnson, Lyndon, 32

Jones (deserter), 63–65
Jordon, Shug, 105
justifications for behavior, 8, 13

K
Kaczynski, Ted, 206
Kelley, Clarence M.
  bank sign and, 105
  Coleman and, 101–102
  Crime Resistance and, 106, 107
  description of, 83–84
  as Director, 84–85, 207–208
  report for, 103
  resignation of, 86
  Webster and, 121–122, 127
Kelly, Gerald, 220*ph*
Kennedy, John, 188, 192
KGB, 140–141, 143–145, 148,
  154–155, 183
King, Martin Luther, 25, 77
Ku Klux Klan, 45–47, 192, 194,
  199–200, 207

L
laundry stamp, 152
law school graduates, recruiting,
  230–232
Lee, Ed, 48*ph*
Lewis, Joe, 239–240
Lincoln, Abraham, 187–189,
  194–195
Lincoln, The War Years, Vol. 1 (Sandburg), 187–189
line-ups, 40
local law enforcement
  collaboration with, 101–108,
    110–111
  early impressions of, 10
  opinions regarding, 58–59
  relations with, 44, 61, 63, 66, 167

M
MacDonald, Jeff, 220*ph*

mail bomb, 193–194, 196, 198
Malone, Bill, 40
marriage
  to Ginni, 8–9
  to Patricia, 106
Martinez, George, 213
Martinez, Martha Dixon, 213–219,
  220*ph*
Melton, Earl, 100*ph*, 102
Mexican Joe, 113, 114–115, 117
Miles, Ralph, 66–67, 83, 124
Miller, John, 213
minorities (agents), 75, 82, 181–
  185, 205, 229–232
minorities (SAC), 111–112
Moody, Walter Leroy, Jr., 198–201,
  199, 203
Moore, Tom, 124
Morse, Wray, 134*ph*
Moses, Cecil, 122–123, 124, 127
mothers of deserters, 68–70
motivation, definition, 65
murders
  in Atlanta, 109–119, 125
  of civil rights workers, 45–47
  of Coler and Williams, 85
  of King, 25
  of Vance, 191–198, 199–200, 203
Murphy, Audie, 33–34
Murrah Federal Building bombing,
  206

N
NAACP (National Association for
  the Advancement of Colored
  People), 198
NAC #17 (New Agents Class #17)
  in FBIHQ, 15
  firearms training and, 19–24
  first days with, 11–14
  graduation, 27–30
  Hogan's Alley and, 25–26
  letters from classmates, 242

photo of, 42*ph*
Tickel and, 17
National Crime Information Center, 246
Navy, 36, 146
Nelson, "Red", 40
Nelson, Willie, 85
New York office, complaints about, 57–58
nine/eleven, 206
Nixon, Richard, 12, 83–84
novels, writing of, 235, 240

O
O'Farrell, Robert Wayne, 200
Oklahoma City bombing, 206
OP (Office of Preference list), 49–50
Operation Desert Storm, 236
OPO (Old Post Office)
  classes at, 11, 27–28, 29
  move from, 15
  paper airplane and, 30
organized crime
  in Denver, 39–40
  expansion of FBI and, 12
  Freeh and, 203
  Procop and, 31, 36, 40
  in Russia, 225
Owens, Bob (brother), 166–170
Owens, Brett (son), 8, 9, 108
Owens, Deke (son), 57, 108, 161, 215
Owens, Duanne (son), 8, 9, 108, 207, 244–245
Owens, Ginni (wife)
  affairs and, 59–60
  in Birmingham, 57
  courtship of and marriage to, 8–9
  custody and, 108
  in Denver, 31
  divorce from, 60
  furniture burglary and, 8
  move with, 52–53

relationship with during basic training, 14, 17
Owens, Jack (father), 169–170, 245–246
Owens, Laura Kathyn (daughter), 129–130, 186*ph*, 244–245
Owens, Mary Helen (mother), 169–170, 194, 245–246
Owens, Molly (daughter), 135–137, 185, 186*ph*, 244–245
Owens, Stacey 106, 186*ph*, 244–245
Owens, Patricia (wife)
  in Australia, 234
  courtship of and marriage to, 104–106
  Laura and, 129–130
  Molly and, 135–137
  photo of, 186*ph*
  at retirement breakfast, 244
  Sessions and, 185

P
Pare, George, 142, 143, 145, 217
Parkis, Charles, 11, 15, 27, 42*ph*
Parsons, James, 102
Patton, David, 48*ph*
payday procedures, 65
Payne, Jimmy Ray, 119
Peltier, Leonard, 85
Pentagon, 140, 209, 212
photos of author, 10*ph*, 42*ph*, 48*ph*, 54*ph*, 100*ph*, 134*ph*, 164*ph*, 180*ph*, 186*ph*, 190*ph*, 202*ph*, 220*ph*
physical fitness
  coordinator, 234, 242
  importance of, 204
  in-service training, 204–205
  test, changed to voluntary, 208
Pierce, Chuck, 157–163
pinhead rumor, 29
Pittman, Alethea, 229–230, 231, 232

politics of Directorship, 83
Postal Inspectors, 193
post-traumatic stress conference,
    162–163
Powell, Colin, 209–212
Powell, Mrs., 209
practical jokes
    brother's, 166
    children's photos, 168
    colored shirt day, 27–28
    credentials and, 241–242
    desk deception, 57
    elevator incidents, 56, 81, 125
    during target practice, 24
    target practice and, 42
prison
    entry into alone, 176–179
    food, 176
    siege in Atlanta, 171–180
    uprising in Talladega, 213–219
Procop, Richard, 12, 42*ph*, 31, 40,
    50–51
Procopio, Jim, 12, 42*ph*, 54*ph*
profile of Atlanta murderer, 109
provocation, definition, 147
psychic, use of, 199
psycholgists, FBI, 161–163
pursuit angles, definition, 65

Q
Quantico, FBI Academy at
    firearms training at, 18–24, 54*ph*
    post-traumatic stress conference
        a, 162
    profilers, 109, 118, 182, 199
    staff cuts at, 206
    SWAT training at, 84
    training at, 14, 17

R
radios, FBI
    theft of, 238
    trouble with, 3, 188

Rahman, Omar Abdel, Sheik, 206
Ramsey, Wilbur, 20
raquetball
    against Ben, 45–47
    at the Presidio, 107
    against Rogers, 36, 38, 39, 41
Ray, James Earl, 25, 77
Reagan, Ronald, 110, 139, 146
reckless behavior, 87–100
recordkeeping. *see* statistics/record-
    keeping
recruiting, 107, 140, 229–232, 236
Red Cross, 174
Redford, Robert, 85
reliable source, definition, 132
Republicans, 131–133
retirement, 241–247
Rickwood Field, 222
Ridlehoover, Marshall, 220*ph*
roadblock, to catch fugitive, 131–
    133
Robinson, Robert, 198
Rogers, Bob
    birth of daughter, 52
    confrontation of supervisor by, 41
    meeting of in Denver, 31
    physical fitness and, 204–205
    softball and, 43–44
    transfer news from, 51
    working with, 36–39, 40–41
Rolen, Bob, 243
Ruby Ridge, 207
Russian police, 225–228
    see also Soviet Union, dissolution of
Russian studies students, 235
Ryder Truck Company, 206

S
SAC (Special Agent in Charge)
    communication with press, 74
    in Denver, 35, 51
    see also Glover, John; Lewis, Joe;
        Miles, Ralph; Moses, Cecil;

Whitaker, Allen

Sadat, Anwar, 126–127
Salameh, Mohammed, 206
salaries, 74
Salvation Army, 174
Samford University, 122, 126–127
San Francisco, work in, 105,
    106–107
Sandburg, Carl, 187
Schmidle, Harold, 220*ph*
search, in woods, 4
security, for Webster, 122–127
Sessions, William S., 181, 184–185,
    186*ph*, 207, 219
Sherman, 195
shooting. *see* firearms training
shooting incident
    during drug bust, 160
    paperwork for, 160–161
shotgun lead, definition, 62
Sievers, Bill, 216, 221–224
Singleton (fugitive), 1–5
Sixteenth Street Baptist Church
    bombing, 194
Sizemore, Leon
    absence of, 64, 88
    Crime Resistance program and,
        101–102, 105, 106–107
    elevator incident and, 56
    Hoover and, 72–73
    introduction to, 55
    photo of, 100*ph*
    retired, 237–238, 241–242
    SWAT teams and, 84
    working with, 57–58, 59, 68–70
Sligh, Bob (the Fox)
    counterintelligence and, 141–142,
        217
    joking with, 167
    photo of, 134*ph*
    retired, 238
    undercover assignment and, 146,
        148, 152

working with, 143, 184
snow, Powell's visit and, 211–212
softball
    in Denver, 43–44
    fight, 44, 48
    team members, 116, 142, 158
    team photo, 48*ph*
SOG (Seat of Government), 16
Soviet Union, dissolution of,
    155–156, 225, 236
    see also Russian police
Special Agent Advisory Committee,
    205, 230–231
special interest groups, within FBI,
    181–185
Special Surveillance Group (SSG),
    207, 245
spying. *see* FCI (Foreign Counterin-
    telligence)
Stallings, Gene, 210
Starr, Bart, 210
state troopers. *see* local law enforce-
    ment
statistics/recordkeeping
    Hoover's system of, 73
    importance of, 61
    posting of, 58
    TIO (time-in-the-office), 82
stolen cars, 244
    Alabama title law and, 58, 89
    recovery of, 61
    searching for, alone, 90–92
Supan, Jim, 48*ph*
supervisor confrontations, 41, 92
Surprise Target Course (Hogan's Al-
    ley), 25–26
surveillance
    in Atlanta, 110–113, 125
    botched, 144–145
    description of, 1–2
    of KGB agent, 143–145
    of King, 77
    Special Surveillance Group (SSG),

207, 245
of Williams, 118
SWAT (Special Weapons and Tactics) teams
  at Atlanta prison siege, 171–180
  Birmingham, 175, 180*ph*
  BuCars and, 239
  compensation for, 180
  continued participation in, 142, 146
  drug bust with, 157–163
  formation of, 84
  HRT (Hostage Rescue Team) and, 218
  Knoxville, 214
  photos of, 164*ph*, 190*ph*, 202, 220*ph*
  resignation from, 235
  at Talladega prison uprising, 213–219
  training, 172–173
  women and, 122, 214–215

T
Talladega prison uprising, 213–219, 221, 242
Talladega roadblock, 131–133
target practice, 19–20, 23–24
telephone directory, as reminder, 52
Temple, Bill, 190*ph*
tennis
  at Georgia Tech, 113, 125
  Webster's game, 122–124, 127
terrorism, 206–207, 236–237
The Club, 124
the *eye*, 145
The Greatest Generation (Brokaw), 245
Thompson (fugitive), 1–5
Thompson machine gun, 22–23
Tickel, Ed
  in basic training, 9, 12, 14, 16–17
  conviction of, 238–239

in firearms training, 20, 21
  graduation, 42*ph*
  Thompson machine gun and, 22–23
  transfer to Tampa, 52
ticket, definition, 68
TIO (time-in-the-office), 82
title law, 58, 89
Tolson, Clyde, 77, 78–79
training agents, in Denver, 32–34
transfers, procedure, 49–50
trash cans, pristine nature of, 17–18
typewriter, as evidence, 200
typist, uncooperative, 103

U
UFAP (unlawful flight to avoid prosecution), 62–63
undercover assignment
  end of, 155–156, 219, 225
  expansion of, 153–154
  first encounter with, 146–149
  memory of, 244
  relationship with target during, 149–151, 152–153
  reports during, 151–152
  travel to Washington for, 149
Unibomber, 206
University of Alabama
  changes in, 234
  speeches at, 235
  visit to, 165–166
University of Alabama School of Law
  birth of sons while enrolled at, 9
  burglary at, of furniture, 7–8
  Pittman and, 229–230, 232
  Procopio and, 12
  recruiting from, 229
  Vance and, 192
  yearbook photo, 10*ph*
U.S. Marshals
  prisoner and, 38
  softball and, 43

Wounded Knee and, 84–85
USSR, dissolution of, 155–156, 225, 236
see also Russian police
V
Vance, Charles, 196
Vance, Helen, 193, 196–197, 199
Vance, Joyce, 199
Vance, Robert, 191–198, 198–200, 203
Vance, Robert, Jr., 196, 199
Vance, Stacey, *see* Owens, Stacey
Vance, Patricia, *see* Owens, Patricia
Vietnam War
    deserters and, 93
    effect on early career, 85
    impact of, 32
    Kelley and, 85
    support for, 13
VIN (vehicle indentification number), 90–91, 206
Voice of America, 11
Volkswagen arrest, 93–99
Vulcan, statue of, 87, 144

W
Waco, 207
wall, hitting the, 233
Wallace, George, 105, 192
Warden, Joe, 100*ph*, 102, 104
Washington Field Office, 11
watch, theft of, 107
Watkins, Jerry Dale, 93–99
Watmon, Tom, 48*ph*
Webster, William H., 121–127, 176, 207
Westberg, Bill, 134*ph*, 141, 146
WFO (Washington Field Office), 11
Whitaker, Allen, 193–194, 216, 218, 219, 221, 239
Williams, Ron, 85
Williams, Wayne
    arrest and conviction f, 119

discussion of with Webster, 125
first encounter with, 114
Gilliland, Gregg and, 115–116
surveillance of, 118
suspicion of, 116–117
Windham, Janice, 184
Wiseman, Tom, 234
Wizard of Transfers, 49–50
women (agents)
    hiring of, 82, 205
    Hoover and, 75
    Iraqi nationals and, 236–237
    recruiting, 229–232
    special interest groups and, 181–185
    in SWAT, 214–215
Wounded Knee, 84–85
Wright, Don, 172–174
WTC (World Trade Center) bombing, 206

Z
Zapalac, Frank "Zappy", 29
Zeiss, George, 25–26